MAKING CONNECTIONS

LOW INTERMEDIATE

A Strategic Approach to Academic Reading and Vocabulary

Jessica Williams

With
Daphne Mackey

CAMBRIDGE
UNIVERSITY PRESS

CAMBRIDGE UNIVERSITY PRESS
Cambridge, New York, Melbourne, Madrid, Cape Town, Singapore,
São Paulo, Delhi, Dubai, Tokyo, Mexico City

Cambridge University Press
32 Avenue of the Americas, New York, NY 10013-2473, USA

www.cambridge.org
Information on this title: www.cambridge.org/9780521152167

© Cambridge University Press 2011

First published 2011

Printed in Hong Kong, China, by Golden Cup Printing Company Limited

A catalog record for this publication is available from the British Library.

Williams, Jessica, 1957–
  Making connections low intermediate : a strategic approach to academic
reading and vocabulary / Jessica Williams.
       p. cm.
  Includes bibliographical references and index.
  ISBN 978-0-521-15216-7 (student's book : alk. paper)
1. Reading (Higher education) 2. College reading improvement programs.
3. Vocabulary--Study and teaching (Higher) I. Title.

LB2395.3.W56 2011
428.4071'1--dc22

2010040537

ISBN 978-0-521-15216-7 Student's Book
ISBN 978-0-521-15217-4 Teacher's Manual

Book design: Adventure House, NYC
Realia design and layout services: Page Designs International, Inc.
Photo research: Elizabeth Blomster

TABLE OF CONTENTS

INTRODUCTION
TO THE INSTRUCTOR

LEVEL

Making Connections Low Intermediate is a low intermediate–level academic reading and vocabulary skills book. It is intended for students who need to improve their strategic reading skills and build their academic vocabulary.

APPROACH

Making Connections Low Intermediate incorporates the following insights from second language reading theory and practice:

- Reading is an interactive process, in which readers use their knowledge of language, text organization, and the world to understand what they read.
- Reading is goal-oriented and strategic; good academic readers are metacognitively aware readers.
- While reading, good readers engage in a search for coherence; that is, they look for the propositional and rhetorical connectedness of text.
- Readers are ultimately judged by the product of their reading; that is, the accuracy of the picture they are able to produce of a text.

CONTENT AND ORGANIZATION

Each of the eight units of *Making Connections Low Intermediate* focuses on one general topic, with each of the three readings in a unit focusing on a specific aspect of the topic. Thus, as students work through a unit, they increase their knowledge of the topic, which in turn facilitates their processing of the later readings in the unit.

Each of the eight units of the book is organized into a number of sections:

- Two Skills and Strategies sections, interwoven with the readings, introduce and practice specific skills and strategies. The first Skills and Strategies section in each unit addresses strategies for understanding vocabulary in a text and developing vocabulary acquisition strategies. The second Skills and Strategies section in each unit focuses on reading comprehension and text-processing strategies. For easier orientation and reference, all Skills and Strategies pages are lightly colored.
- The three readings in each unit are of increasing length, ranging from approximately 470 to 930 words. The readings are accompanied by associated activities in pre-reading, reading, comprehension, vocabulary building and review, research, discussion, and writing.
- A final section provides coherence-building tasks and a review of the vocabulary, skills, and strategies introduced in the unit.

The structural, lexical, and organizational forms targeted in a given section recur in subsequent readings and activities throughout the remainder of the book. Similarly, after certain text-processing strategies are introduced and practiced in a Skills and Strategies section, students are cued to use these strategies while reading the texts in the rest of the book.

READING ACTIVITIES

The readings in **Making Connections Low Intermediate** are accompanied by the following activities:

Getting into the Topic

This pre-reading activity gives students the opportunity to activate their knowledge of the general topic of the reading by introducing elements of the reading or connecting them to students' current knowledge.

Getting a First Idea about the Reading

This previewing activity enables students to develop expectations about the content and organization of the reading before they begin to read it.

While You Read

This activity consists of a set of tasks that students complete while reading the texts. Each task sets a short-term goal and activates an appropriate text-processing strategy introduced in an earlier Skills and Strategies section. The tasks are cued by boldface text and appear in colored boxes in the margin of the page. Students signal their completion of a task by highlighting, circling, numbering, or underlining parts of the reading or by writing notes in the margin.

Main Idea Check

This activity requires students to read for the main idea of the entire text in the first five readings of the book, and of each paragraph in all readings thereafter. It is recommended that reading for main ideas be the goal of the first read-through of each reading. It is also recommended that students pause after each paragraph and choose its main idea before reading the next paragraph.

A Closer Look

This activity requires students to look for specific information in each reading and its accompanying graphics. Typically, students respond to True/False, fill-in-the-blank, matching, or multiple-choice questions. Other tasks include identifying the elements in a chronological process and filling in items in a chart.

Vocabulary Study and Review

This set of activities always begins with *Vocabulary Study: Definitions*, which uses contexts provided by the accompanying reading to focus student attention on eight of the vocabulary items selected as key vocabulary for that reading. The remaining key vocabulary items for the reading are reviewed in one of three activities: (1) *Vocabulary Study: Word Families*, which allows students to build their vocabulary by recognizing different word forms with similar meanings; (2) *Vocabulary Study: Words in Context*, which gives students practice applying the strategies introduced in the first Skills and Strategies section in each unit; or

(3) *Vocabulary Study: Synonyms*, which uses students' current lexical knowledge to expand their vocabulary. There are two additional vocabulary activities: *Vocabulary Review: Same or Different*, which offers opportunities to review the vocabulary of the two preceding readings, and *Vocabulary Review: Academic Word List*, which reviews items from the Academic Word List that occur in the entire unit. The Academic Word List consists of words that appear in a broad range of academic contexts. Familiarity with these words will prepare students for future encounters with academic texts.

Beyond the Reading

These activities give students an opportunity to explore the topic in greater depth by doing some basic research on the topic, engaging in discussion, and completing a short writing assignment.

VOCABULARY

The key vocabulary items introduced in **Making Connections Low Intermediate** have been selected for their usefulness in general academic English. After its introduction, each vocabulary item is reused as often as possible in readings and activities within the same unit and in subsequent units. These words and phrases are listed alphabetically, by reading number, in Appendix 1 [page 251]. Each entry contains a simple definition and an example, making this section of the book a useful resource for students expanding their academic vocabulary. Academic Word List items are noted with the icon ⓐ in Appendices 1 and 2.

COURSE LENGTH

Making Connections Low Intermediate has enough material for a reading course of 50 to 70 class hours, assuming a corresponding number of hours available for homework assignments. Completing all the *Beyond the Reading* tasks that accompany each reading might make the course longer.

GUIDELINES FOR USING *MAKING CONNECTIONS LOW INTERMEDIATE*

Through its sequencing of materials, **Making Connections Low Intermediate** helps students gradually integrate knowledge, skills, and strategies into a strategic approach to academic reading and vocabulary.

- To enable students to derive the greatest benefit from the sequenced materials, we recommend that you use each unit and each section within that unit in the order of their appearance in the book.
- Most of the activities are suitable for both in-class work and homework assignments. However, it is best if they are introduced, modeled, and practiced in class – in some cases repeatedly – before they are assigned for completion as homework.
- There are more suggestions for the use of specific materials included in the *Teacher's Manual*, which also includes a complete set of answers.

TO THE STUDENT

WHAT YOU WILL LEARN IN *MAKING CONNECTIONS LOW INTERMEDIATE*

Welcome to *Making Connections Low Intermediate*. We have created this book to help you develop a strategic approach to academic reading and vocabulary building.

This book will help you do the following:

1. Build your academic vocabulary

Like most students of English, you probably believe that a better knowledge of vocabulary will make you a better reader. You are right. In this book, you have the opportunity to expand your vocabulary by more than three hundred and fifty nontechnical words and phrases that are common in academic English. Some of the words in each unit come from the Academic Word List. To help you remember and learn these words after they have been introduced, they are reused in later readings and activities.

In the first Skills and Strategies section of each unit, you will be introduced to many strategies for learning new vocabulary words. You will have many opportunities to practice these new strategies while you are reading this book.

2. Understand how academic texts are written

A larger vocabulary, however, is not enough to make you the best reader you can be. You will also improve by developing your knowledge of English academic writing, especially the way information is organized in texts.

In the second Skills and Strategies section of each unit, you will have many opportunities to learn about the organization of information in texts in academic English.

3. Develop effective reading strategies

In addition, research has shown that good readers use a number of effective reading strategies. These are techniques that they use to improve their understanding of what they are reading.

The second Skills and Strategies section of each unit also introduces you to many helpful reading strategies. You will have a large number of opportunities to practice these new strategies while you are reading this book.

HOW *MAKING CONNECTIONS LOW INTERMEDIATE* IS ORGANIZED

Making Connections Low Intermediate contains eight units. Each unit deals with one general topic of interest and has the same internal organization.

- Two Skills and Strategies sections: one focused on vocabulary, and the other focused on reading strategies
- Three readings of increasing length and related activities in reading, vocabulary study, research, discussion, and writing

- A final Making Connections section that helps you review vocabulary and understand connections between sentences

At the end of the book, you will find Appendix I. This is similar to a dictionary. It explains and gives examples of the academic vocabulary items that you will study from each reading. Appendix 2 is an index that allows you to find the entry for any of the more than 350 vocabulary items introduced in the book.

HOW TO GET THE MOST OUT OF *MAKING CONNECTIONS LOW INTERMEDIATE*

What can you do to get the greatest benefit from using **Making Connections Low Intermediate**? Here are a few suggestions:

- Whenever you read, use the reading and vocabulary strategies introduced in the Skills and Strategies sections of the book.
- Successful academic reading is hard work! Study hard and expect to be tired after class work or homework.
- Outside of class, read as much English as you can. Balance the hard work of academic reading with other reading that is just for your own personal interest and enjoyment.

ACKNOWLEDGMENTS

Many people helped bring this text from an idea to the page. First, I would like to thank Bernard Seal. This is our second *Making Connections* project together, and Bernard's insight and advice have always been constructive and thoughtful. I also acknowledge the singular contribution of Daphne Mackey, for her assistance in writing several key parts of this manuscript. A very special thanks goes to Karen Shimoda, my development editor. Karen's dedication to this project, even when there were other demands on her time and energy, and her attention to its smallest detail were what kept it on target and on deadline. For their invaluable work in moving the project toward completion, I would also like to thank Mandie Drucker, our diligent fact checker and copy editor; and Caitlin Mara, in-house Development Editor.

For turning the raw manuscript into a finished book, I would also like to acknowledge the hard work of the production team, including Heather McCarron and Alan Kaplan. Special thanks are due to Don Williams, who once again was the compositor extraordinaire.

I also appreciate the contributions of the following reviewers for their thoughtful comments:

Susan Boland, Tidewater Community College, Virginia
Mike Sfiropoulos, Palm Beach Community College, Florida
Harry Holden, El Centro Community College, Texas
Claudia Kupiec, DePaul University, Illinois
Mike Lee, Clara Song, et al., CDI Holdings Inc., Seoul, South Korea
Susan Niemeyer, Los Angeles Community College, California

Finally, I acknowledge Ken Pakenham, author of *Making Connections High Intermediate*, whose fine work began the *Making Connections* series.

PHOTO CREDITS

Crossing Borders

SKILLS AND STRATEGIES 1
FINDING THE MEANINGS OF WORDS (1)

Writers sometimes use words that a reader may not know. To help readers understand a difficult word, writers may explain what the word means by giving its definition. Writers often use clues to do this. These clues can be other words, phrases, or punctuation. They can signal, or show you, that a definition is coming next. Good readers pay attention to these clues. This helps them find the meanings of words.

EXAMPLES & EXPLANATIONS

Examples

Computers can scan, **or** take pictures of, travelers' faces.

Explanations

Sometimes writers give the definition of a difficult word immediately after the word. They may use the word *or* to signal, or show you, that a definition is coming next. Notice that a comma will come before *or* at the end of the definition.

scan = take pictures

Governments want to be able to use their countries' natural resources, **that is**, the natural materials in the water, on land, and underground.

Writers may use phrases, such as *that is* or *in other words*, to explain the meaning of a word.

natural resources = materials in the water, on land, and underground

National borders **–** the places where one country ends and another country begins **–** can be physical or political.

Writers may also use punctuation around definitions. They may use parentheses, dashes, and commas. Here the writer uses dashes (–).

national borders = the places where one country ends and another begins

A new development in technology is the **computer chip**. A **computer chip** is a very small electronic part that can store information.

Sometimes writers repeat the word in the next sentence and then give a definition there.

computer chip = a very small electronic part that can store information

STRATEGIES

These strategies will help you find the meanings of words while you read.

- Look for words and phrases that signal, or show you, that a definition for a difficult word is coming next. Read the definition carefully.
- Pay attention to punctuation. Look for parentheses, commas, and dashes.
- If there is no definition immediately after the difficult word, look in the next sentence. Writers sometimes repeat the word in the next sentence and give the definition there.

SKILL PRACTICE 1

Read the following sentences, and find the clues that signal the meaning of each word in **bold**. Circle the clues. The first one has been done for you.

1 Gold and sugar are two of Mexico's important **exports** (items sold by one country to another country).

2 The officials told the travelers about the dangerous **infection** – a disease or sickness in a person's body – that was spreading in South America.

3 It is important to use different **strategies**, or plans for success, when you play chess.

4 The speaker talked for 15 minutes, and then he gave his **conclusion**. A conclusion is the final part of something.

5 At international soccer matches, fights are quite **frequent**; in other words, they occur often.

6 Since we do not know how much the tickets cost, we have to **guess**, that is, give an answer that we are not sure about.

7 The man was not sure of the **value** of the painting. In other words, he was not sure how much money to pay for it.

8 Some toys are dangerous. They can seriously **injure**, or harm, the children who play with them.

SKILL PRACTICE 2

Read the sentences in Skill Practice 1 again. Look at the clues you circled for each sentence. Use the clues to figure out the meaning of each word in **bold**. Write a short definition or synonym – a word that means the same or almost the same thing – on the blank lines. The first one has been done for you.

1 Gold and sugar are two of Mexico's important **exports** (items sold by one country to another country).

exports = _items sold by one country to another country_

2 The officials told the travelers about the dangerous **infection** – a disease or sickness in a person's body – that was spreading in South America.

infection = _____

3 It is important to use different **strategies**, or plans for success, when you play chess.

strategies = _____

4 The speaker talked for 15 minutes, and then he gave his **conclusion**. A conclusion is the final part of something.

conclusion = _____

5 At international soccer matches, fights are quite **frequent**; in other words, they occur often.

frequent = _____

6 Since we do not know how much the tickets cost, we have to **guess**, that is, give an answer that we are not sure about.

guess = _____

7 The man was not sure of the **value** of the painting. In other words, he was not sure how much money to pay for it.

value = _____

8 Some toys are dangerous. They can seriously **injure**, or harm, the children who play with them.

injure = _____

READING 1

BORDERS ON THE LAND, IN THE OCEAN, AND IN THE AIR

GETTING INTO THE TOPIC

Thai–Laos Border

China–Pakistan Border

Look at the two photographs. Then discuss the following questions with a partner.

1 What is a national border?
2 How are the borders in the two photographs different?
3 Where are the borders in your country? Are they like the first photo, the second photo, or both photos?

GETTING A FIRST IDEA ABOUT THE READING

The first few sentences of a reading can give you a good idea about the content of the whole reading.

Read the title above and the first seven sentences of Reading 1 below. Then answer the questions that follow.

> Long ago, there were no national borders. People moved freely from place to place. Today, countries have national borders. National borders are where one country ends and another country begins. There are two kinds of national borders. The first kind is a physical border. Physical borders between countries can be rivers or mountains.

1 Find the definition of *national border* in the fourth sentence. Highlight it.
2 Look back at the photographs. Which photo do you think shows an example of a physical border? What are other examples of physical borders?
3 What do you think this reading will discuss next?

WHILE YOU READ

As you read, stop at the end of each sentence that contains words in **bold**. Then follow the instructions in the box in the margin.

Borders on the Land, in the Ocean, and in the Air

Look in the next two sentences for a definition of *physical border*. Highlight it.

Long ago, there were no national borders. People moved freely from place to place. Today, countries have national borders. National borders are where one country ends and another country begins. There are two kinds of national borders. The first kind is a **physical border**. Physical borders between countries can be rivers or mountains. You can see them. The Rio Grande River is a physical border between Mexico and the United States. The Pyrenees Mountains are a physical border between Spain and France.

Look in the third sentence for a definition of *political border*. Highlight it.

The second kind of border is a **political border**. If there is no physical border between countries, governments must decide on one. Political borders are lines between countries like physical borders, but governments decide where these borders will be. The political borders of many North African countries are a good example of this. In the nineteenth and early twentieth centuries, European countries had power over many parts of Africa. They decided on the borders. Many of these borders were just straight lines on a map. They were not physical features, such as rivers or mountains. (See Figure 1.1.)

FIGURE 1.1 Countries of North Africa

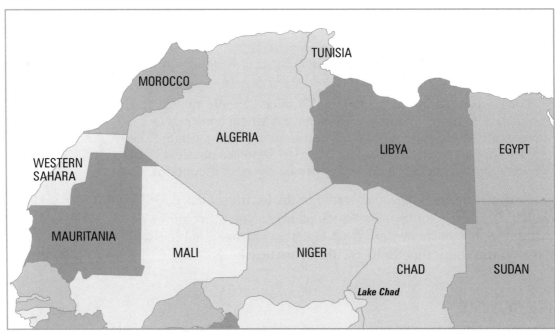

Many North African countries have political borders that are straight lines.

Governments want to control their borders. They want to decide *who* is coming into their country. Government officials at the borders **check**, that is, take a careful look at, everyone who enters. Only people who have permission to enter the country can come in. The government also wants to know *what* is crossing the border, so officials also check everything that enters the country. Most governments make money on the things that people bring into their countries. In many countries, there is a tax on things that enter the country. A **tax** is money that you must pay to the government. For example, when Brazilians bring a new computer from the United States into Brazil, they have to pay money to Brazil's government.

Governments also want to control the ocean near their borders. They want to be sure their country is safe, so they do not want dangerous people to come near their country. There is an international law about this. It says that a country owns the ocean within 13.8 miles (22.2 kilometers) of that country's **shore**. However, there is another important reason why countries want to control the ocean near their shores. The ocean and the land under the ocean have many natural resources, such as fish and oil. Countries want to use these resources, and they do not want other countries to use them. There is an international law that says that a country may use the natural resources within 124.3 miles (200 kilometers) of its shore. Other countries may not use them. However, no country controls the ocean or its resources more than 124.3 miles from its shore. (See Figure 1.2.)

3

Find a clue in this sentence that signals a definition of *check*. Circle the clue, and highlight the definition.

Look in the rest of this sentence for a definition of *tax*. Highlight it.

4

Look at the map to help you guess the meaning of *shore*. Write a definition in the margin.

FIGURE 1.2 The Area in the Ocean that a Country Controls

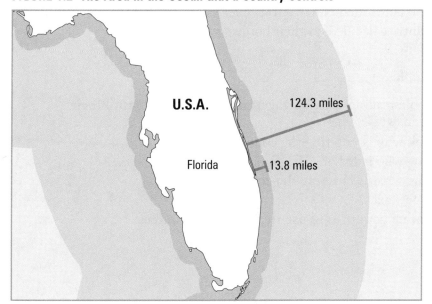

U.S.A.

124.3 miles

Florida

13.8 miles

There are international laws about who controls the ocean near a country's shore.

What about the air near a country's border? Can a country 5
control that, too? The international law that controls the air
around a country is the same as the law about the ocean. Every
country controls the airspace within 13.8 miles of its borders.
A plane must ask permission to fly in that space. International
laws like this are another way to control national borders.

MAIN IDEA CHECK

The main idea of a reading is what the whole reading is about.

Which sentence gives the main idea of Reading 1?
   a Long ago there were no physical or political borders.
   b There are different laws about borders on the land, in the ocean, and in
      the air.
   c Borders help governments control who and what comes into a country.
   d If two countries cannot decide on their borders, they often go to war.

A CLOSER LOOK

Look back at Reading 1 to answer the following questions.

1 A river can be a physical border. True or False? (Par. 1)

2 How did many of the borders in North Africa begin? (Par. 2)
   a The borders followed the rivers, which are very straight.
   b The borders were physical features.
   c The Europeans who controlled North Africa decided on the borders.
   d North African countries decided on their borders when they
      became independent.

3 Fish and oil are examples of _____. (Par. 4)

4 According to the whole reading, why do governments want to control their
   borders? Circle four answers.
   a They want to know who is entering the country.
   b They want to know who is leaving the county.
   c They want to know what is entering the country.
   d They want to collect taxes.
   e They don't want other countries to use their natural resources.

5 Draw a line from the beginning of a sentence in Column A to its correct ending in Column B. (Pars. 4 and 5)

COLUMN A	COLUMN B
No country controls the water that is	within 13.8 miles of the shore.
Each country owns the ocean	within 124.3 miles of the shore.
Every country controls the airspace that is	more than 124.3 miles from the shore.
Every country controls natural resources that are	within 13.8 miles of the border.

VOCABULARY STUDY: DEFINITIONS

Find words in Reading 1 that can complete the following definitions. If you need help, use Key Vocabulary from the Readings on page 251.

1 Something that you can see or touch is _____. (adj) Par. 1

2 A/An _____ line is the closest distance from one place to another place. (adj) Par. 2

3 _____ are an important part of something and are easy to notice. (n pl) Par. 2

4 To _____ something is to have power over it. (v) Par. 3

5 To _____ something is to look at it carefully to make sure it is correct. (v) Par. 3

6 The _____ is the land at the side of an ocean, lake, or large river. (n) Par. 4

7 _____ are valuable things that belong to a person, group, or country. (n pl) Par. 4

8 If you allow people to do something, you give them _____ to do it. (n) Par. 5

VOCABULARY STUDY: WORD FAMILIES

Word families are different *parts of speech* that have similar meanings. Some parts of speech are *verbs*, *nouns*, *adjectives*, and *adverbs*. When you learn a word, learn the other words in its word family, too. This will help you to increase your vocabulary.

WORD FORM	PART OF SPEECH
to accept	verb
acceptance	noun
acceptable	adjective
acceptably	adverb

Read the words in the following chart. The words in **bold** are the parts of speech that appear in Reading 1. Find these words in the reading. If you need help, use Key Vocabulary from the Readings on page 251.

NOUN	ADJECTIVE
care	***careful***
danger	***dangerous***
nation	***national***
official	*official*
safety	***safe***

Choose the correct form of the words from the chart to complete the following sentences. Use the correct verb tenses and subject-verb agreement. Use the correct singular and plural noun forms.

1 Most countries have a/an _____ song. Children sing the song in school.

2 The government _____ at the border watched the travelers when they entered the airport.

3 It is _____ to drive when you are very tired.

4 She kept the important papers in a/an _____ place where no one could find them.

5 The workers checked the machines with great _____. They wanted to be sure the machines were working correctly.

6 There are 13 _____ in South America.

7 He left the country because of the _____ of war.

8   The city of Bombay changed its _____ name to Mumbai
    in 1996.

9   The factory has many rules about _____, so that workers do
    not get injured.

10 If you are _____ when you take tests, you might not make
    any mistakes.

BEYOND THE READING

Research
Find a map of your own country or a country you know well. Study the borders.
Look for any physical borders, like mountains or rivers. Find answers to the
following questions:
- Which countries share a border with the country you chose to research?
- Are there any physical borders? What are they?
- What is the history of the borders?

Discussion
Share your research with a partner or your classmates.

Writing
Write a short description of the borders in the country you researched.

READING 2
WALLS AS BORDERS

GETTING INTO THE TOPIC

A  B  C

Look at the three photographs of famous walls. Which photo matches each of the walls? (The answers are on page 18.)

1 _____ Great Wall, China (fifth century BCE)

2 _____ Hadrian's Wall, England (second century CE)

3 _____ Berlin Wall, Germany (1961)

GETTING A FIRST IDEA ABOUT THE READING

Read the title above and the first four sentences of Reading 2 below. Then answer the questions that follow.

> Today most national borders are lines on a map. Two countries agree on the line between them. However, in the past, some countries had walls or fences on their borders. Walls had several purposes.

1 What do you think this reading will be about? Circle four answers.
   a Border walls that were built a long time ago
   b Famous walls
   c How to build a strong border wall
   d The reason that countries build walls at their borders
   e Walls that are at the border of some countries today

2 Why do you think countries built walls on their borders long ago?
3 Why do you think countries build walls on their borders today?

WHILE YOU READ

As you read, stop at the end of each sentence that contains words in **bold**. Then follow the instructions in the box in the margin.

Walls as Borders

Today, most national borders are lines on a map. Two countries agree on the line between them. However, in the past, some countries had walls or fences on their borders. Walls had several purposes. They helped to prevent **invasions**, that is, the arrival of enemies. Walls were also a good way to make money. There were often only a few entrances in a wall. People had to pay taxes when they went through these entrances. In more recent times, walls also have had other purposes. Some walls prevent people from leaving their country. Other walls stop people from entering a country. These people are often looking for jobs and are hoping for a better life on the other side of the wall.

Two of the most famous walls in history are the Great Wall of China and Hadrian's Wall. The Great Wall of China is 5,500 miles (8,850 kilometers) long and more than 29.5 feet (9 meters) wide in some places. The Chinese built it to stop invaders from entering China. Along the top of the wall, there were thousands of **guards**. These guards were men who could see anyone who came near the wall. In England, the Romans built Hadrian's Wall in the second century CE. Like the Great Wall of China, its major purpose was also to stop invaders. However, it had another purpose: People had to pay the Romans to come through Hadrian's Wall.

The most famous twentieth-century wall is the Berlin Wall. After World War II, East and West Germany became separate. The Soviet Union controlled East Germany. At first, people could still travel between East and West Berlin. However, the Soviet Union wanted to stop this, so in 1961, it built the Berlin Wall. The purpose of this wall was not to stop invaders. It was to prevent the people of East Berlin from leaving. On August 13, 1961, all travel between East and West Berlin suddenly stopped. No one could cross the border. Some people tried to climb over the wall, but this was dangerous. East German guards killed some of these people. More than one hundred people were killed trying to cross the border before the Berlin Wall came down in 1989.

1

2

3

Find a clue in this sentence that signals a definition of *invasion*. Circle the clue, and highlight the definition.

Look in the next sentence to help you guess the meaning of *guards*. What do guards do: (a) keep people safe or (b) build walls? Circle the answer.

A guard at the Berlin Wall prevents people from crossing the border.

Look in the rest of this sentence for a definition of *electronic fence*. Highlight it.

Today, the newest walls are electronic. For example, many people attempt to enter the United States from Mexico without permission every year. Many of these people are searching for jobs in the United States. The United States has tried to stop them with fences and walls at the border. However, the border is very long, and in some places there are no physical walls or fences. Instead, there is an electronic fence in some places. An **electronic fence** is a group of computers and cameras that can tell the guards when people are crossing the border, so the guards can stop them. The United States continues to build both physical and electronic fences.

4

People cross into the United States without permission every day.

Walls and fences **divide** people. Often people with more money and easier lives are on one side. Poorer people with more difficult lives are on the other side. However, walls and fences cannot always stop people from crossing the border. For example, the fence at the Mexican border does not stop everyone from crossing. Government officials believe that half a million people enter the United States from Mexico without permission every year. People wanting a better life will continue to try to cross borders.

Look in the next two sentences for a definition of *divide*. Highlight it.

MAIN IDEA CHECK

The main idea of a reading is what the whole reading is about.

Which sentence gives the main idea of Reading 2?

a Walls can stop people from entering a country.

b Walls and fences help governments to make money and keep people safe.

c The most famous walls in history are the Great Wall of China and the Berlin Wall.

d In the past and today, walls at borders have had different purposes.

A CLOSER LOOK

Look back at Reading 2 to answer the following questions.

1 Which of the following is *not* a purpose for a wall on a border? (Par. 1)
   a Walls can give people a better life.
   b Walls stop enemies from entering the country.
   c Walls stop people from leaving the country.
   d Walls help the government collect money from people when they enter
     the country.

2 Hadrian's Wall protected China in the second century CE. True or False?
   (Par. 2)

3 Which of the following statements are correct? Circle two answers. (Par. 3)
   a East German guards killed some people who tried to climb over the wall.
   b The Soviet Union killed some Germans who tried to enter East Berlin.
   c The wall stopped invaders from the Soviet Union.
   d The purpose of the wall was to stop travel between East and West Berlin.
   e The Berlin Wall was built during World War II.

4 What is the main reason why many people try to enter the United States
   from Mexico even if they do not have permission? (Par. 4)
   a They don't like living in Mexico.
   b They think the wall is unfair.
   c They don't want to pay taxes.
   d They want to find good jobs.

5 Reread paragraph 4. Write two differences between an electronic fence and
   an ordinary fence.

   _____

   _____

6 Draw a line from the name of the wall in the left column to the purpose of
   the wall in the right column. In one case, a wall has two purposes. Draw
   two lines from that wall to the two different purposes.

WALL	PURPOSE
The Great Wall of China	to stop people from leaving
Hadrian's Wall	to stop people from entering without permission
The Berlin Wall	to stop enemy invaders
Fences on the Mexico–United States border	to make money from taxes

VOCABULARY STUDY: DEFINITIONS

Find words in Reading 2 that can complete the following definitions. If you need help, use Key Vocabulary from the Readings on page 251.

1 To _____ about something is to think the same thing about it. (v) Par. 1

2 _____ are walls made of metal or wood. (n pl) Par. 1

3 People who work against other people and try to hurt them are _____. (n pl) Par. 1

4 Something that happened a short time ago is _____. (adj) Par. 1

5 People who watch or protect a person or a place are _____. (n pl) Par. 2

6 Something that is independent or apart from something else is _____. (adj) Par. 3

7 When something happens very quickly, it happens _____. (adv) Par. 3

8 Machines that use computers or part of computers are _____. (adj) Par. 4

VOCABULARY STUDY: WORDS IN CONTEXT

Complete the following sentences with words from the list below. If necessary, review the words in Key Vocabulary from the Readings on page 251.

purpose	prevented	invasion	entrance
major	attempt	searched	divide

1 Dogs _____ for the man who was lost in the mountains.

2 The _____ of the new machine is to make our work easier.

3 There was a/an _____ by an army of 20,000 men.

4 Guards closed the doors and _____ people from entering the bank after 5:00 p.m.

5 Mountains _____ the country into two parts.

6 She stood at the _____ of her house and said hello to her friends when they arrived.

7 The teacher explained the two _____ causes of the war.

8 Travelers should not _____ to climb mountains during the winter.

VOCABULARY REVIEW: SAME OR DIFFERENT

The following pairs of sentences contain vocabulary from Readings 1 and 2 in this unit. Write *S* on the blank line if the two sentences have the same meaning. Write *D* if the meanings are different.

_____ 1 Officials searched the building for the dangerous man.

The guards checked visitors as they entered the country.

_____ 2 The cat tried to climb over the fence.

The cat attempted to get under the wall.

_____ 3 The purpose of the wall is to prevent enemies from coming into our country.

The wall is for our safety. It stops invasions.

_____ 4 The map showed the country's physical features.

The map showed the country's rivers, mountains, lakes, and shores.

_____ 5 The little boys agreed to divide their food.

Both little boys wanted to eat their food slowly.

BEYOND THE READING

Research

Find out if there are any fences or walls on the border of your country or a country that you know well. Find answers to the following questions:

- What is the purpose of the wall or fence?
- When was it built?
- How successful has it been?

Discussion

Share your research with a partner or your classmates.

Writing

Write a short summary of your research. Describe the wall or fence and its history.

Answers to the question on page 12.

1 A
2 C
3 B

SKILLS AND STRATEGIES 2
FINDING THE TOPIC OF A PARAGRAPH

Most paragraphs have one topic. The topic is the general subject of the paragraph. It is what the paragraph is about. Usually you can find the topic at the beginning of the paragraph. Sometimes, however, you will have to read the whole paragraph to find the topic. Finding the topic of a paragraph is an important reading skill.

EXAMPLES & EXPLANATIONS

Examples

Today people cross national borders much more often than they did one hundred years ago. Cars and planes help us move easily from one country to another. You can get on a plane and a few hours later arrive in another country on the other side of the world.

Explanations

The topic is often at the beginning of the paragraph. In this paragraph, the topic is *crossing national borders*.

However, this easy movement can also cause problems. The spread of disease is the most serious problem. When people move around the world, diseases sometimes move with them. As a result, at many borders, government officials check to see if travelers are sick. Sick travelers may have to see a doctor or take some medicine before they can enter the country.

The topic is not always in the first sentence. The first sentence in this paragraph says there are problems, but the second sentence gives the topic: *the spread of disease*. In addition, many of the words in this paragraph, such as *sick*, *doctor*, and *medicine*, give clues to the topic. These words can help you understand that the topic is *the spread of disease*.

One example of this is SARS. In 2003, this serious disease appeared in China. It spread quickly around Asia and to Canada. More than 8,000 people became sick, and more than 700 people died. Government officials at borders around the world checked travelers, especially from China and Canada, to see if they were sick. Travelers with SARS were prevented from entering the country.

The topics of the first two paragraphs are *crossing borders* and *disease*. In this paragraph, there are a lot of specific details about one disease. The topic of this paragraph is *the spread of a disease called SARS*.

STRATEGIES

These strategies will help you find the topic of a paragraph while you read.

- As you read the paragraph, ask yourself: *What is this paragraph about?*
- Pay attention to the first sentence. It often gives the topic of the paragraph.
- Look for words and phrases that are all connected to the same topic. They can help you figure out the topic of the whole paragraph.

SKILL PRACTICE 1

Read the following paragraphs. Then look at the four possible topic choices for the paragraph. Circle the best choice. Discuss your answers with a partner.

1   In the early 1800s, many people came to the United States from different countries. These people are called *immigrants*. The United States wanted immigrants to come to work on farms and factories. The government did not check the immigrants' health. In the 1880s, the number of immigrants increased quickly. The government began to worry about diseases. It worried that the immigrants were bringing diseases.

Topic:
a The history of immigration
b Health and immigration
c Immigrant workers
d Health in the United States

2   In 1891, the government began to check the health of all immigrants. There were doctors and hospitals at the border. The largest number of immigrants – about 70 percent of them – came through New York, so the largest hospital was there. The doctors looked for two kinds of diseases. The first were dangerous diseases that might spread from one person to another. The second were diseases that might prevent the person from working. The government only wanted immigrants who were healthy enough to work hard.

Topic:
a Immigrants in New York
b Checking immigrants' health
c Dangerous diseases
d Government doctors on the U.S. border

3   If immigrants had either of these kinds of diseases, they could not enter the country. If the doctors believed that the people would get better, they sent them to a hospital. The people stayed in the hospital until they were healthy again. Their friends and families had to wait for them. If the doctors believed the immigrants would not get better, sometimes they sent them back to their countries.

Topic:

a Immigrants with diseases

b Immigrant families

c Two diseases

d Immigration and immigrants

SKILL PRACTICE 2

Read the following paragraphs. After each paragraph, stop and think about the topic. Then write the topic on the blank line.

1   Computer chips are very small, but they can store a lot of information. Many credit cards and passports have computer chips inside of them. These are called *smart cards*. Look at a credit card. It may have a black line on the back. Computers can read this black line. It tells the computer a lot of important information.

Topic: _____

2   Many people use passwords. A password is a secret number, word, or group of letters. You may use a password to get into your computer, your bank, or the school library. You should never use your telephone number or birthday as your password, because other people may know them. You should also choose different passwords for different purposes. Have you ever forgotten a password? When people have a lot of different passwords, they sometimes forget them.

Topic: _____

3   People often worry about their pet dogs and cats. They worry that their pet will run away or get lost. How will they be able to find their pet? Some pets wear something around their necks that has information about them. For example, the information might give the pet's name and address. What happens if the pet loses this information? The pet may never come home. Because some people worry about this, they put a computer chip under their pet's skin. The chip has the information about the pet. If someone finds the pet, a computer can read the information on the chip. This helps the dog or cat return home.

Topic: _____

READING 3
BORDER CONTROL

GETTING INTO THE TOPIC

Discuss the following questions with a partner.

1 What usually happens when people cross a border into a different country? Do they have to show anything to the officials at the border? Do they have to answer any questions? Can they take what they want with them over the border?

2 Have you or someone you know ever had an unusual experience crossing a border? What happened?

GETTING A FIRST IDEA ABOUT THE READING

It is a good idea to look at a reading quickly before you read it carefully. This is called *previewing*. Previewing gives you information about what you are going to read. One way to do this is to read the title and look at any pictures, photographs, or charts.

Read the title and the headings in Reading 3. Then look at the photographs on pages 24 and 25. What do they tell you about the content of the reading? Complete the chart and discuss your answers with a partner.

	POSSIBLE CONTENT OF THE READING
TITLE	
HEADINGS	
PHOTOGRAPHS	

WHILE YOU READ

As you read, stop at the end of each sentence that contains words in **bold**. Then follow the instructions in the box in the margin.

Border Control

I. DOCUMENTS AT THE BORDER

What happens when you cross a national border? The answer is not the same in every country. When you enter most countries, you need a **passport** – a document that governments give to their citizens that allows them to travel to other countries. Passports include important information such as name, birth date, and birthplace. Most passports also include a photograph. When you enter most countries, you must show a passport. However, this is not true for many countries in Europe. When Europeans cross a national border between countries in the European Union, they do not need to show a passport.

A passport is not the only type of travel document. A visa is another important travel document. Many countries require travelers to have a visa when they enter. The type of visa depends on which country you come from and the reason for your visit. There are several types of visas. If you go for a short visit, you may need a tourist visa. If you want to study, you need a student visa. If you want to find a job in the country, **you probably need a business or work visa**.

II. NEW TECHNOLOGY AT THE BORDER

Government officials at national borders look very carefully at passports and visas. They want to be sure that the people who are entering the country are not dangerous. They use technology to help them decide who may enter the country. For example, when travelers enter the country, officials at the border check their computers for important information about these travelers. They can check if travelers have been in the country before and if they have done something wrong. Officials also examine each traveler's documents to see if they are real. Some people try to cross the border without permission. They use fake passports or visas. Officials at the border can use computer technology to check whether these documents are real or fake.

Technology has been helpful in other ways, too. In the second half of the twentieth century, passports were the major form of identification for travelers. Now there are new forms of identification that use technology. One example is a machine that can read fingerprints. When travelers enter the country, they put their fingers on a machine that **scans** them. In other words, the machine takes a picture of the fingerprints and saves the picture in a computer. It can also send the picture

Find a clue in this sentence that signals a definition of *passport*. Circle the clue, and highlight the definition.

What is the topic of paragraph 2? Write it in the margin.

Look in the next sentence for a clue that signals a definition of *scan*. Circle the clue, and highlight the definition.

to government officials who are far from the border. Those officials can compare the picture to fingerprints of many other people. If the traveler's fingerprints are the same as fingerprints of a dangerous person, the traveler may not enter the country. In 2007, about 30 airports around the world began to use this technology.

A fingerprint. Officials compare travelers' fingerprints to keep dangerous people out of the country.

One person's fingerprints are different from another person's fingerprints. Therefore, many countries use fingerprints as a good form of identification. However, it is possible to trick the machines that scan them. In 2008, a woman at a Japanese airport put tape on her fingers. The tape had another person's fingerprints on it, so she was able to enter Japan without permission.

As a result of these problems, some airports are using another part of the body for identification – the **iris**. The iris is the colored part of the eye. New machines can scan travelers' irises and save the pictures. Several airports have started to use this technology, including Heathrow Airport in England. Irises work better than fingerprints for identification. The iris has hundreds of very small lines in it. These lines are **unique**. In other words, everyone's iris is different. Even twins have different irises. These new forms of technology have another advantage. They are fast. This makes lines at airports and borders shorter and helps travelers move more quickly.

Look in the next sentence for a definition of *iris*. Highlight it.

Look in the next sentence for a clue that signals a definition of *unique*. Circle the clue, and highlight the definition.

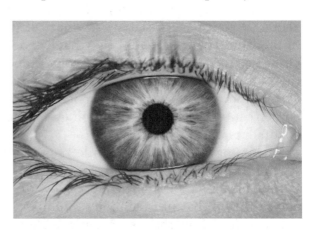

An Iris. New machines can quickly scan irises for identification.

III. CROSSING BORDERS IN THE FUTURE

Passports, visas, fingerprint scans, and iris scans are all forms of identification that governments can use today. Sometime in the future, there might be new forms of identification. You might not need paper documents. You may not need to scan your fingers or eyes. You will store all of your important information on a computer chip. This computer chip will be inside a small card, or perhaps under your skin. Computers will quickly read, save, and send the information on the card when you **cross the border**.

What is the topic of paragraph 7? Write it in the margin.

Long ago, there were no national borders. People moved around freely. They moved to find food or somewhere to live. They did not think about borders or documents. Some people believe that in the future, national borders will become less important. Some borders may disappear. People will move freely again. They will travel quickly and easily around the world for education, for work, or simply to see new places.

New technology will help travelers cross borders more quickly in the future.

MAIN IDEA CHECK

The main idea of a reading is what the whole reading is about.

Which sentence gives the main idea of Reading 3?

    a Paper documents are not important anymore.

    b It is important to have correct documents when you cross a national border.

    c In the future, there will be no national borders.

    d The way that officials check travelers at the borders is changing.

A CLOSER LOOK

Look back at Reading 3 to answer the following questions.

1 Which of the following is *not* information on most passports? (Par. 1)

    a Birth date

    b Birthplace

    c Name

    d Address

    e Photograph

2 If you want to visit a country for one week, you will probably need a/an _____ visa. (Par. 2)

3 According to section II, how has technology helped government officials? Circle three answers.

    a Computers can check if travelers have done anything wrong.

    b Machines can scan travelers' eyes.

    c Computers can make fake documents.

    d Computers can tape travelers' fingerprints.

    e Machines can scan travelers' fingerprints.

4 What happens if computers show that a traveler's fingerprints are the same as fingerprints of a dangerous person? (Par. 4)

    a The traveler needs a new passport.

    b The traveler must have an iris scan.

    c The traveler may not enter the country.

    d The traveler must give his passport to officials at the border.

5 How did the woman at the Japanese airport trick the fingerprint scanner? (Par. 5)

    a Her fingerprints were not on her passport.

    b She used a fake passport.

    c She taped another person's fingerprints onto her fingers.

    d She used the iris scanner instead of the fingerprint scanner.

6 Twins have the same lines in their irises. True or False? (Par. 6)

7 Reread paragraphs 5 and 6. Write two reasons why iris scanners may be better than fingerprint scanners.

_____

_____

8 What might be the next step in technology at borders? (Par. 7)
   a Borders will disappear.
   b People will store all their information on a computer chip.
   c People will move freely everywhere.
   d Passports will disappear.

VOCABULARY STUDY: DEFINITIONS

Find words in Reading 3 that can complete the following definitions. If you need help, use Key Vocabulary from the Readings on page 251.

1 A/an _____ is an official piece of paper. (*n*) Par. 1

2 _____ are people who belong to a country. (*n pl*) Par. 1

3 A person who visits a place for fun is a/an _____. (*n*) Par. 2

4 The knowledge and methods used in science and industry is _____. (*n*) Par. 3

5 Your _____ is a card or piece of paper that says who you are. (*n*) Par. 4

6 _____ is something you can use to attach one thing to another thing. (*n*) Par. 5

7 Two brothers, two sisters, or a brother and a sister who are born at the same time are _____. (*n pl*) Par. 6

8 When things _____, people can no longer see them. (*v*) Par. 8

VOCABULARY STUDY: SYNONYMS

Read the sentences below. The words or phrases in parentheses mean the same or almost the same as the words in the list. For each sentence, replace the words in parentheses with a word (or phrase) from the list. Write it on the blank line. If necessary, review the words in Key Vocabulary from the Readings on page 251.

examine	require	unique	advantages
depends on	store	fake	trick

1 This painting is (not real) _____.

2 They are very sick, and they (need) _____ a doctor.

3 The price of airplane tickets (changes with) _____ the cost of oil.

4 This is a/an (very, very unusual) _____ flower. There are no others like it.

5 The girl tried to (fool) _____ her parents. She broke a plate, but she told her parents that her sister broke it.

6 My new computer has two (good things) _____. It is very fast, and it is not expensive.

7 We will need to (look at) _____ the situation very carefully.

8 They (keep) _____ bread and cake in a box in the kitchen.

VOCABULARY REVIEW: ACADEMIC WORD LIST

As you read academic texts, you will find some words appear frequently, even if the topics of the texts are very different. These words are part of an important list of words called the Academic Word List (AWL). Learning words on the Academic Word List will help you to improve your reading, writing, and test taking.

The following are AWL words from all the readings in Unit 1. Complete the sentences below with these words. If necessary, review the AWL words in Key Vocabulary from the Readings on page 251.

identification (n)	tape (n)	technology (n)	features (n)	major (adj)
resources (n)	require (v)	documents (n)	physical (adj)	unique (adj)

1 She put important _____, such as her passport, under her bed.

2 The country's most important natural _____ are oil, gas, and gold.

3 _____, especially the use of computers, has changed many things in business, government, and education.

4 On a trip to Antarctica, you will _____ warm clothes.

5 Scientists said the fish was _____. It was the only one in the world.

6 The teacher used _____ to put the children's pictures on the wall.

7 All citizens must carry a/an _____ card when they leave the country.

8 One of the most famous _____ of Egypt is the Nile River.

9 During the twentieth century, there were several _____ wars.

10 As children grow, their _____ abilities increase. They can run, jump, and throw things.

BEYOND THE READING

Research
Find out about border control in your country or a country that you know well. Find answers to the following questions:
- Do all visitors need a visa to visit?
- Do citizens of the country need a visa to visit other countries? Which countries?
- Do officials at the airports use technology? What kind of technology?

Discussion
Share your research with a partner or your classmates.

Writing
Write a short summary of your research. Describe border control in the country you researched.

MAKING CONNECTIONS

The vocabulary in these exercises comes from all the readings in Unit 1. The exercises will help you see how writers make connections across sentences in a paragraph.

One way that writers make connections is by referring to the same thing in more than one sentence. They can do this with pronouns. A *pronoun* refers to a noun that comes before it. In the following example, the pronoun is in **bold**, and the thing it refers to is underlined. The arrow shows the connection.

Government officials work at the border. **They** check all passports.

Sometimes pronouns refer to ideas. In the following example, the pronoun is in **bold**, and the idea it refers to is underlined. The arrow shows that the pronoun refers to the whole idea in the first sentence.

There was a long line of trucks and cars at the border crossing. **This** delayed the tour bus for three hours.

Here is a list of some common pronouns that help make connections. When you see a pronoun, ask yourself: *What does this pronoun refer to?*

he	she	it	they	this	that	these	those

EXERCISE 1

Read the following groups of sentences. Highlight the pronoun in the second sentence in each group. Underline the noun or idea the pronoun refers to. Draw an arrow from the pronoun to the underlined item. The first one has been done for you.

1 I gave my passport to the official. He examined the photo carefully.

2 Everyone is required to show some kind of identification. The guard at the entrance will ask for it.

3 All the documents are electronic. They are stored on one computer.

4 There were three attempts to guess the password. They all failed.

5 Each person's iris is unique. That is the reason irises are good forms of identification.

6 There were separate lines for visitors and citizens. This made it faster for citizens to come back into the country.

EXERCISE 2

Make a clear paragraph by putting sentences A, B, and C into the best order after the numbered sentence. Look for pronouns to help you. Write the letters in the correct order on the blank lines.

1 The fence along the border prevents people from entering. ___ ___ ___

A	These help officials see if anyone is trying to come across the fence at night.	B	It is very high and has a lot of lights.	C	That is the time when most people try to cross the border without permission.

2 All Americans need to know about recent changes at the Mexican border.

___ ___ ___

A	They began in January.	B	The most important change affects American tourists.	C	They now have to show passports as identification instead of drivers' licenses.

3 Tourists should check the government Web site before they travel.

___ ___ ___

A	These could make travel in those countries difficult for foreign citizens.	B	This helps people understand when there are dangerous political situations.	C	It has information about safety in different countries.

4 The invasion was a complete surprise. ___ ___ ___

A	Enemy soldiers crossed the border at night.	B	They took control of the major city.	C	It happened suddenly, with no warning.

5 The information is stored on a computer chip in your passport.

___ ___ ___

A	They worry that someone with the right technology can steal the information.	B	A computer can then scan it when you go through customs.	C	Some people don't like this.

Names

SKILLS AND STRATEGIES 3-4
- Noticing Parts of Words (1)
- Finding the Main Idea of a Paragraph

READINGS
- Where Does Your Name Come From?
- Changing Names
- Names in Business

SKILLS AND STRATEGIES 3
NOTICING PARTS OF WORDS (1)

One way to understand the meaning of a word you don't know is to notice the parts of the word. Sometimes a group of letters is added to the beginning or the end of a word to change its meaning. A group of letters added to the beginning of a word is called a *prefix*. A prefix creates a new word. A group of letters added to the end of a word is called a *suffix*. A suffix can tell you what part of speech a word is. For example, it can tell you if the word is a *noun*, a *verb*, or an *adjective*. Good readers can use prefixes and suffixes to help them figure out a word's meaning.

EXAMPLES & EXPLANATIONS

Examples

I have an **un**usual name. People often **mis**pronounce it.

Explanations

When you add a prefix to a word, it creates a new word. This new word has a different meaning from the old word.

unusual = not usual
mispronounce = pronounce the wrong way

The teach**er** asked for his name and checked his identifica**tion**.

Many suffixes help you identify nouns.

teacher = a person who teaches
identification = someone or something used to identify

Many cities are named after other cities that are more fam**ous**. Twenty-three towns in the United States are named after the beauti**ful** city of Paris, France.

Suffixes also help you identify adjectives.

famous = having fame
beautiful = full of beauty

They want to modern**ize** the name of their store. They are going to short**en** it to GT.

Suffixes also help you identify verbs.

modernize = make modern
shorten = make short

THE LANGUAGE OF PREFIXES AND SUFFIXES

Here are some common prefixes and suffixes and their meanings.

PREFIXES	NOUN SUFFIXES	ADJECTIVE SUFFIXES	VERB SUFFIXES

in-, un-, dis-
not
 	
inter-
between
 	
mis-
wrong
 	
re-
again, back
	-er, -ist, -or
	a person or thing
	  that does
	  something
	
	-tion, -ment
	an action, idea,
	  or process
		-al, -an, -ish, -ous
		connected to
		  something
		
		-less
		without something
		
		-ful
		with something
			-en, -ify, -ize
			make or cause
			  something to be

STRATEGIES

These strategies will help you notice parts of words. They will help you understand the meanings of words while you read.

- Study and learn the meanings of the prefixes and suffixes in the chart.
- To learn more prefixes and suffixes, find a dictionary or a source on the Internet that lists prefixes and suffixes.
- If you see a word you don't know, notice if the word has a prefix or a suffix.
- If the word has a prefix, does the prefix help you understand the meaning of the word?
- If the word has a suffix, does the suffix help you identify the word as a *noun* (a person or thing), an *adjective* (a description of a person or thing), or a *verb* (an action)?
- Look at the whole sentence. Notice how the word connects to the other words and the general meaning of the sentence.

SKILL PRACTICE 1

Read the following sentences, and notice the different parts of the words in **bold**. Circle any prefixes or suffixes you see in the words. The first one has been done for you.

1 The **act(or)** changed his name after he became famous.

2 The baby's parents **disagreed** about what to name their baby.

3 The teacher was **careless** and always called his students by the wrong names.

4 They **renamed** their store last year, but everyone still calls it by its old name.

5 The **unofficial** name of their football team is the "Green Men."

6 Their name was difficult to spell, so they decided to **simplify** it.

7 In some **African** countries, the day when you are born becomes part of your name.

8 Some **interstate** highways in the United States are named after famous people.

SKILL PRACTICE 2

Read the sentences in Skill Practice 1 again. Look at the prefixes or suffixes you circled in each sentence. Then figure out the definitions for the words in **bold**. Write the definitions on the blank lines. The first one has been done for you.

1 The **actor** changed his name after he became famous.

   actor = <u>a person who acts</u>

2 The baby's parents **disagreed** about what to name their baby.

   disagreed = _____

3 The teacher was **careless** and always called his students by the wrong names.

   careless = _____

4 They **renamed** their store last year, but everyone still calls it by its old name.

   renamed = _____

5 The **unofficial** name of their football team is the "Green Men."

   unofficial = _____

6 Their name was difficult to spell, so they decided to **simplify** it.

   simplify = _____

7 In some **African** countries, the day when you are born becomes part of your name.

   African = _____

8 Some **interstate** highways in the United States are named after famous people.

   interstate = _____

READING 1

WHERE DOES YOUR NAME COME FROM?

GETTING INTO THE TOPIC

Discuss the following questions with a partner.

1 What is your full name?
2 Which part of your name is your family name?
3 Does your family name come first or last?
4 Does your name mean something? If so, what does it mean?
5 How did you get your name?

GETTING A FIRST IDEA ABOUT THE READING

As you learned in Getting a First Idea about the Reading on page 22, *previewing* is a good way to get an idea of what the reading will be about.

Read the title, and look at the photograph and table on pages 38 and 39 in Reading 1. What do you think this reading will be about? What topics do you think will be in the reading? Write your answers below.

1 I think this reading will be about _____

_____ .

2 Circle the topics that you think might be in the reading.
   a The history of names
   b Names of famous people
   c How to say people's names
   d Common names around the world
   e How people choose names

WHILE YOU READ

As you read, stop at the end of each sentence that contains words in **bold**. Then follow the instructions in the box in the margin.

Where Does Your Name Come From?

Naming customs are different around the world. For example, not everyone has the same number of names. In some countries, such as Indonesia, many people have just one name. In most cultures, however, people have at least two names: a family name and a **given** name. Your given name is the name you receive when you are born. Your family name is the name you share with other people in your family.

Look in the next sentence for a definition of *given name*. Highlight it.

In English, the family name is often called the *last name*, and the given name is often called the *first name*. However, the order of the two names is not the same everywhere. For example, in many Asian countries, the family name is first and the given name is second. When people from different cultures meet, sometimes they use the **incorrect** name. When this happens, it can be very embarrassing.

Circle the prefix in *incorrect*. Then write a definition for *incorrect* in the margin.

People from different countries meet and learn each other's names.

What is the origin of family names? Many come from the name of a place, like *London*, or a job, such as *Farmer* or *Shoemaker*. In some countries, there are many different family names. In other countries, there are only a few. In South Korea, there are only about 250 family names. About half of all Koreans have one of the three most common family names – Kim, Park, or Lee. This can cause a problem, because most Koreans believe you should not marry a person with the same last name. This means Koreans must be careful whom they fall **in love with**!

What do you think the topic of this paragraph will be? Write it in the margin.

Was the topic you wrote in the margin correct? Put a check (✓) next to it if it was correct.

TABLE 2.1 The World's Most Common Family Names by Country

Country	Most Common Family Name
Brazil	Silva
China	Wang
France	Martin
Germany	Müller
Japan	Sato
South Korea	Kim
Mexico	Hernández
Poland	Nowak
Spain	García
United Kingdom	Smith
United States	Smith
Vietnam	Nguyen

Source: Wikipedia

There is generally no choice about a family name, but there 4 is much more choice about given names. Parents choose their child's name for many different reasons. They may select a name that sounds beautiful or means something special. These names may have meanings like *peace* or *strong*. In some cultures, parents may pay money to a professional to help them find a good name. They want to find a name that will be lucky for their child.

It is also common to give a child a name that is the same 5 as the name of a parent or grandparent. Another common choice is to name the child after a famous **religious** person. For example, many Mexicans have names such as Jesús or María. Many Egyptians have the name of the Muslim leader, Muhammed. Some parents choose the name of a famous political leader. After the election of President Barack Obama, some parents in the United States and Kenya chose the name Barack.

Sometimes names become popular for a short time. Parents 6 may choose the name of a popular actor or singer. For example, the singer Madonna made that name popular in the 1980s. However, some parents want a name that is unique. They might invent a new name for their child. In China, many people have the same family name, so some parents invent new given names. They want their children to be a little different from other children.

Circle the suffix in *religious*. Is *religious* (a) a noun, (b) a verb, or (c) an adjective? Circle the answer.

There are many different naming customs, and parents all 7
over the world choose their children's names very carefully.
Your name may show your history and culture, or it may be
unusual. It may be the name of a family member or a famous
person. It may have a special meaning. Do you know why your
parents chose your name?

MAIN IDEA CHECK

The main idea of a reading is what the whole reading is about.

Which sentence gives the main idea of Reading 1?
  a The order of names may be different in different countries.
  b Parents may have many different ideas when they choose their
     child's name.
  c Names have an interesting history.
  d There are many different naming customs around the world.

A CLOSER LOOK

Look back at Reading 1 to answer the following questions.

1 Most people have more than two names. True or False? (Par. 1)

2 What are two common origins of family names? (Par. 3)
  a A job
  b A religious leader
  c A place
  d A famous singer

3 South Korea does not have a lot of family names. Why is this a problem?
   (Par. 3)
  a Soon there will not be enough family names.
  b Koreans prefer not to marry a person with the same last name.
  c Many Koreans do not like these names.
  d Koreans must ask their parents for permission to marry.

4 According to Table 2.1 on page 39, _____ is the most common
   family name in two countries.

5 Some parents pay a professional to help them choose a name. True or False?
   (Par. 4)

6 According to the whole reading, some parents give their children the name of someone famous. Draw a line from the type of famous person in the left column to the example in the right column.

FAMOUS PERSON	EXAMPLE
A religious leader	Madonna
A singer	Barack Obama
A political leader	Muhammed

VOCABULARY STUDY: DEFINITIONS

Find words in Reading 1 that can complete the following definitions. If you need help, use Key Vocabulary from the Readings on page 251.

1 To _____ something is to have the same thing as another person. (v) Par. 1

2 Something that makes you uncomfortable in front of other people is _____. (adj) Par. 2

3 A/An _____ name is a very frequent and usual name. (adj) Par. 3

4 If something is _____ true, this means it is usually true. (adv) Par. 4

5 To _____ something is to choose it. (v) Par. 4

6 A/An _____ is a person who uses special knowledge and training in a job. (n) Par. 4

7 A/An _____ is a person who controls a group or country. (n) Par. 5

8 To _____ something is to create something new. (v) Par. 6

VOCABULARY STUDY: WORD FAMILIES

Read the words in the following chart. The words in **bold** are the parts of speech that appear in Reading 1. Find these words in the reading. If you need help, use Key Vocabulary from the Readings on page 251.

NOUN	ADJECTIVE
culture	cultural
luck	**lucky**
origin	original
popularity	**popular**
religion	**religious**

Choose the correct form of the words from the chart to complete the following sentences. Use the correct verb tenses and subject-verb agreement. Use the correct singular and plural noun forms.

1 The most _____ girls' name in the United States in 1910 was Mary.

2 Hinduism is one of the major _____ of the world.

3 Many English words have a Latin _____.

4 The _____ of given names changes every year. Not many Americans choose the name Mary today.

5 When she went to live in India, she had to learn the rules of a different _____.

6 Many Chinese people like the number eight, because they believe that it is _____.

7 The _____ name for the Internet was "ARPANET." The name changed to "Internet" in the 1980s.

8 Some parents choose _____ names, such as Abraham, Muhammed, or Jesus, for their children.

9 Some people believe it is bad _____ to name a baby before it is born.

10 The teacher planned many different _____ activities for the children to help them understand people from all over the world.

BEYOND THE READING

Research
Find out about naming customs in your country or in another country. Find answers to the following questions:
- What are the three most popular family names in the country?
- What is the most popular given name for baby boys in the country today?
- What is the most popular given name for baby girls in the country today?
- What are some of the naming customs in the country?

Discussion
Share your research with a partner or your classmates.

Writing
Write a short explanation of naming customs in the country you researched. Be sure to give examples.

READING 2
CHANGING NAMES

GETTING INTO THE TOPIC

 Bono
(Paul David
Hewson)

 Mother Teresa
(Agnesë Gonxhe
Bojaxhiu)

 Muhammed Ali
(Cassius Clay)

Read the title of this reading, and look at the photographs of these famous
people. Read their new and original names. Then discuss the following
questions with a partner.

1 Why do you think these people changed their names? Write two
possible reasons.

   a _____

   b _____

2 Would you ever change your name? Explain your answer.

GETTING A FIRST IDEA ABOUT THE READING

As you learned in Skills and Strategies 2 on page 19, most paragraphs
have one topic, and you can usually find the topic at the beginning of
the paragraph.

The following are the first sentences of the paragraphs in Reading 2. Read
these sentences. Then, with a partner, discuss what you think the paragraphs
will be about.

1 Everyone begins life with a name. (Par. 1)
2 In some cultures, a name change is a natural part of life. (Par. 2)
3 Some people change their names when they change their religion. (Par. 3)
4 Immigrants sometimes change their names. (Par. 4)
5 Names that are unusual or different can sometimes make life difficult. (Par. 5)
6 People change their names for many reasons: marriage, a new religion, or a
  new country. (Par. 6)

WHILE YOU READ

As you read, stop at the end of each sentence that contains words in **bold**.
Then follow the instructions in the box in the margin.

Changing names

Everyone begins life with a name. A name becomes an important part of a person's identity. However, sometimes a person's name changes. There are many reasons for name changes, but the most common reason is marriage. Many women change their family name to their husband's family name when they get married. This has been a tradition in the western part of the world for a long time. However, it is more **uncommon** today in North America and Europe. Many women in those places want to keep their own family names, because they are part of their identity. Some couples prefer to use both names. For example, if James Smith marries Sarah Taylor, they could become James and Sarah Smith-Taylor.

Circle the prefix in uncommon. *Then write a definition for* uncommon *in the margin.*

When a couple gets married, sometimes the woman changes her name.

In some cultures, a name change is a **natural** part of life. Some Native Americans get a name when they are born and then get a new name when they are older. Their new name may tell something about them. For example, it may describe a special talent or something important they have done. They could get a new name like Runs Fast or Little Hunter.

Circle the suffix in natural. *Is* natural *(a) a noun, (b) a verb, or (c) an adjective? Circle the answer.*

Some people change their names when they change their religion. The American boxer,[1] Muhammad Ali, changed his name from Cassius Clay when he became a Muslim. Other people change their names when they become famous. Many

---

[1] *boxer*: a person who plays the sport of boxing, in which two people fight with their closed hands or with special gloves

movie **stars**, in other words, famous actors, have changed their names. They may believe that their name is too ordinary. They want a name that sounds more exciting. Martial arts[2] star Jet Li's original name was Li Lian Jie. Singers often change their names, too. Rap singer Queen Latifah's original name was Dana Owens.

Find a clue in this sentence that signals a definition of *stars*. Circle the clue, and highlight the definition.

Jet Li (Li Lian Jie) and Queen Latifah (Dana Owens)

Immigrants sometimes change their names. They want their name to sound more like the names in their new country. Their original names may be difficult to pronounce. They believe it will be easier for them and for their children if their names are not so unusual. During the nineteenth and early twentieth centuries, many immigrants to the United States and parts of Canada gave their children English first names. Many also changed their family names. One Polish immigrant with the family name Sochaczewski brought her child to school in New York. The teachers told her the name was too difficult. They told her to find a new name. She chose her aunt's name, Wachtel, which was easier for the teachers to pronounce. Soon, the whole family changed to the new name.

What is the topic of this paragraph? Write it in the margin.

Names that are unusual or different can sometimes make life difficult. Names can reveal a person's religious or ethnic group. As a result, in some places, people with certain names may face discrimination. This means it may be difficult for them to get an education, find a job, or find a place to live.

---

2 *martial arts*: traditional skills of fighting or defending yourself, such as judo or karate

During periods of religious or ethnic conflict, some names can become dangerous. Therefore, sometimes people change their name because a different name is safer for them and their family.

People change their names for many reasons: marriage, a 6 new religion, or a new country. In some cases, they change their names just because they want a change. For example, one person may think his name sounds **childish**. He may want something more serious. Another person may think her name is too serious. She may want a name that sounds more fun and exciting. Because a name is part of a person's identity, a change in a name can also mean a change in identity.

Circle the suffix in *childish*. Is *childish* (a) a noun, (b) a verb, or (c) an adjective? Circle the answer.

MAIN IDEA CHECK

The main idea of a reading is what the whole reading is about.

Which sentence gives the main idea of Reading 2?
  a People change their names for many different reasons.
  b People need a very good reason to change their names.
  c Name changes can happen at different times in life.
  d A name change is a serious decision.

A CLOSER LOOK

Look back at Reading 2 to answer the following questions.

1 Marriage is the most common reason for a family name change.
   True or False? (Par. 1)

2 What is the reason for a double family name such as Smith-Simpson?
   (Par. 1)
   a Some women have two family names.
   b It includes both the husband's and wife's family names.
   c It shows a family's ethnic or religious group.
   d It shows a wife's identity.

3 Reread paragraph 2. Write two things a Native American's name may tell about the person.

4 Which types of people often change their names? Circle three answers.
   (Pars. 3 and 4)

   a Immigrants
   b Movie stars
   c Children
   d Politicians
   e Singers

5 Reread paragraph 5. Write two reasons why an unusual or different name
   may cause problems.

   _____

   _____

6 According to the whole reading, why do people change their names? Circle
   four answers.

   a People want a name that is more exciting.
   b People want a name that is easier to say.
   c People want a name that reveals their identity.
   d People change their name because of a new religion.
   e People want a new name that is safer than their original name.

VOCABULARY STUDY: DEFINITIONS

Find words in Reading 2 that can complete the following definitions. If you
need help, use Key Vocabulary from the Readings on page 251.

1 All of the unique features that make one person different from other people
   are his or her _____. (n) Par. 1

2 _____ are two people, usually a husband and a wife. (n pl) Par. 1

3 Something that is expected and usual is _____. (adj) Par. 2

4 A/An _____ is a person who finds animals and kills them for
   food. (n) Par. 2

5 _____ are people who come from one country to live in another
   country. (n pl) Par. 4

6 A/An _____ group is a group of people with the same race or
   national origin. (adj) Par. 5

7 _____ is treating people badly because of their religion, race, or
   age. (n) Par. 5

8 Someone who thinks carefully about everything and does not laugh a lot is
   _____. (adj) Par. 6

VOCABULARY STUDY: WORDS IN CONTEXT

Complete the following sentences with words from the list below. If necessary, review the words in Key Vocabulary from the Readings on page 251.

traditions	pronounce	period	revealed
ordinary	prefer	talent	conflict

1 The president's name is very long and difficult to _____.

2 Some students _____ to study in the morning; other students like to study in the evening.

3 Sometimes a small _____ between two countries can become a war.

4 There was a short _____ of silence, and then everyone began to speak.

5 The students learned about the national _____ and holidays of Vietnam.

6 The children in the new school have special _____ in music, art, or sports.

7 It was a very _____ day. Nothing special happened.

8 After a long time, she finally _____ the secret.

VOCABULARY REVIEW: SAME OR DIFFERENT

The following pairs of sentences contain vocabulary from Readings 1 and 2 in this unit. Write *S* on the blank line if the two sentences have the same meaning. Write *D* if the meanings are different.

_____ 1 The two countries share many traditions.　　　The two countries have similar cultures.

_____ 2 There was a long period of conflict in the country during the nineteenth century.　　　During the nineteenth century, there was discrimination against ethnic and religious groups.

_____ 3 The leader revealed his plans to only a few people.　　　The leader told only a few people about his ideas for the future.

_____ 4 The husband and wife selected a common name for their child.　　　The couple chose a lucky name for their child.

_____ 5 Some people think they have embarrassing names.　　　Some people have names that are difficult to pronounce.

BEYOND THE READING

Research

Find some information about an important person who has changed his or her name. Find answers to the following questions:

- What was his or her original name?
- Why did the person change his or her name?
- Do you think it was a good decision? Explain your answer.

Discussion

Share your research with a partner or your classmates.

Writing

Write a short summary of your research. Describe the reasons for the name change.

SKILLS AND STRATEGIES 4
FINDING THE MAIN IDEA OF A PARAGRAPH

As you learned in Skills and Strategies 2 on page 19, each paragraph has a topic. However, each paragraph also has a main idea. The main idea is what the writer wants to say about the topic. Sometimes you can find the main idea in the first sentence of the paragraph. Sometimes you must read the whole paragraph before you can find the main idea. Finding the main idea of each paragraph will help you understand what the whole reading is about.

EXAMPLES & EXPLANATIONS

Examples

Places get their names in many different ways. Sometimes they have the names of famous people. Sometimes they have the names of a physical feature. For example, Hillside is a common name for a town near a hill.

Some places have very amusing names – they make people laugh. For example, there is a town in the United States called Boring, Oregon. Another town is called Why, Arizona.

Why do some places have unusual names? Sometimes one person calls a place something, and that becomes its name. A town in the U.S. state of Tennessee did not have a name. The people made many suggestions for the name, but they couldn't agree on one. Finally, one person said, "I guess our town will remain nameless." This is how Nameless, Tennessee, got its name.

Explanations

The topic of this paragraph is *names of places*.

The main idea is what the writer wants to say about names of places. Here, the writer wants to say that places get their names in many different ways.

In this paragraph, both the topic and the main idea are in the first sentence.

The topic in this paragraph is also *names of places*.

This time the writer's main idea is that some places have very amusing names.

In this paragraph, both the topic and the main idea are also in the first sentence.

The main idea is not always in the first sentence. In this case, the first sentence is a question. The answer to the question is the main idea.

The topic of this paragraph is *how places get unusual names*. The topic is in the question that begins the paragraph.

The main idea is the answer to the question, which is in the second sentence: *One person starts to use a name*.

STRATEGIES

These strategies will help you find the main idea of a paragraph while you read.

- As you read a paragraph, ask yourself questions: *What is the topic? What does the writer want to say about this topic?*
- Pay attention to the first sentence of a paragraph. It often contains both the topic and the main idea.
- Look for the answer to a question. This may tell you the main idea.
- Read the whole paragraph to find out what the writer is trying to say about the topic.

SKILL PRACTICE 1

Read the following paragraphs. Then look at the four possible main idea choices for the paragraph. Circle the best choice. Discuss your answers with a partner.

1   Sometimes the names of towns are not amusing to the people who live there. The citizens of Boring, Oregon, do not think the name of their town is amusing. It was named after Mr. Boring, an important man in town.

Main idea:

a Many towns are named after important people.

b Mr. Boring was so important that people named a town after him.

c Many towns have unusual names.

d The people who live in a town may not think its name is amusing.

2   How do places get such amusing names? They often happen by accident. Long ago, the town of Why, Arizona, was only a place where a few streets met. The point where the streets met was in the shape of the letter *Y*. Later, the place with the Y became "Why."

Main idea:

a Arizona has a town called Why.

b Some places get their names by accident.

c The town of Why was named after two streets.

d People in Why, Arizona, changed the name of their town.

3   In the United States, *Jr.* (junior) and *Sr.* (senior) after a name show that the two people are son and father, but in Germany this is not true. The *Jr.* just shows that a person is named after someone else. The two people may not be close relatives.

Main idea:

a In the United States, *Jr.* and *Sr.* show that two people are related.

b Two people with *Jr.* and *Sr.* may not be close relatives in Germany.

c *Jr.* and *Sr.* may show different things in different countries.

d Someone named *Jr.* is named after his father.

4   When countries change their names, the governments of other countries do not always use the new name. Myanmar is an example of this. When a new government took over the country of Burma (the old name), the new rulers called it *Myanmar*. Governments that wanted to work with the new rulers started to call the country *Myanmar*. Other governments continued to call it *Burma*.

Main idea:

a Myanmar and Burma are names of the same country.

b Governments sometimes do not like the new rulers of a country.

c The use of a country's name is a big decision for other governments.

d When a country changes its name, other governments do not always use the new name.

SKILL PRACTICE 2

Read the following paragraphs. Write the main idea of each paragraph on the blank lines.

1   How important is a name in a person's life? A recent study shows that it is very important. Boys with certain names get into trouble and go to jail much more often than boys with other names. The names Alec, Ivan, and Luke are not a good choice of names, according to this research.

Main idea: _____

2   People often like to visit towns with unusual names. In the Grand Cayman Islands, you can visit Hell. It is a popular place for tourists to buy postcards. In Germany, a lot of people visit the town of Kissing. They like to take pictures of the official town sign.

Main idea: _____

3   In the United States, many small towns are named after famous places in other countries. Some of the towns got their names because people came from those places. Others were just named for beautiful cities. For example, 23 towns in the United States are named Paris.

Main idea: _____

4   Some towns change their names to attract visitors. The town of Truth or Consequences is named after an old American television game show. In 1950, the TV show asked for a town to change its name in order to host the game show. The 7,300 people in Hot Springs, New Mexico, agreed to change their town's name. Many visitors go to this town just because of its name.

Main idea: _____

READING 3
NAMES IN BUSINESS

GETTING INTO THE TOPIC

Look at the photographs on pages 54, 55, and 56. Then discuss the following questions with a partner.

1 What do you know about the companies or products in the photographs?
2 Why do you think companies chose those names for their businesses or products?
3 Which names do you think are good? Which names do you think are not good? Explain your answers.
4 Do you think the name of a company or product is important? Explain your answer.

GETTING A FIRST IDEA ABOUT THE READING

Read the title, the section headings, and the first sentence of each paragraph of Reading 3. Then read the questions below. Write the number of the section (*I*, *II*, or *III*) next to the question or questions it will answer.

SECTION	QUESTIONS THAT EACH SECTION WILL ANSWER
	How do companies choose their names?
	Why are names important in business?
	How do people feel when they hear or read a company or product name?
	How do names change people's ideas about a company or product?
	How are names connected to companies and products?

WHILE YOU READ

As you read, stop at the end of each sentence that contains words in **bold**. Then follow the instructions in the box in the margin.

Names in Business

I. THE IMPORTANCE OF NAMES

The names of companies and products have many different
origins. Older companies often got their names from people.
Car companies are a good example. Many car companies, such
as Ford, Toyota, and Tata,[1] all have the names of the men who
started them. Other car companies, such as SAAB, FIAT, and
BMW have names that are **initials**. For example, BMW are the
initials for Bavarian Motor Works. Today, most new companies
do not choose names like these. They want more interesting
names, because they know that company and product names
are very important.

Look in the next
sentence for clues to
a definition of *initials*.
Circle the clues, and
write the definition in
the margin.

Many companies have
names that are initials.

A new company must choose its name carefully. It must
also think carefully when it names its products. A name can
influence what people think about a company or a product.
People will remember a good name. They may choose that
company or product because of its name. This means that a
company or a product with a good name may not need many
advertisements. This can save the company a lot of money.

II. CONNECTING A NAME TO A COMPANY

Some companies choose their own name. However, because
this is a very important decision, other companies hire
professionals to help **them**. There are businesses that do
just one thing: they think of names for new companies and
products. They research names and give advice about how
people will respond to them. If it is an international company,
they consider international factors. Companies want to know

What is the topic of this
paragraph? Write it in
the margin.

---

[1] *Tata*: the largest Indian automobile company

how people all over the world will respond to their company or product name. International companies have to be careful. Sometimes a good name in one language could also mean something bad or embarrassing in **another language**.

Companies consider many things when they choose a name. They want a name that customers will connect with the company. If a company makes shoes for running, it should consider names that are related to feet or shoes. *Green Moon* or *Crazy Cow* would not be good names for shoes. A good name should also be easy to remember. However, the name should not be too ordinary. It is probably not a good idea to choose a name like *Best Shoes* or *The Shoe Company*. These names are boring and do not show how the company is unique.

Think about the topic of paragraph 3. What does the author want to say about it? Write the main idea in the margin.

4

A good name for a company should be easy to say and easy to spell. Correct spelling is especially important, because customers often look for the company on the Internet. If the company sells cheese, the name should use the correct spelling of *cheese*. It should not use a name like *Cheez Pleez!*

5

III. EMOTIONAL RESPONSE TO NAMES

Perhaps the most important factor that a company must consider is the emotion that people will feel when they hear the name of the company. What will they think about when they hear the name? A good name tells a story. If a shoe company chooses a name like *Fast Feet*, this explains the business to the customers. There is a clear connection between shoes and feet, but the name is a little ordinary. Two companies that make running shoes chose names that are more interesting: *Nike* – the Greek goddess of victory – and *Reebok* – a large animal from Africa that runs very **fast**. These names tell good stories. The companies hope their customers will think about victory and speed when they buy their shoes.

6

Find a clue in this sentence that signals a definition of *reebok*. Circle the clue, and highlight the definition.

A company name, like Reebok, can make customers think about its meaning.

The names of some electronic products and medicines also provide good examples of responses to products. The names for these products should make people think about modern science and technology. Sometimes this choice relates to sounds. For example, words that begin with *e-* or *i-*, like *e-mail* and *iPhone*, make people think about technology. In English, words that begin or end with *x*, such as *x-ray*, often sound very scientific or technical. A good example of a product name is *Xerox*. It sounds very technical, but it is also easy to remember. Another good example is the company name *Google*. This name comes from the word *googol*, which means a very large number: 10^{100}. The company chose this name because it makes the company sound scientific and powerful. Today, Google is a very **successful company**.

What is the main idea of paragraph 7? Write it in the margin.

Finally, sometimes businesses want to find a new name. Kentucky Fried Chicken sells lots of fried chicken. Today, many customers worry that they eat too much fat. Kentucky Fried Chicken didn't want its customers to just think about its fried food. The company decided to change its name to KFC. KFC wanted customers to think about its other products, which are not fried. A company may also change its name when something bad happens. For example, there was an airplane crash in Florida in 1997. The company that owned the airplane, Valujet, wanted its customers to forget the crash, so it changed its name to AirTran.

Choosing and changing names is an important part of any business. Names can have a **powerful** influence on customers. With a good response from customers, a company can make a lot of money. With a bad response, a company may lose a lot of money.

Circle the suffix in *powerful*. Is *powerful* (a) a noun, (b) a verb, or (c) an adjective? Circle the answer.

Some companies choose scientific-sounding names.

MAIN IDEA CHECK

Here are the main ideas of each paragraph in Reading 3. Match each paragraph to its main idea. Write the number of the paragraph on the blank line.

Paragraphs 1–2

_____ A A name can have a strong influence on the success of a product.

_____ B Company and product names are chosen in different ways.

Paragraphs 3–5

_____ C Companies should think carefully about the spelling of product names.

_____ D A name should have a clear connection to a product.

_____ E Many companies hire professionals when they need to choose a name.

Paragraphs 6–9

_____ F Many electronic products and medicines have names that sound scientific.

_____ G Product names can influence how much money a company makes.

_____ H Companies sometimes need to change their name.

_____ I Different names result in different emotional responses.

A CLOSER LOOK

Look back at Reading 3 to answer the following questions.

1 Reread paragraph 1. Write two common choices for company names in the past.

_____

_____

2 A good name can save money for a company. True or False? (Par. 2)

3 What do some professionals do to find names for new businesses or products? Circle three answers. (Par. 3)

   a They do research about how people will respond to a name.
   b They give advice about names.
   c They find customers for the company.
   d They think about international factors.

4 The most important factor that companies must consider is the _____ that people feel when they hear a product name. (Par. 6)

5 What do you think companies hope that customers will think about when they see these product names? Draw a line from the product in the left column to an idea in the right column. (Pars. 6 and 7)

PRODUCT	IDEA
Nike shoes	The power of large numbers
Xerox	Victory
Google	Speed
Reebok shoes	Modern technology

6 The name *Google* is a new word that the company invented to sound technical and powerful. True or False? (Par. 7)

7 Which three letters sound technical or scientific in English? (Par. 7)

a *i*

b *z*

c *x*

d *e*

8 Why do some companies decide to change their name? (Par. 8)

a They want customers to change their ideas about the company or product.

b They think customers will be more interested in a new name.

c They think the old name has become too boring.

d They hope that the new name will save the company money.

VOCABULARY STUDY: DEFINITIONS

Find words in Reading 3 that can complete the following definitions. If you need help, use Key Vocabulary from the Readings on page 251.

1 _____ are things that companies make and sell. (*n pl*) Par. 2

2 To _____ people is to change what they think or do. (*v*) Par. 2

3 _____ are pictures, songs, or other information that may make people buy something. (*n pl*) Par. 2

4 To _____ someone is to give her or him a job. (*v*) Par. 3

5 _____ is an idea or opinion someone gives you to help you make a decision. (*n*) Par. 3

6 _____ is when you win a race or a game. (*n*) Par. 6

7 Something that is connected to the knowledge, machines, or methods used in science and industry is _____. (*adj*) Par. 7

8 Something that has the results you want is _____. (*adj*) Par. 7

VOCABULARY STUDY: SYNONYMS

Read the sentences below. The words and phrases in parentheses mean the same or almost the same as the words in the box. For each sentence, replace the words or phrases in parentheses with a word from the box. Write the word on the blank line. If necessary, review the words in Key Vocabulary from the Readings on page 251.

considered	emotions	researched	factor
crash	related to	response	modern

1 There was a good (reaction) _____ to my idea. Everyone said they liked it very much.

2 She (studied) _____ the new company on the Internet. She wanted to find all the important facts about it.

3 There was a terrible car (accident) _____ on the street in front of my house.

4 The president wanted to bring (new) _____ ideas and technology to her country.

5 She had many different (feelings) _____ when she saw her father in the hospital.

6 The good weather in Los Angeles was one thing that made him decide to stay there, but his job was the most important (reason) _____ .

7 The parents (thought carefully about) _____ it for a long time before they made a decision about what to name their baby.

8 Discrimination is sometimes (connected to) _____ a person's religion or ethnic group.

VOCABULARY REVIEW: ACADEMIC WORD LIST

The following are Academic Word List (AWL) words from all the readings in Unit 2. Complete the sentences below with these words. If necessary, review the AWL words in Key Vocabulary from the Readings on page 251.

selected (v)	factor (n)	period (n)	reveal (v)	professional (n)
response (n)	researched (v)	immigrants (n)	ethnic (adj)	couple (n)

1 _____ arrived in New York from many different countries in the early twentieth century.

2 The most important _____ in their decision to leave their country was safety.

3 She was not sure where to sell her company's products, so she hired a
_____ to help her.

4 The student _____ the origins of the city's traditions.

5 There was a strong _____ to the leader's ideas. Many people
did not like them.

6 The soldier did not _____ his name. He said nothing.

7 There was a short _____ of peace between the two wars.

8 The _____ got married last year. Now they are going to have
a baby.

9 He looked at all the computers in the store and finally _____ a
very expensive one.

10 There are many different _____ groups in Nigeria. They speak
different languages and have different traditions.

BEYOND THE READING

Research
Choose a company or a product. Do some research on the origin of its name.
Find answers to the following questions:
- When did the company get its name?
- How did it get its name?
- Has the company or product been successful?

Discussion
- Share your results with a partner or your classmates.
- Discuss whether or not you think the name is a good name. Explain
  your reasons.

Writing
Write a short summary of your research. Include your opinion of
the name.

MAKING CONNECTIONS

The vocabulary in these exercises comes from all the readings in Unit 2. The exercises will help you see how writers make connections across sentences in a paragraph.

One way that writers make connections is by adding information about an earlier idea, person, or thing. Some words that signal this addition are *another*, *others*, and *also*.

In the following example, the word that signals additional information is in **bold**. The earlier idea, person, or thing is underlined. The additional information is also underlined. The arrow shows the connection.

Smith is the most common family name in the United

States. **Another** common family name is Williams.

EXERCISE 1

Read the following groups of sentences. Highlight the word that signals additional information. Underline the original idea, person, or thing in the first sentence. Underline the additional information. Draw arrows from the highlighted word to the underlined items. The first one has been done for you.

1 Some parents name their children after family members. Others name their children after famous people.

2 Names often reveal a person's ethnic group. They sometimes also reveal a person's religious group.

3 One popular name for girls in Japan in the 1990s was Akiko. Another was Tomoko.

4 Some immigrants' names are often difficult to spell. They are also difficult to pronounce.

5 Some immigrants changed the spelling of their names. Others changed their names to something completely new.

6 All the girls in the family have Maria in their names. One daughter is Maria Angela. Another daughter is Anna Maria.

EXERCISE 2

Make a clear paragraph by putting sentences A, B, and C into the best order after the numbered sentence. Look for pronouns (see page 30) and words that signal addition to help you. Write the letters in the correct order on the blank lines.

1 There are a lot of ways to find out more about family history. ___ ___ ___

| A There are also professionals who will do the research for you. | B Another possibility is to research the origin of your name on the Internet. | C Talking to older family members is a good way to begin. |

2 If you meet an American woman named Linda, she is probably not young. ___ ___ ___

| A This is because the name Linda was popular in the United States in the 1950s. | B Now, it is not as common as the name Jennifer. | C Another popular modern name is Jessica. |

3 The most common family names in Canada have changed in the last 20 years. ___ ___ ___

| A It has a lot more people from different ethnic groups than it used to. | B They used to be British names, but now names like Patel and Li are more common. | C This shows very clearly the change in the Canadian population. |

4 We have different naming traditions in our family. ___ ___ ___

| A Some of us give children religious names such as Sarah and Matthew. | B Others like more unusual names for children. | C They prefer unique names with uncommon spellings. |

5 Young people need to be careful when they select their e-mail names. ___ ___ ___

| A Some are not serious names. | B This is a problem when answering an advertisement for a job. | C Others are quite childish. |

Food

SKILLS AND STRATEGIES 5-6
- Collocations (1)
- Finding Supporting Details

READINGS
- Food from the Old World and the New World
- Fast Food
- Table Manners

SKILLS AND STRATEGIES 5
COLLOCATIONS (1)

When you read in English, you will notice that sometimes the same words often go together. For example, when you see the word *meal*, it often appears in a group of words, such as *make a meal* or *have a meal*. When two or more words often go together, we call this a *collocation*. Many collocations have a verb and a noun. Good readers know these collocations. This helps them read more quickly.

EXAMPLES & EXPLANATIONS

Examples

If I **have time** in the mornings, I eat a big breakfast with eggs, bacon, toast, and fruit. However, a big breakfast **takes time**, so I usually only eat cereal.

When my family eats dinner together, everyone **makes** a lot of **noise**.

Explanations

A noun such as *time* may appear with different verbs in collocations. Learn the words together, for example, **have time** and **take time**.

Notice that sometimes there are other words between the words that go together. For example, *a lot of* is in the middle of the collocation **makes noise**. *A lot of* is not part of the collocation.

THE LANGUAGE OF COLLOCATION

Here are some common collocations with verbs and nouns.

VERB + NOUN			
have	*make*	*take*	*tell*
• *lunch*	• *a difference*	• *a break*	• *a story*
• *time*	• *a meal*	• *time*	• *the truth*
• *fun*	• *noise*	• *a shower*	• *a lie*

STRATEGIES

These strategies will help you learn collocations.

- When you are reading, try to notice verbs and nouns that often go together. These may be useful collocations. Be careful. Sometimes other words are between the verb and noun. These words may not be part of the collocation.
- When you look up a noun in a dictionary, notice the verbs that can go together with it.
- When you make a list of new vocabulary to study, write the collocations. Learn the words that go together, not just the single words.

SKILL PRACTICE 1

Read the following paragraphs. Choose words from the list above each paragraph to complete the collocations. Write the words on the blank lines. The first one has been done for you.

take	win	follow	make

1   Learning to cook is easy. You just need to find a recipe and
   _____*follow*_____ the directions. _____ care when you measure,
         a   b
   but don't worry if you _____ a mistake. Some cooks
                                 c
   _____ prizes for recipes that they made with mistakes.
         d

have	meet	offer	take

2   If you _____ trouble learning how to cook, you may want to
                  a
   _____ a cooking class. Some grocery stores _____
         b   c
   cooking lessons. This can also be a great way to _____ people.
                                                            d

do	get	have	spend

3   Students _____ a lot of time sitting in classes every day.
                     a
   Many students _____ classes from 8:30 a.m. until 3:30 p.m.
                        b
   every day. Most students also need to _____ homework as soon
                                                 c
   as they get home. This means that many students don't _____
                                                                  d
   enough exercise.

take	makes	does	tell

4 Many married couples _____ turns cooking. Each night, one
                         a

person _____ dinner, and the other person _____ the
          b   c

dishes. This is a great system. If you don't like what your husband or wife

cooks, this is a good time *not* to _____ the truth!
                                              d

SKILL PRACTICE 2

Read the following paragraphs. Highlight any verb and noun collocations you
see. Then write the collocations on the blank lines next to their meanings.
The first one has been done for you.

1   In the past, families ate together every night. They were able to have
dinner at the same time each night. Today, both parents usually have a job.
It may be difficult for them to have the time to make dinner.

   a work somewhere _____

   b cook a meal _____

   c eat a meal in the evening *have dinner* _____

   d be available _____

2   Young people often rent a house together to save money. Some people
call this a "share house." Sometimes sharing the kitchen can cause
problems, and housemates have arguments.

   a fight _____

   b create difficulties _____

   c reduce expenses _____

   d pay money for a place to live _____

3   When housemates take turns cooking, they often make a mess.
Sometimes they don't do the dishes. Sometimes they fight over which food
is theirs in the refrigerator. Housemates need to solve problems like these
to make a share house successful.

   a cause things to be untidy or dirty _____

   b find answers or solutions _____

   c go one after another _____

   d wash things that you use for eating _____

READING 1
FOOD FROM THE OLD WORLD AND THE NEW WORLD

GETTING INTO THE TOPIC

Study the map, and discuss the following with a partner.

1 We often call one half of the world "the Old World" and the other half "the New World." Why?

2 Label the map. Label the Old World with an *O*. Label the New World with an *N*.

3 People from the Old World began to visit the New World in the fifteenth century. Name one food or animal that people from the Old World brought to the New World.

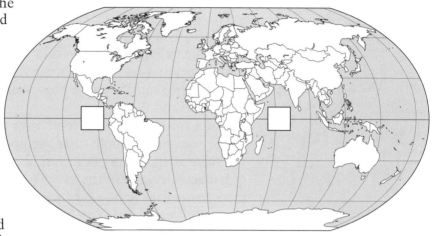

4 Name one food or animal that people brought back from the New World to the Old World.

GETTING A FIRST IDEA ABOUT THE READING

Read the title, and look at the photographs on page 68 in Reading 1. What do you think this reading will be about? Write your answers below.

1 What do you think this reading will say about Old World and New World food?

_____

2 Which of the photographs do you think are food of the Old World?

_____

3 Which of the photographs do you think are food of the New World?

_____

WHILE YOU READ

As you read, stop at the end of each sentence that contains words in **bold**. Then follow the instructions in the box in the margin.

Food from the Old World and the New World

What do you eat for breakfast? Coffee and eggs? Perhaps a banana? What about your favorite dinner? Pizza and chocolate cake? Chicken and rice? Meat and potatoes? Today, many people in the world can buy all of these foods easily. However, this has not always been possible. In the past, these familiar foods were not available **everywhere**.

A big change occurred about 500 years ago, when people from the Old World began to explore the New World. They found many unfamiliar kinds of food in the New World. They found potatoes, peanuts, tomatoes, chilies, corn, and chocolate. Today, many of these New World foods are very common in Europe and Asia.

The explorers brought food from the Old World with them. There were many foods that the people in the New World did not have at that time. For example, there was no milk, cheese, or bananas. People of the New World did not raise animals for food. Instead, they hunted animals, as well as birds and insects. They did not have chickens, cows, pigs, or sheep. These animals came to the New World with **European explorers**.

What is the main idea of paragraph 1? Write it in the margin.

Look back in paragraph 3 for two collocations with verbs and the noun *animal*. Highlight the collocations.

Five hundred years ago, many familiar foods were not available everywhere.

Between the fifteenth and seventeenth centuries, explorers 4 from Europe and Asia brought crops, that is, useful plants, from their countries to the New World. They planted crops like wheat, apples, and sugar cane. Today, these crops are very common in North and South America. The United States is the second largest producer of apples and wheat, and Brazil is the world's largest producer of sugar cane.

The **explorers** also brought new foods back to their coun- 5 tries. Some foods, such as corn and potatoes, became very important in the Old World. Many New World crops are easy to grow even when the soil and weather are not good. New World crops like potatoes could also feed a lot of people. This increase in food helped the world's population to grow quickly in the eighteenth and nineteenth centuries.

Some New World foods, like corn and potatoes, were avail- 6 able to almost everyone in the Old World. However, other foods from the New World, like chocolate and pineapples, were only for rich people. They did not grow in the Old World, so they were rare. Poor people could not pay for them. In the seventeenth century, pineapples were so valuable that people did not eat them. They put them on their tables, like **flowers**.

Many different foods are available all over the world today, 7 so it is sometimes difficult to remember that this was not always true. Thirty percent of all food plants in the world today came from the New World. Think about ice cream. Three of the most popular flavors of ice cream are vanilla, chocolate, and strawberry. All three of these flavors are from plants. Five hundred years ago, these plants grew only in the New World.

> Circle the suffix in *explorers*. Is *explorer* (a) a noun, (b) a verb, or (c) an adjective? Circle the answer.

> What is the main idea of paragraph 6? Write it in the margin.

MAIN IDEA CHECK

Here are the main ideas of each paragraph in Reading 1. Match each paragraph to its main idea. Write the number of the paragraph on the blank line.

Paragraphs 1–4

_____ A Before explorers came to the New World, many familiar foods of today were not available in the New World.

_____ B People from the Old World planted crops in the New World.

_____ C Before explorers came to the New World, many familiar foods of today were not available in the Old World.

_____ D Some familiar foods of today were not always available everywhere.

Paragraphs 5–7

_____ E Some New World crops were very successful in the Old World.

_____ F Many familiar foods of today were not available 500 years ago.

_____ G Some New World crops were very expensive in the Old World.

A CLOSER LOOK

Look back at Reading 1 to answer the following questions.

1 Before the fifteenth century, many familiar foods were not available to everyone in the world. True or False? (Par. 2)

2 What kinds of animals did people in the New World raise for food? (Par. 3)
   a Sheep
   b Pigs
   c Chickens
   d None of these

3 The United States is the largest producer of sugar cane. True or False? (Par. 4)

4 What were some reasons for the success of potatoes in the Old World? Circle three answers. (Par. 5)
   a They are easy to grow.
   b They are not expensive.
   c They can grow in bad weather.
   d They can feed a lot of people.

5 What was one result of the success of these New World crops? (Par. 5)
   a No one was hungry.
   b The population increased.
   c Some foods became too expensive for poor people.
   d People stopped planting Old World crops.

6 _____ is one New World food that was available only to rich people. (Par. 6)

7 According to the whole reading, were the following foods originally from the Old World or the New World? Write O (for *Old World*) or N (for *New World*) on the blank lines.

   a _____ corn   e _____ potatoes
   b _____ chocolate   f _____ sugar cane
   c _____ bananas   g _____ tomatoes
   d _____ apples

VOCABULARY STUDY: DEFINITIONS

Find words in Reading 1 that can complete the following definitions. If you need help, use Key Vocabulary from the Readings on page 251.

1 Something that you have often seen or heard before is _____. (*adj*) Par. 1

2 Something that is possible to get is _____. (*adj*) Par. 1

3 To _____ people or things is to take care of them as they grow, for example, children, plants, or animals. (*v*) Par. 3

4 _____ are plants that grow on farms, often for food. (*n pl*) Par. 4

5 The _____ is dirt, where plants grow. (*n*) Par. 5

6 Something that is unusual and hard to find is _____. (*adj*) Par. 6

7 Something that is worth a lot of money is _____. (*adj*) Par. 6

8 _____ are the way that things taste. (*n pl*) Par. 7

VOCABULARY STUDY: WORD FAMILIES

Read the words in the following chart. The words in **bold** are the parts of speech that appear in Reading 1. Find these words in the reading. If you need help, use Key Vocabulary from the Readings on page 251.

NOUN	VERB
exploration	***explore***
increase	*increase*
occurrence	***occur***
plant	*plant*
population	*populate*

Choose the correct form of the words from the chart to complete the following sentences. Use the correct verb tenses and subject-verb agreement. Use the correct singular and plural noun forms.

1 The _____ of cities is rising all over the world.

2 There was a large _____ in the number of tourists all over the world last year.

3 The accident _____ at three o'clock yesterday afternoon.

4 They have many beautiful _____ in their garden.

5 There was a period of _____ between the fifteenth and seventeenth centuries.

6 Oil prices _____ by 10 percent last year.

7 She _____ tomatoes and potatoes in her garden.

8 New immigrants _____ American cities and towns in the eighteenth century.

9 The tourists _____ the pretty villages along the shore.

10 Rain is a common _____ in northeastern India in July and August.

BEYOND THE READING

Research
Choose one of the foods from this list and find out if it was originally from the Old World or the New World. Then find the answer for your favorite food.
- popcorn
- squash
- olives
- chilies

Discussion
Share your research with a partner or your classmates.

Writing
Write a short summary about the food that you researched.

READING 2
FAST FOOD

GETTING INTO THE TOPIC

Look at the photograph of the fast-food restaurant on page 74. Then discuss the following questions with a partner.

1 Do you enjoy fast food?
2 Why do you think so many people like fast food?
3 How often do you eat fast food? Once a week? Once a month?

GETTING A FIRST IDEA ABOUT THE READING

The following are the first sentences of the paragraphs in Reading 2. Read these sentences. Then, with a partner, discuss what you think the paragraphs will be about.

1 Fast food is global. (Par. 1)
2 Although the first fast-food restaurants were in the United States, the fast-food business is growing all over the world. (Par. 2)
3 Not all fast-food companies serve the same food all over the world. (Par. 3)
4 Not all fast-food restaurants sell burgers and pizza, and not all fast-food companies are American. (Par. 4)
5 Fast food is convenient, inexpensive, and tastes good, but it may not be good for you. (Par. 5)
6 It is likely that the number of fast-food restaurants will continue to increase. (Par. 6)

WHILE YOU READ

As you read, stop at the end of each sentence that contains words in **bold**. Then follow the instructions in the box in the margin.

Fast Food

Fast food is global. People all over the world love to eat ₁ fast food. They like hamburgers, fried chicken, and pizza, and thousands of fast-food restaurants are on every continent. The popularity of fast food is increasing. There are several reasons for this popularity. Many people don't want to cook their own food, so fast food makes their lives easier. Fast food is not expensive. It tastes good, and it is also – fast!

Although the first fast-food restaurants were in the United ₂ States, the fast-food business is growing all over the world. Today, many fast-food companies make more money in other countries. More than half of all of McDonalds's 31,000 restaurants are outside the United States. China has more than 800 McDonalds restaurants, and there are 200 more in **Hong Kong**.

Look back in paragraph 2 for a collocation with a verb and the noun *money*. Highlight the collocation.

McDonalds is in many countries all over the world, including Thailand as shown here.

Not all fast-food companies serve the same food all over ₃ the world. They serve different foods in different countries because they want to satisfy their customers. For example, in the United States, KFC restaurants serve white chicken meat and potatoes. In China, KFC serves dark chicken meat and rice instead of potatoes. Most Chinese customers prefer these choices. In India, most people do not eat beef, so McDonalds serves burgers made from chicken and vegetables. In Japan, some of the burgers are made from **shrimp**.

What is the main idea of paragraph 3? Write it in the margin.

Not all fast-food restaurants sell burgers and pizza, and ₄ not all fast-food companies are American. Many successful fast-food companies started in other countries. They sell food that is popular in those countries. Some of them have become popular in the United States. One example is the chicken restaurant, Pollo Campero. It began in Guatemala. On the first day of business in the Pollo Campero in Chicago, 200 people waited outside for more than six hours for the restaurant to open. Many of them were immigrants from Guatemala who loved the Pollo Campero chicken. They wanted to be the first people to eat in the restaurant.

Fast food is convenient, inexpensive, and tastes good, but it may not be good for you. Many people worry about the effect of fast food on their health. Most fast food has a lot of fat, salt, and sugar in it. Some scientists and doctors believe there is a connection between fast food and health problems. Many doctors tell us not to eat fast food too often. People who eat a lot of fast food often **gain weight**; that is, they get heavier. This may be one reason that many young people today are heavier than young people in the past. As a result of these concerns, many fast-food restaurants now offer other foods, such as fruit, salad, and yogurt. They do not have so much fat, salt, and sugar. However, many customers still prefer the flavor of meals that have a lot of fat, salt, and sugar in them.

It is likely that the number of fast-food restaurants will continue to increase. American companies, such as McDonalds, will continue to expand. Fast-food consumption across the world will also grow as more people eat at fast-food restaurants instead of at home. In 2005, Americans spent almost $600 per person on fast food. In 2008, half of all Americans ate in a fast-food restaurant once a week. The percentage is even higher in some Asian countries. Although fast food may not be good for your health, people all over the world love it and **will continue to eat it**.

5

6

Find a clue in this sentence that signals a definition of *gain weight*. Circle the clue, and highlight the definition.

What is the main idea of paragraph 6? Write it in the margin.

FIGURE 3.1 Global Fast-Food Consumption in 2005

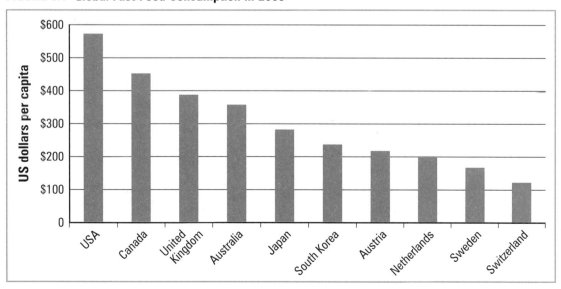

Source: Euromonitor

MAIN IDEA CHECK

Here are the main ideas of each paragraph in Reading 2. Match each paragraph to its main idea. Write the number of the paragraph on the blank line.

Paragraphs 1–3

_____ A Fast-food companies make most of their money outside of the United States.

_____ B Some fast-food companies serve the same food everywhere; others serve different things in different countries.

_____ C There are several reasons why fast food is popular all over the world.

Paragraphs 4–6

_____ D More and more people will eat fast food in the future.

_____ E Most fast food is not very good for your health.

_____ F There are many popular fast-food restaurants that have started outside of the United States.

A CLOSER LOOK

Look back at Reading 2 to answer the following questions.

1 Why is fast food popular? Circle three answers. (Par. 1)
   a It tastes good.
   b It is inexpensive.
   c It is international.
   d It makes people's lives easy.

2 Almost all of the fast-food business is in the United States. True or False? (Par. 2)

3 Why are the burgers in India made from chicken? (Par. 3)
   a Most Indians do not like shrimp.
   b Most Indians prefer dark chicken meat.
   c Most Indians like rice, and chicken is better with rice.
   d Most Indians do not eat beef.

4 Some Japanese burgers are made of _____. (Par. 3)

5 What one fact in paragraph 4 suggests that Pollo Campero is popular?
   a Customers waited for hours.
   b Customers bought a lot of chicken.
   c Customers liked Pollo Campero better than KFC.
   d Customers traveled a long way.

6 Why do doctors think most fast food is not good for your health? Circle two answers. (Par. 5)

    a It has a lot of fat, salt, and sugar.

    b Young people eat too much fast food.

    c Yogurt is not good for you.

    d Eating a lot of fast food can make you too heavy.

7 According to Figure 3.1 on page 75, who eats the most fast food?

    a Americans

    b Japanese

    c South Koreans

    d Europeans

8 In 2008, Americans ate at fast-food restaurants more often than they ate at home. True or False? (Par. 6)

VOCABULARY STUDY: DEFINITIONS

Find words in Reading 2 that can complete the following definitions. If you need help, use Key Vocabulary from the Readings on page 251.

1 Something that is in every part of the world is _____.
(adj) Par. 1

2 A/An _____ is a large piece of land with water all around it.
(n) Par. 1

3 To _____ people is to give them what they want or need.
(v) Par. 3

4 A/An _____ is the result of an influence. (n) Par. 5

5 To _____ something is to give or provide it. (v) Par. 5

6 _____ is a kind of food made from milk. It is thick and often has a sweet or fruit flavor. (n) Par. 5

7 Something that will probably happen is _____. (adj) Par. 6

8 _____ is eating or using something. (n) Par. 6

VOCABULARY STUDY: WORDS IN CONTEXT

Complete the following sentences with words or phrases from the list below. If necessary, review the words in Key Vocabulary from the Readings on page 251.

gain weight	instead of	health	serves
convenient	worry	percentage	expand

1 There is a higher _____ of women than men in American universities.

2 If you eat a lot of candy, you will _____.

3 She ate a salad _____ a sandwich because she was not very hungry.

4 The restaurant _____ dinner between 5:30 and 9:00 p.m.

5 She liked her new apartment because it was so _____. It was very close to her job.

6 You should eat lots of fruits and vegetables. They are good for your _____.

7 Modern cities are growing, and they will continue to _____ in the twenty-first century.

8 Parents often _____ about their children when they are out with their friends. They want them to be safe.

VOCABULARY REVIEW: SAME OR DIFFERENT

The following pairs of sentences contain vocabulary from Readings 1 and 2 in this unit. Write *S* on the blank line if the two sentences have the same meaning. Write *D* if the meanings are different.

_____ 1 You are likely to get heavy if you choose to eat sweet things and not vegetables.   You will probably gain weight if you eat food with sugar instead of vegetables.

_____ 2 She planted many rare trees and flowers in her garden.   She could raise many different plants because the soil was very good.

_____ 3 At this restaurant, most of the food is good for your health.   This restaurant serves lots of food that is good for you.

_____ 4 The percentage of people in the world who are hungry increased last year.   The number of hungry people in the world expanded last year.

_____ 5 The hotel manager offered the couple the only room that was available.   Their room was not large, but it was inexpensive and convenient.

BEYOND THE READING

Research

Do some research in your class about fast food. Ask your classmates the following questions:

- How often do you eat in fast-food restaurants?
- How much money do you spend in fast-food restaurants every week?
- What is your favorite kind of fast food?

Discussion

Discuss your results as a class.

Writing

Use your class's results to create a chart like the one below. Use answers to one of the questions above to create your chart. Then write a few sentences about the information in the chart.

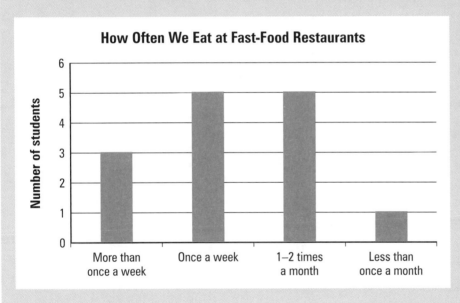

How Often We Eat at Fast-Food Restaurants

SKILLS AND STRATEGIES 6
FINDING SUPPORTING DETAILS

As you learned in Skills and Strategies 4 on page 50, each paragraph has a
main idea. The main idea tells you what the writer wants to say about the
topic. A well-written paragraph also has *supporting details*. Supporting details
are statements with specific information to support the main idea. Supporting
details are usually facts, examples, or reasons. Finding supporting details will
help you understand what you read.

EXAMPLES & EXPLANATIONS

Example

[1]At certain points in history, being
overweight was a sign of good health.
[2]Now, research shows that too much
food is not a good idea. [3]For example, a
study of people over 100 years old shows
that they eat very little. [4]Research also
shows that people who eat too much
often have health problems. [5]They do
not live as long as other people.
[6]Eating less helps people live long
and healthy lives.

Explanation

Sentence 2 contains the main idea of the paragraph: *Too
much food is not a good idea.*

Sentence 3 provides the first supporting detail: *People over
100 years old eat very little.*

Sentence 4 provides the second supporting detail: *People who
eat too much often have health problems.*

Sentence 5 provides the third supporting detail: *People who
eat too much do not live as long as other people.*

Sentence 6 is a conclusion sentence. It restates the
main idea.

THE LANGUAGE OF SUPPORTING DETAILS

Sometimes writers use words or phrases to signal a list of supporting details.
Here are some common words and phrases that signal supporting details.

WORDS AND PHRASES THAT SIGNAL SUPPORTING DETAILS			
for example	*first*	*one reason*	*research shows*
for instance	*next*	*one example*	*a study shows*
	finally	*one explanation*	

STRATEGIES

These strategies will help you find supporting details while you read.

- First, identify the main idea. Use the strategies you learned in Skills and Strategies 4 on page 51.
- Look for examples, facts, and reasons that support the main idea.
- Notice specific words or phrases that signal these supporting details.
- Number or underline supporting details as you read. Check that these details support the main idea by looking back and rereading the main idea.

SKILL PRACTICE 1

Read the following pairs of sentences. Write *M* next to the sentence in each pair that is a main idea. Write *S* next to the sentence that is a supporting detail.

1 _____ A Research shows that people started to grow rice over 5,000 years ago.

_____ B Rice is one of the oldest crops in the world.

2 _____ A Some people use it in soaps; some people use it for cooking.

_____ B The almond has many uses all over the world.

3 _____ A It was the first place where people sat at tables and ordered from a menu.

_____ B The first restaurant started in 1765 in Paris.

4 _____ A People all over the world celebrate the New Year by eating special types of food.

_____ B For example, in Spain and Portugal, people eat 12 grapes at midnight for good luck in each month of the new year.

5 _____ A It is a good idea to eat fish at least twice a week.

_____ B Research shows that the type of fat in fish is good for your heart.

6 _____ A Some restaurants in the past were "family style."

_____ B Guests helped themselves to food that the host put on a table.

SKILL PRACTICE 2

Read the following paragraphs. The main ideas are given to you. Find the supporting details in each paragraph, and write them on the blank lines.

1   Pasta is easy to cook, but it is important to follow these steps for perfect pasta. First, choose a pot that is large enough for a lot of water. If you don't have enough water, the noodles will stick together. Next, make sure the water is boiling before you add the noodles. Stir the noodles as soon as you put them in the water. This will separate the noodles. These steps will help you have delicious pasta.

Main idea: It is possible to cook perfect pasta if you follow certain steps.

Supporting detail: _____

Supporting detail: _____

Supporting detail: _____

2   Foods with certain colors or shapes have special meanings at the new year. For example, in Peru people eat gold-colored food on New Year's Day. In the Philippines, people eat food that is green. Another New Year's custom is to eat different types of beans that are shaped like coins. The idea of all these different customs is the same: At the beginning of the new year, eat food that is the color of money or that looks like money, and you will have enough money all during the year.

Main idea: People eat food of certain shapes or colors on New Year's Day.

Supporting detail: _____

Supporting detail: _____

Supporting detail: _____

3   Rice is one of the most important food crops in the world. Research shows that about half of the people in the world depend on rice for a major part of their diet. It takes a lot of work and a lot of water to grow rice, but one seed of rice produces about 3,000 grains of rice. Rice is the basis of the diet in Asia, but people grow it everywhere in the world except for Antarctica. Few crops are as important as rice.

Main idea: Rice is a very important crop.

Supporting detail: _____

Supporting detail: _____

Supporting detail: _____

READING 3
TABLE MANNERS

GETTING INTO THE TOPIC

Look at the photographs on pages 85 and 86. Then discuss the following questions with a partner.

1 Do you usually use a fork, chopsticks, or your hands when you eat?
2 When you visit someone for dinner, how do you know when to begin eating?
3 How do you politely show that you have had enough to eat?
4 Is the way we act during meals important? Explain your answer.

GETTING A FIRST IDEA ABOUT THE READING

Read the title, the section headings, and the first sentence of each paragraph of Reading 3. Then read the questions below. Write the number of the section (*I*, *II*, or *III*) next to the question or questions it will answer.

SECTION	QUESTIONS THAT EACH SECTION WILL ANSWER
	What are table manners?
	How do table manners show that we enjoy food?
	How do people show their appreciation of food in different ways in different cultures?
	Why are table manners important?
	What are some examples of how table manners keep us safe?
	How are table manners related to health?

WHILE YOU READ

As you read, stop at the end of each sentence that contains words in **bold**. Then follow the instructions in the box in the margin.

Table Manners

I. THE IMPORTANCE AND HISTORY OF TABLE MANNERS

Mealtimes are important in every culture. Meals give friends and family a chance to sit down, enjoy food, and talk together. When you visit a different country, mealtimes can help you learn a new language and culture. However, it is important to know how to act at mealtimes. **Table manners**, that is, how people act at mealtimes, are different around the world. [1]

Should you use your hands or a fork to pick up your food? Is it polite to make noise when you eat? Should you leave any food on your plate? If you make an error in your mealtime behavior, people may think you are impolite. In order to understand these customs, it is helpful to understand more about their origins. There are cultural and historical explanations for many of our table manners today. [2]

Table manners have changed throughout history. We call them table manners, but long ago, people did not eat at tables. In ancient Rome, people lay down at meals. They leaned on one hand and ate with the other hand. In Europe, until about 1500, there were no plates and no forks. Instead of plates, people ate their food from a piece of old, dry bread. They ate with their fingers or used pieces of bread to bring food to their mouths. [3]

II. TABLE MANNERS AND SAFETY

One explanation for our table manners today is safety. Knives were the first things that people used to eat their food. In the past, men brought their own knives to the table. They used the same knives for hunting and protection. These knives were very useful, but they were also dangerous. There were often fights at mealtimes, and sometimes people died. As a result, the King of France gave an order that all table knives had to have round **ends**. [4]

The danger of knives may explain table manners today in some countries such as Spain. There were also fights during meals in Spain. Men carried knives and also guns. Sometimes they held these weapons under the table. However, it is difficult to hide a weapon in your hands if your hands are visible. In Spain and some other countries today, it is polite to keep your hands above the table where everyone can see them. Although most people are not worried about guns and knives at meals anymore, this custom remains. [5]

Find a clue in this sentence that signals a definition of *table manners*. Circle the clue, and highlight the definition.

Look back in paragraph 4 for a collocation with a verb and the noun *order*. Highlight the collocation.

Another explanation for our table manners is the safety of the food. Germs can spread easily at mealtime. Some table manners help stop germs from spreading, and this can keep people healthy. For instance, in most cultures, it is impolite to put your own fork, chopsticks, or your hands into a central dish, because this can spread germs. Instead, you should use another fork or the opposite end of your chopsticks. In some countries, for example, India, many people eat their food with their hands. Hosts in India provide a place for people to wash their hands before and after the meal. These customs help prevent germs from spreading during **meals**.

What is the main idea of paragraph 6? Write it in the margin.

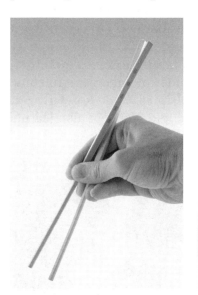

Ways of eating food may be different across cultures.

III. SHOWING APPRECIATION OF OUR FOOD

A final explanation for table manners is the way we show appreciation of the food we eat. **We show this appreciation in different ways in different cultures.** In Japan, for example, it is fine to make noise when you are eating soup or noodles. In China, it is fine to burp[1] after a large meal. These noises show that you are enjoying your meal. In most western countries and some other Asian countries, however, people think these noises are impolite.

Hosts like to know that their guests have enjoyed their food. However, even more important, they want to be sure their guests have had enough to eat. How can you show that you

As you read this paragraph, look for a phrase that signals the first supporting detail for this main idea. Circle the phrase, and underline the detail. Then look for two more supporting details. Underline them.

---

[1] *burp*: to allow air from the stomach to come out through the mouth in a noisy way

enjoyed the meal but you do not want to eat more? In most western countries, you can show that you enjoyed your meal if you finish all the food on your plate.

In other countries, however, if you eat everything on your plate, you might offend the host. In these countries, you should leave a little bit of food on your plate. This shows that you are satisfied. It also shows that you are finished. If you finish everything on your plate, this says that you are still hungry. Your hosts may try to give you more food. Guests who **misunderstand** these customs about food may eat too much, or they may go home hungry!

Mealtimes are a good time to observe another culture. You can learn more than just good table manners. You can learn what is important in other cultures, too. For example, you may observe that the oldest member of a family receives food first. This can show you how important older members are in some cultures. Observe carefully at mealtimes, and you will not embarrass yourself or offend other people. You can also learn a lot about another culture.

Circle the prefix in *misunderstand*. Then write a definition for *misunderstand* in the margin.

9

10

Learning table manners in a new culture can be an important thing to do.

MAIN IDEA CHECK

Here are the main ideas of each paragraph in Reading 3. Match each paragraph to its main idea. Write the number of the paragraph on the blank line.

Paragraphs 1–3

_____ A It is important to learn about table manners.

_____ B There are historical explanations for today's table manners.

_____ C Mealtime behavior has changed throughout history.

Paragraphs 4–6

_____ D Spanish table manners provide a good example.

_____ E Some table manners can stop germs from spreading.

_____ F In the past, some customs made mealtimes less dangerous.

Paragraphs 7–10

_____ G In some cultures, you should finish everything on your plate.

_____ H We show our appreciation of food in different ways.

_____ I Table manners can tell you a lot about a culture.

_____ J In some cultures, it is polite to leave a little bit of food on your plate.

A CLOSER LOOK

Look back at Reading 3 to answer the following questions.

1 What might happen if you make an error in your table manners? (Par. 2)
   a It will be hard to understand the culture.
   b You will use the wrong fork.
   c People will think you are impolite.
   d It will be more difficult to learn the language.

2 The ancient Romans did not sit at a table for meals. True or False? (Par. 3)

3 Before 1500, Europeans used bread for plates. True or False? (Par. 3)

4 The main idea of paragraph 3 is *Table manners have changed throughout history*. Write three details from paragraph 3 to support this idea.

_____

_____

_____

5 What is the origin of the Spanish custom described in paragraph 5?

   a People could not take food and hide it under the table.

   b People could hide their dirty hands.

   c People could keep their knives under the table.

   d People could not hide weapons under the table.

6 If you put your fork or chopsticks in the central dish after you have used it, _____ can spread easily. (Par. 6)

7 What are some ways to show appreciation of food in different cultures? Circle three answers. (Pars. 7–9)

   a Make noises.

   b Finish everything.

   c Don't finish everything.

   d Leave your fork on your plate.

8 In some cultures, if you finish everything on your plate, this may offend your host. Why? (Par. 9)

   a It shows appreciation of your food.

   b Your host will want you to eat more food.

   c Your host will not know what to say.

   d It tells the host you are still hungry.

VOCABULARY STUDY: DEFINITIONS

Find words in Reading 3 that can complete the following definitions. If you need help, use Key Vocabulary from the Readings on page 251.

1 _____ is keeping people or things safe and away from danger. (n) Par. 4

2 A/An _____ is a very strong request or demand. (n) Par. 4

3 To _____ something is to put it where no one can see it. (v) Par. 5

4 Something that you can see is _____. (adj) Par. 5

5 If things _____, they move across a bigger area and have a stronger effect. (v) Par. 6

6 _____ are people who invite you to their homes. (n pl) Par. 6

7 Something that is the last thing in a list is _____. (adj) Par. 7

8 _____ are a long thin food made from water and flour. Spaghetti is an example. (n pl). Par. 7

VOCABULARY STUDY: SYNONYMS

Read the sentences below. The words in parentheses mean the same or almost the same as the words in the list. For each sentence, replace the words in parentheses with a word from the list. Write it on the blank line. If necessary, review the words in Key Vocabulary from the Readings on page 251.

appreciation	offended	error	leaned
observed	behavior	germs	impolite

1 Her (actions) _____ at the party made everyone angry.

2 He (rested) _____ his back against the tree and looked up at the sky.

3 They showed their (thanks) _____ by bringing gifts to their hosts.

4 It is (rude) _____ to call people after ten o'clock at night.

5 The student made one (mistake) _____ on the test.

6 The scientist (watched) _____ the animals in the forest.

7 (Bacteria) _____ are very small, but they can make you sick.

8 The president said some things that (angered) _____ the visitors. He said bad things about their country.

VOCABULARY REVIEW: ACADEMIC WORD LIST

The following are Academic Word List (AWL) words from all the readings in Unit 3. Complete the sentences below with these words. If necessary, review the AWL words in Key Vocabulary from the Readings on page 251.

occurs (v)	errors (n)	available (adj)	expanding (v)	consumption (n)
final (adj)	global (adj)	appreciation (n)	visible (adj)	percentage (n)

1 He used a large _____ of the money to pay for his education.

2 She made many _____ on the test, so she got a bad grade.

3 The _____ of chocolate around the world increased in the nineteenth century.

4 Bad weather often _____ during the summer months.

5 He gave two reasons for his decision to sell his house, but the third and _____ one was the most important.

6 The sun was still _____ between the clouds.

7 Many businesses today are _____. They have offices all over the world.

8 The fast-food business is _____ quickly. New restaurants are opening every month.

9 The children and their parents showed their _____ by bringing gifts to the teacher.

10 This coat is _____ in three different colors.

BEYOND THE READING

Research

Interview a classmate or someone from outside of your classroom about table manners. Ask the following questions:

- What are two table manners that you think are the most important?
- Why do you think they are important?

Discussion

Share your research with a partner or your classmates.

Writing

Write a short description of your research on table manners.

MAKING CONNECTIONS

The vocabulary in these exercises comes from all the readings in Unit 3. The exercises will help you see how writers make connections across sentences in a paragraph.

In *Making Connections* for Unit 2 on page 61, you learned that writers use words such as *another*, *other*, and *also* to add information to an earlier idea, person, or thing.

Writers can also add information by using *transition* words or phrases such as *for example*, *for instance*, or *in addition*. They use these words or phrases when they want to add a specific fact or example to support a main idea. You learned some of these transition words and phrases in Skills and Strategies 6 on page 80.

EXERCISE 1

Read the following groups of sentences. Highlight any transition words or phrases that signal additional facts or examples. Underline the original idea, person, or thing in the first sentence. Underline the additional fact or example. The first one has been done for you.

1 Many young people gain weight when they go to college. For instance, many students gain about 15 pounds in their freshman year of college.

2 Today, tourists can find familiar food anywhere they go. For example, there are many KFC restaurants in China.

3 A research study in France found that consumption of tea has health benefits for women. For instance, it may protect them from heart attacks.

4 We waited for 20 minutes before the waiter offered to take our order. In addition, he was impolite when we complained.

5 Shoppers can find food from all over the world in grocery stores now. For example, in Japan, you can buy apples from the United States and cookies from France.

6 The cold weather killed a large percentage of the crops. In addition, the price of seeds increased. Farmers had a very bad year.

EXERCISE 2

Make a clear paragraph by putting sentences A, B, and C into the best order after the numbered sentence. Look for pronouns and words or phrases that signal additional facts and examples to help you. Write the letters in the correct order on the blank lines.

1 Government health officials sometimes warn people not to eat a certain kind of food. ___ ___ ___

A	B	C
This usually occurs because of germs in the food.	If the germs spread, many people get sick.	In addition, they tell grocery stores to stop selling the food.

2 Customs for tipping are different all over the world. ___ ___ ___

A	B	C
For example, in most Asian countries, no one leaves a tip for the waiter or waitress.	In the United States and Canada, waiters and waitresses depend on tips for most of their salary.	If you want to get good service in the United States or Canada, pay a tip of 20 percent.

3 The word *tea* usually refers to something you drink. ___ ___ ___

A	B	C
In Britain, it also refers to a meal.	Other British people make tea the main meal of the day instead of a light meal.	For example, it can mean a light meal in the late afternoon.

4 Consumption of sugar has increased a great deal in the past 50 years.
___ ___ ___

A	B	C
For example, many people get a disease called *diabetes* because they eat too much sugar.	This has a bad effect on people's health.	Studies show that each person in the United States now consumes about 140 pounds of sugar every year.

5 All over the world, there are different customs for eating rice. ___ ___ ___

A	B	C
It's important to learn these customs before you travel.	For example, in some countries it is impolite to pick up a bowl of rice and eat from it.	In other countries, it is polite to do this.

Urban Transportation

SKILLS AND STRATEGIES 7
PHRASES (1)

As you learned in Skills and Strategies 5, on page 64, some verbs and nouns often go together. These are collocations. Another group of words that go together are *phrases*, for example, *on the whole* and *all of a sudden*. These phrases are fixed, that is, they don't change any of their parts. All the words are always the same. Good readers notice fixed phrases and learn them. If you can find fixed phrases in a reading, it can help you understand a reading better and read more quickly.

EXAMPLES & EXPLANATIONS

Examples

In general, the bus system works well.

The passengers got on the train **one by one**.

Explanations

Fixed phrases are very common in English.

in general = usually

You can't change anything in a fixed phrase. For example, in this sentence, you cannot change *by* to *after*. You can't say, "one after one."

one by one = separately, one after the other

THE LANGUAGE OF FIXED PHRASES

Here are some common fixed phrases and their meanings.

FIXED PHRASES	MEANINGS
all in all	thinking about everything
all of a sudden	something happens quickly without warning
for the time being	for the present time only
in general	usually
in no time	very soon, very quickly
in the beginning	during the first part, before now
in the long run	at a time far away in the future
one by one	separately, one after the other
on the whole	in most cases
on time	something happens at the expected time
quite a few	a large number
so far	until now

STRATEGIES

These strategies will help you identify and learn fixed phrases.

- When you read, look for words that often go together.
- When you make a list of new vocabulary to study, write words that go together, not just the single words.
- When you look up a word in a dictionary, notice any fixed phrases that are listed with the word.

SKILL PRACTICE 1

Read the following paragraphs. Fill in the blank lines with fixed phrases from the list above each paragraph. If you need help, use the Language of Fixed Phrases chart on page 94. The first one has been done for you.

all in all	in general	on time
all of a sudden	in no time	quite a few

1   In the past, public transportation was not popular in my city. Buses were

never _____*on time*_____ , so people were often late to work.
                  a

_____ , it was not a great way to get to work. Then,
          b

_____ , gas prices became very high.
          c

_____ , people began to appreciate public transportation.
          d

_____ people decided to leave their cars at home and
          e

take the bus. _____ , people are very happy with the
                              f

public transportation system today.

for the time being	in the long run	on the whole
in the beginning	one by one	so far

2   Last month, the city started to build a new subway.

_____ , it isn't causing a lot of problems. However, the
          a

city has closed many streets _____ while they work on
                                          b

the subway. _____ , everything is very confusing.
                          c

_____ , people didn't want a new subway.
          d

_____ , they felt it was too expensive.
          e

_____ , however, people will enjoy the convenience.
          f

SKILL PRACTICE 2

Here are some other common fixed phrases. Read them. Then read the paragraph that follows the phrases. Look at the words in parentheses in each paragraph. Try to guess which of the fixed phrases in the list above the paragraph they match. Write them on the blank lines. The first one has been done for you.

a great deal of	according to	all over the world
as a result	in fact	in the meantime

1   Cities (everywhere) __all over the world__ have traffic problems, but
      a
no city in the world has more problems than São Paolo, Brazil. There are

too many cars in the city. People spend (a lot of) _____
                                                                    b
time trying to get places. (Actually) _____, some people
                                                          c
spend almost three hours a day getting to work and home again. (Because of

this) _____, there is also a lot of pollution. This situation
          d
is not getting any better. (As we read in) _____ *Time*
                                                                e
Magazine, people in Brazil buy almost 1,000 new cars every day. City

leaders need to act soon to solve this problem. (Until something else

happens) _____, drivers have to sit in their cars and wait.
                      f

as a matter of fact	before too long	by plane
instead of	more and more	these days

2   It is not very far from Paris to London (in the air)

_____. (The truth is) _____, it only
          a   b
takes about one hour. Unfortunately, (now) _____ it
                                                                      c
takes (a larger amount of) _____ time to get to the
                                              d
airport and go through security. A lot of people are now taking the train

(not) _____ a plane. (Soon) _____,
          e   f
airlines may stop flying between cities that are this close to each other.

READING 1
A SHORT HISTORY OF PUBLIC TRANSPORTATION

GETTING INTO THE TOPIC

Read the two definitions below and look at the photographs of *public transportation* on pages 98 and 99. Then discuss the following questions with a partner.

- **public transportation** (*n*) a group of buses and trains that run at regular times on regular routes and are used by the public
- **urban** (*adj*) of or in a city or town

1 When do you think the photographs were taken?
2 What do you think people used before these forms of public transportation?
3 What are some advantages of these forms of public transportation?
4 What other types of transportation do people use today?

GETTING A FIRST IDEA ABOUT THE READING

The following are the beginnings of the first sentences of each paragraph in Reading 1. Read them. Then, with a partner, discuss what you think the paragraphs will be about.

1 In the past, most people lived far from cities . . . (Par. 1)
2 The first modern form of public transportation was . . . (Par. 2)
3 At the end of the nineteenth century, a new form of transportation appeared . . . (Par. 3)
4 In the early twentieth century, elevated trains and subway systems were . . . (Par. 4)
5 In older cities, especially in Europe and Asia, driving a car was . . . (Par. 5)
6 In the United States, the government spent lots of money to build these roads . . . (Par. 6)
7 Public transportation systems in other parts of the world . . . (Par. 7)

WHILE YOU READ

As you read, stop at the end of each sentence that contains words in **bold**. Then follow the instructions in the box in the margin.

A Short History of Public Transportation

Look back in this sentence for a fixed phrase. Circle it.

In the past, most people lived far from cities in small groups or on farms. When they went from place to place, they walked or rode **animals**. Then people began to move to towns and cities, where there were a lot more people. They needed to get to work, to school, to shops, or to the doctor. Because many people were going to the same places, it was easier for them to travel together. This was the beginning of public transportation.

The first modern form of public transportation was the electric streetcar in the early nineteenth century. These streetcars operated along rails in the street. They were the major form of public transportation for many years. Streetcars were faster than horses. However, they had one big problem. They operated in the street, where there were also many horses, carts, and bicycles. The streets were crowded, so the streetcars could not move very quickly.

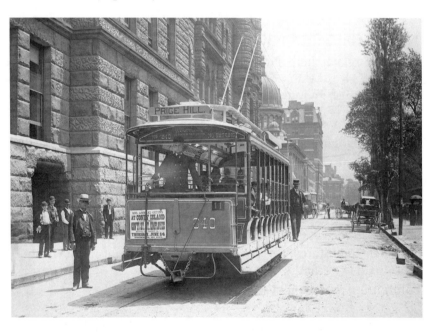

Streetcars were a common form of transportation in the nineteenth century.

At the end of the nineteenth century, a new form of transportation appeared: electric railways. Some electric railways operated above the streets. These are called **elevated trains**. Others ran though tunnels under the ground. These underground trains are sometimes called subways. The first major subway system was the London Underground. Soon, other cities, including Budapest, Paris, Berlin, and New York, built subway systems. For a long time, New York had the biggest subway system in the world.

Look back in the last sentence for a definition of *elevated trains*. Highlight it.

Elevated trains first appeared at the end of the nineteenth century.

In the early twentieth century, elevated trains and subway systems were very popular in major cities. However, soon they had competition from new forms of transportation, such as buses and cars. These used gasoline instead of electricity. Everyone wanted a car. People could go anywhere they wanted in their cars. They could go at any time they wanted. They did not have to wait for a streetcar, a train, or a bus. However, cars were very expensive. In the beginning, only rich people could buy them. Soon, however, cars became much cheaper. As a result, lots of people began to buy **cars**.

In older cities, especially in Europe and Asia, driving a car was not always easy. The streets were narrow and crowded. There were no streetlights. Many newer cities, especially in North America, were different. They were built for cars. They had wide roads and streetlights.

In the United States, the government spent lots of money to build these roads, especially in locations like California. All these roads encouraged more people to buy cars. Cities like Los Angeles had public transportation, but people preferred to drive their own cars. People with cars moved to homes far outside of the cities. The public transportation system did not reach these homes, so people needed cars to go everywhere. Because more people chose to drive, public transportation systems in cities like Los Angeles began to lose money. Today, these cities still have public transportation systems, but on the whole, they are not very **successful**.

What is the main idea of paragraph 4? Write it in the margin.

Look back in this sentence for a fixed phrase. Circle it.

Public transportation systems in other parts of the world, especially subways, have been very successful (see Figure 4.1). Moscow and Tokyo, for example, have very large systems. Millions of people use them. In many countries, the governments spend a lot of money on public transportation. They understand that it is more efficient than cars. Public transportation also uses less energy, and it produces less **pollution**. 7

Look back in paragraph 7 for a collocation with a verb and the noun *money*. Highlight the collocation.

FIGURE 4.1 Top Twelve Subway Systems in 2009

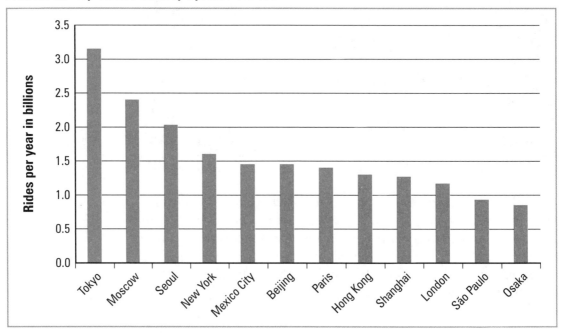

Source: Wikipedia

MAIN IDEA CHECK

Here are the main ideas of each paragraph in Reading 1. Match each paragraph to its main idea. Write the number of the paragraph on the blank line.

Paragraphs 1–3

_____ A Electric streetcars were fast, but they also had some problems.

_____ B Electric railways worked better because they ran above or below the street.

_____ C Public transportation began when many people needed to go to the same places.

Paragraphs 4–7

_____ D Public transportation systems in Asia and Europe have been successful.

_____ E Some American public transportation systems lost lots of money when more people chose to drive cars.

_____ F It is often easier to drive cars in new cities than in old cities.

_____ G Cars began to be a popular form of transportation.

A CLOSER LOOK

Look back at Reading 1 to answer the following questions.

1 How did people get to places far from their homes before public transportation? Circle two answers. (Par. 1)
   a They walked.
   b They did not go anywhere.
   c They rode animals.
   d They rode bicycles.

2 What was the problem with electric streetcars? (Par. 2)
   a They often broke.
   b The streets were crowded, so the street cars could not move quickly.
   c Electricity made them very expensive.
   d They were very noisy and dirty, so they were not popular.

3 New York has the biggest subway system in the world. True or False? (Par. 3 and Figure 4.1)

4 What are some advantages of public transportation over cars? Circle two answers. (Par. 7)
   a It is less expensive.
   b It causes less pollution.
   c It uses less energy.
   d It is faster.

5 According to Figure 4.1 on page 100, the subway system in _____ has more than three billion rides per year.

6 Number the different forms of transportation in the correct order in which they first appeared. Write the correct numbers on the blank lines. Put _1_ next to the earliest form and _4_ next to the most recent form.

   a _____ cars

   b _____ horses

   c _____ electric trains

   d _____ streetcars

VOCABULARY STUDY: DEFINITIONS

Find words in Reading 1 that can complete the following definitions. If you need help, use Key Vocabulary from the Readings on page 251.

1 A place that is full of people and things is _____. (*adj*) Par. 2

2 _____ are long roads that run under the ground. (*n pl*) Par. 3

3 A/An _____ is a group of connected things that work together. (*n*) Par. 3

4 Something that has a short distance between one side and the other is _____. (*adj*) Par. 5

5 Something that has a long distance between one side and the other is _____. (*adj*) Par. 5

6 _____ are places. (*n pl*) Par. 6

7 Something that works well without waste is _____. (*adj*) Par. 7

8 _____ is the power from something like oil or electricity, which brings light, heat, and transportation. (*n*) Par. 7

VOCABULARY STUDY: WORD FAMILIES

Read the words in the following chart. The words in **bold** are the parts of speech that appear in Reading 1. Find these words in the reading. If you need help, use Key Vocabulary from the Readings on page 251.

NOUN	VERB
competition	*compete*
encouragement	***encourage***
operation	***operate***
pollution	*pollute*
transportation	*transport*

Choose the correct form of the words from the chart to complete the following sentences. Use the correct verb tenses and subject-verb agreement. Use the correct singular and plural noun forms.

1 Many teachers _____ their students to write about their own experiences.

2 The factories near the town _____ its air and water.

3 Public _____ in many Asian and Europeans cities is very convenient.

4 A central computer controls the _____ of the trains and buses across the city.

5 Air _____ can make it difficult for some people to breathe.

6 The child did not get very much _____ from his parents or teachers, so he did not do well in school.

7 At the end of the year, the 10 best runners will _____ for a prize.

8 Elevated trains _____ on rails above the street.

9 The company uses trucks to _____ their products to stores that are far away.

10 There is a lot of _____ among airlines. Each airline tries to offer low prices so people will buy tickets from them.

BEYOND THE READING

Research

Find out about public transportation in your city or a city you know well. Find answers to the following questions:

- What are the main forms of transportation in the city?
- How much does a single ride cost?
- Does public transportation go outside of the city?
- How many people in the city use public transportation every day or every year?

Discussion

Share your research with a partner or your classmates.

Writing

Write a short description of the public transportation system you researched.

READING 2
BICYCLES AS TRANSPORTATION

GETTING INTO THE TOPIC
Discuss the following questions with a partner.

1 Do you have a bicycle? How often do you ride it?
2 Do a lot of people in your city or town ride bicycles to school or to work?
3 Does your town or city have special roads for bicycles?
4 What are the advantages and disadvantages of bicycles as a form of transportation?

GETTING A FIRST IDEA ABOUT THE READING
Read the title and the first sentence of each paragraph in Reading 2. Then look at the photographs on pages 106 and 107. What do you think this reading will be about? Write your answers below.

1 I think this reading will be about _____

_____.

2 Put a paragraph number in the chart next to the topic that you think will be in the paragraph.

PARAGRAPH	TOPIC
	How bicycles can help cities
	How riders can improve bicycle safety
	Advantages of bicycles and bicycle-sharing programs
	The popularity of bicycles
	Bicycles and safety
	The global increase in cars
	Bicycle use around the world

WHILE YOU READ
As you read, stop at the end of each sentence that contains words in **bold**. Then follow the instructions in the box in the margin.

Bicycles as Transportation

All over the world, more and more people are buying cars. 1
An increase in cars means more roads, more traffic, and more
pollution. One solution to these problems is more bicycle
use. **Bicycles have many advantages.** They do not pollute,
they are inexpensive, and they can improve health. Of course,
bicycles also have disadvantages compared to cars. They are
slower than cars. Cars can also carry more people and more
things. However, some city leaders believe bicycles have more
advantages than disadvantages. As a result, these cities are
trying to increase the use of bicycles.

As you read, look for
supporting details
for this main idea.
Number them.

Bicycles are already popular in many countries. There are 2
more than a billion bicycles around the world. That number
continues to rise. Bicycle production has increased significantly
since the middle of the twentieth century. In 1960, the rate of
production was 20 million bicycles every year. In 2007, it was
more than 130 million (see Figure 4.2). China makes more
bicycles than any other country. Two thirds of all bicycles are
made in **China**.

What is the main idea
of paragraph 2? Write it
in the margin.

FIGURE 4.2 Bicycle Production (in millions)

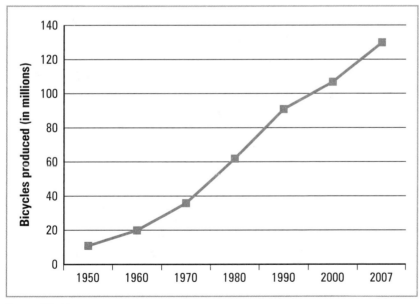

Source: Worldometers

The Chinese also ride their bicycles more than people in 3 other countries. In several cities in China, people use their bicycles for more than half of the trips they take to work, to school, or to go shopping. In contrast, Australians and Americans use bicycles on only one percent of their trips. In the poorest countries, the percentages are also low. In those countries, many people do not have enough money to buy bicycles.

Bicycles are a popular form of transportation in many countries.

Bicycles can help cities. In many cities around the world, 4 traffic and pollution are serious concerns. Some cities have started bicycle-sharing programs. More programs will start soon in other cities. These cities hope they will help reduce traffic and pollution. These programs encourage people to leave their cars at home and use bicycles instead. The programs provide hundreds or thousands of bicycles across the city. Everyone shares them. People can pick up a bicycle in one place, pay some money, ride it for a short time, and leave it in another place. Then someone else can use it. In 2009, there were more than 100 bicycle-sharing programs in cities all over the world, including Barcelona, Mexico City, Paris, and Rio de **Janeiro**. The program in Paris is one of the biggest and most successful. Today it has more than 42 million users and 21,000 bicycles.

Look back in this sentence for a fixed phrase. Circle it.

More people are riding bicycles, so bicycle safety is becom- 5 ing an important issue. Most bicycle accidents occur with cars. As a result, many cities and towns try to separate bicycles and cars. They have created paths for bicycles that are not on the street. However, research shows that these paths do not always decrease bicycle accidents. The research shows that riders think they are safer on these paths. Therefore, they sometimes ride less carefully on paths than they do on roads with cars.

Bicycle riders can also do some things to stay safe. All 6 bicycle riders should wear a helmet. A helmet protects a rider's head in an accident. Most people who die in bicycle accidents were not wearing helmets. In addition, riders should follow the same rules as cars. Many accidents occur because riders do not follow the **traffic rules**.

Look back in paragraph 6 for a collocation with a noun and the verb *follow*. Highlight the collocation.

Bicycle safety is very important.

Bicycles and bicycle-sharing programs are good for riders. 7 Riding a bicycle is less expensive than driving a car. Bicycles also give people exercise. This can improve their health. Bicycles are good for cities, too. New bicycle-sharing programs are cheaper than new buses or trains. Bicycle use also reduces the number of cars, so the streets are less crowded. Perhaps the most important thing is their effect on pollution. When more people use bicycles instead of cars, air pollution decreases.

MAIN IDEA CHECK

Here are the main ideas of each paragraph in Reading 2. Match each paragraph to its main idea. Write the number of the paragraph on the blank line.

Paragraphs 1–4

_____ A Bicycle use is different in different parts of the world.

_____ B Bicycles have advantages and disadvantages.

_____ C The number of bicycles in the world is growing.

_____ D Bicycle-sharing programs can reduce pollution and traffic.

_____ E Bicycle riders can do things to stay safe.

_____ F Bicycles can help riders and cities.

_____ G Cities and towns are trying to improve bicycle safety.

A CLOSER LOOK

Look back at Reading 2 to answer the following questions.

1 Fill in the chart below to show the advantages and disadvantages of bicycles. (Par. 1)

ADVANTAGES	DISADVANTAGES

2 According to Figure 4.2 on page 105, bicycle producers made about _____ million more bicycles in 2005 than in 1960.

3 The people of China ride their bicycles more than people in other countries. True or False? (Par. 3)

4 Which statements are true about bicycle-sharing programs? Circle three answers. (Par. 4)

   a People can use the bicycles for a few weeks or months.
   b Riders can pick up a bicycle in one place and leave it in another place.
   c The number of these programs is increasing.
   d The programs can help reduce pollution.

5 Separate paths for bicycles reduce accidents. True or False? (Par. 5)

6 Reread paragraph 6. Write two things bicycle riders should do to stay safe.

_____

_____

7 According to paragraph 7, bicycle-sharing programs are good for riders and for cities. Write three details from paragraph 7 to support this idea.

_____

_____

_____

VOCABULARY STUDY: DEFINITIONS

Find words in Reading 2 that can complete the following definitions. If you need help, use Key Vocabulary from the Readings on page 251.

1 _____ is all of the cars, buses, and trucks on the road. (*n*) Par. 1

2 A/An _____ is an answer to a problem. (*n*) Par. 1

3 If things _____, they go up; they increase. (*v*) Par. 2

4 _____ is the process of making something that will be sold. (*n*) Par. 2

5 To _____ is to make something new. (*v*) Par. 5

6 _____ are small roads, usually for walking, biking, or riding a horse. (*n pl*) Par. 5

7 If things _____, they go down. (*v*) Par. 5

8 A/An _____ is a strong, hard hat that protects the head. (*n*) Par. 6

VOCABULARY STUDY: WORDS IN CONTEXT

Complete the following sentences with words or phrases from the list below. If necessary, review the words in Key Vocabulary from the Readings on page 251.

reduce	exercise	pick up	concerns
trips	significantly	issue	contrast

1 She had a lot of _____ about the house, so she decided not to buy it.

2 They _____ their mail at the post office once a week.

3 This week's warm weather is in _____ with last week's cold rain.

4 Most people should get at least 20 minutes of _____ every day. It will improve their health.

5 Many people believe that the most important _____ in the country today is the economy.

6 The company was not making any money, so it had to _____ the number of workers in the factory.

7 The number of cars in China has increased _____ in the last 10 years.

8 She takes three _____ every week to the nearest town.

VOCABULARY REVIEW: SAME OR DIFFERENT

The following pairs of sentences contain vocabulary from Readings 1 and 2 in this unit. Write S on the blank line if the two sentences have the same meaning. Write D if the meanings are different.

_____ 1 Traffic is a serious issue for cities.

The number of cars and trucks on the street is an important concern for cities.

_____ 2 The train runs through a narrow tunnel.

The transportation system operates on rails in the street.

_____ 3 Many cities are trying to significantly decrease crime.

Many cities are trying to greatly reduce the number of crimes.

_____ 4 Bicycles save energy and don't pollute.

Bicycles are an efficient solution for crowded cities.

_____ 5 The teacher encouraged the children to wear helmets.

The teacher told the children that exercise would improve their health.

BEYOND THE READING

Research

Choose a city. Find out what it does to help bicycle riders. Find answers to the following questions:
- Are there separate paths for bicycles?
- Is there a bicycle-sharing program?
- Can riders take their bicycles on public transportation?
- Do many people ride bicycles?

Discussion

Discuss your research with a partner or your classmates.

Writing

Write a short description of your research.

SKILLS AND STRATEGIES 8
FINDING CONTRASTS

As you learned in Skills and Strategies 6 on page 80, writers use words or phrases to signal supporting details. Writers can also use words or phrases to signal the relationships between ideas, such as a contrast. A *contrast* is the difference between two or more ideas. Often the contrast shows the reader something unexpected or surprising. *However* and *but* are two common words that signal a contrast. Good readers notice these kinds of words or phrases. They help readers find contrasts and understand what a writer is trying to say.

EXAMPLES & EXPLANATIONS

Example

[1]Major car companies introduce new cars every year, **but** some new cars come from very small companies. [2]In the late 1970s, a man named John DeLorean started a company to produce an unusual sports car. [3]**However**, he did not sell enough cars, so he closed the company after only two years. [4]**Although** the company only built 9,000 cars, you can sometimes see a DeLorean sports car on the road.

Explanation

The main idea in this reading is introduced by the word *but*. *But* introduces a contrast between major car companies and very small companies.

However shows another contrast. In sentence 2, DeLorean started a company. In sentence 3, he closed the company.

Although shows an unexpected contrast: The company built very few cars, but some are still on the road.

THE LANGUAGE OF CONTRASTS

Here are some common words and phrases that signal contrast.

WORDS AND PHRASES THAT SIGNAL CONTRASTS			
but	*instead*	*although*	*on the one hand*
however	*in contrast*	*nevertheless*	*on the other hand*

STRATEGIES

These strategies will help you find contrasts while you read.

- Look for words and phrases that signal contrasts.
- When you see a contrast word or phrase, notice the meaning of the next idea. Ask yourself: *What idea is it different from?*
- If the reading is comparing things, make a list of the differences.

SKILL PRACTICE 1

Read the following paragraphs. Circle five words or phrases in each paragraph that signal contrasts. Then answer the questions below. The first one has been done for you.

1   Starting a company is always difficult, (but) starting a car manufacturing company is very difficult. It requires a great deal of money and knowledge. Nevertheless, some people start new companies to build cars. Malcolm Bricklin is one of those people. He started a company in Canada to build cars in 1971. However, he did not know a lot about building cars. He had problems with the design, and it was expensive to make the cars. He sold his first cars in 1974, but the company ran out of money less than two years later. Although the company failed, the cars still win prizes at car shows.

a Is starting a company to manufacture cars easier than starting other companies? It's more difficult.

What word or phrase signaled this contrast? but

b Why is it surprising that people start companies to make cars?

_____

What word or phrase signaled this contrast? _____

c The company started selling cars in 1974. When did it close? _____
What word or phrase signaled this contrast? _____

d The company failed. What is surprising? _____
What word or phrase signaled this contrast? _____

2   Henry Ford's first car was very similar to other cars in the early 1900s. However, he tried to make his cars more cheaply. Ford's ideas about making cars were unique. First, Ford did not design cars for rich people. Instead, he wanted average people to own cars. To make his cars less expensive, he found a new way to make cars. Other car designers made cars one by one. A few workers did all the work to finish one car before they started work on the next car. At Ford's company, on the other hand, the cars moved down a line past workers. Each worker completed one part of a car as it moved down the line. In this way, Ford made more cars quickly and sold them for less money. Ford also cared about his workers. Although other carmakers paid their workers less than $3 a day, Ford paid his workers $5 a day. He even started an English language school for his workers. Ford sold a lot of cars and became very rich, but he never forgot the people who made the cars.

a How were Ford's cars different from other cars in the early 1900s?

_____

What word or phrase signaled this contrast? _____

b Most carmakers designed cars for rich people. Who did Ford design cars for?

_____

What word or phrase signaled this contrast? _____

c Most manufacturers made cars one by one. What was different about the way Ford's company made cars? _____

What word or phrase signaled this contrast? _____

d Did Ford pay his workers the same amount as other carmakers?

_____

What word or phrase signaled this contrast? _____

SKILL PRACTICE 2

Read the following paragraph. Circle the words or phrases that signal a contrast. Write the differences between the two types of cars in the chart. The first one has been done for you.

When you want to buy a car, should you buy a new car or a used car? On the one hand, new cars are clean and beautiful. Old cars don't look as nice. New cars have all the newest technology. In contrast, used cars have older technology. New cars usually don't have problems, but used cars may need repairs. On the other hand, new cars are more expensive. You don't have to pay as much for a used car.

NEW CARS	USED CARS
are clean and beautiful	don't look as nice

READING 3
THE DANGERS OF DRIVING

GETTING INTO THE TOPIC
Look at the photographs on pages 116 and 117. Then discuss the following questions with a partner.

1 Describe what is happening in the photos.
2 Do you think it is safe to eat or drink while you are driving?
3 Do you think it is safe to use the phone while you are driving?
4 Do you do any of the things you see in the photos?

GETTING A FIRST IDEA ABOUT THE READING
Read the title, the section headings, and the first sentence of each paragraph of Reading 3. Then read the questions below. Write the number of the section (*I*, *II*, *III*, or *IV*) next to the question or questions it will answer.

SECTION	QUESTIONS THAT EACH SECTION WILL ANSWER
	How does technology improve car safety?
	What are the dangers of using a mobile phone while driving?
	What are some other distractions for drivers?
	How can drivers prevent injuries?
	What can people do to make travel by car safer?
	Why are there so many accidents?
	Are teenagers dangerous drivers?
	Is eating while driving dangerous?

WHILE YOU READ
As you read, stop at the end of each sentence that contains words in **bold**. Then follow the instructions in the box in the margin.

The Dangers of Driving

I. DRIVING SAFELY

Cars can help us in many ways, but they can also be dangerous. Car accidents cause between 20 and 50 million injuries every year around the world. More than a million people die in car accidents every year; in other words, about 3,500 people every day. Every year, more people drive cars, so this number will probably increase. By 2020, the number of deaths from car accidents will probably rise to almost two million every year.

One cause of car accidents is dangerous driving. First, some people drive too fast. Second, they do not always obey traffic laws. If drivers were more careful about these two things, there would be fewer accidents, and the roads would be safer.

As you read, look for supporting details for this main idea. Number them.

Drivers can also do one easy thing to prevent or reduce deaths and injuries in accidents: They should always wear a seatbelt. Research shows that 50 percent of deaths in car accidents could be prevented by the use of seatbelts. Many countries have laws that require drivers to wear seatbelts. However, not everyone obeys these laws. Many people don't wear their seatbelts because they think they will not have an accident. They think, "I am not driving very far" or "I am not driving very fast." However, most accidents happen when people are driving less than 37 miles per hour (60 kilometers per hour) and when they are near their **homes**.

Look back in paragraph 3 for a word that signals a contrast. Circle the word, and underline the two ideas the writer contrasts.

Wearing a seatbelt helps prevent serious injury in a car accident.

There is one other serious danger for drivers: distraction. Drivers need to be aware of many things when they drive: other cars, people on the street, the weather. It is difficult and dangerous for them to do other things while they are driving.

There are many distractions for drivers, such as the radio, passengers in the car, or even a cup of coffee. All of these distractions can cause accidents.

II. MOBILE PHONES

One recent cause of distraction is mobile phones. The number of mobile phones has increased significantly. Drivers are much more likely to have an accident if they are talking on the phone. Research shows that the problem is not just the phone. The problem is the conversation. Phones that do not require hands are just as dangerous as phones that drivers must hold in their hands. 5

Writing and reading text messages while driving is even more dangerous than talking. When drivers read or write a message on their mobile phone, they are not looking at the road. Instead, they are looking at their phone for four or five seconds. This can lead to an accident. One study in 2003 estimated that mobile phone use causes 2,600 deaths every year in the United **States**. 6

Look back in paragraph 6 for a word that signals a contrast. Circle the word, and underline the two ideas the writer contrasts.

Teenagers are the most likely to use their phones while they are driving. A recent study of American teenagers showed that about a quarter of them send text messages while they are driving. About 40 percent of them talk on the phone while they are driving. 7

It is really dangerous to write and read text messages while driving.

Look back in this sentence for a fixed phrase. Circle it.

According to a recent study, drivers know writing text messages or talking while driving is **dangerous**. Why do they still do it? Some people want to stay connected to their friends and family. Other people want to stay connected to their office. They do not want to miss an important call. They feel they need to continue working while they are driving. 8

III. OTHER DISTRACTIONS FOR DRIVERS

There are other dangerous distractions for drivers. Research 9 shows that eating or drinking while driving is also dangerous. Eating or drinking means that drivers must take their hands off the wheel. When drivers are doing two things at the same time, it is difficult for them to pay attention. However, driving and eating or drinking is very common. One study found that 70 percent of drivers sometimes eat when they drive, and 83 percent sometimes drink when they **drive**.

What makes this man such a dangerous driver?

Look back in paragraph 9 for a collocation with a verb and the noun *attention*. Highlight the collocation.

One final distraction may be surprising. Some people shave 10 or put on makeup while they are driving. Of course, this is dangerous because drivers must take one or both of their hands off the wheel. Also, they have to look away from the road for a few seconds. A study of women drivers in England in 2009 shows that 20 percent of them sometimes put on their makeup while they are driving. The study estimated that this causes a half a million accidents every year in Great Britain.

IV. NEW SAFETY TECHNOLOGY

Scientists and engineers are finding ways to improve safety 11 and decrease the number of accidents. They are using new technology to do this. There are new mobile phones that turn off when the car is moving. Some cars also have new technology that tells drivers if they are too close to another car or if they are not in the center of the road. These cars can also tell when a driver is starting to fall **asleep**.

What is the main idea of paragraph 11? Write it in the margin.

Driving can be dangerous, but people can make it safer. If 12 people drive carefully, wear a seatbelt, and avoid distractions such as mobile phones, food, and putting on makeup, they will be safer. They will also make the roads safer for other people.

MAIN IDEA CHECK

Here are the main ideas of each paragraph in Reading 3. Match each paragraph to its main idea. Write the number of the paragraph on the blank line.

Paragraphs 1–4

_____ A The number of car accidents is increasing.

_____ B Many things can distract drivers.

_____ C Many car accidents occur because drivers do not drive safely.

_____ D It is possible to prevent many deaths and injuries.

Paragraphs 5–8

_____ E Although drivers know some things are dangerous, they still do them.

_____ F Teenagers are the most likely to use a phone while they are driving.

_____ G Reading or writing text messages is a serious distraction.

_____ H Talking on the phone is a serious distraction.

Paragraphs 9–12

_____ I There is new technology to decrease distractions and accidents.

_____ J Drivers can make travel by car safer.

_____ K Eating and drinking while driving is dangerous.

_____ L Shaving or putting on makeup while driving is dangerous.

A CLOSER LOOK

Look back at Reading 3 to answer the following questions.

1 The number of people who die every year in car accidents continues to increase. True or False? (Par. 1)

2 According to paragraph 2, what are some ways in which drivers contribute to accidents? Circle two answers.
   a They don't pay attention when they are driving.
   b They drive too fast.
   c They don't obey traffic laws.
   d They drive after they drink alcohol.

3 According to paragraph 3, what is the most important thing that drivers can do to prevent deaths or injuries in accidents?
   a They should not talk on the phone.
   b They should wear their seatbelts.
   c They should not eat while they are driving.
   d They should drive more slowly.

4 Phones that do not require hands are safer than phones that require hands.
True or False? (Par. 5)

5 _____ are most likely to send or receive text messages while
they are driving. (Par. 7)

6 What are some dangerous distractions for drivers? Circle three answers.
(Pars. 9 and 10)
   a Shaving
   b Eating
   c Singing
   d Talking
   e Putting on makeup

7 How will new technology prevent accidents? Circle three answers. (Par. 11)
   a Cell phones will signal that a driver is starting to fall asleep.
   b Cars will signal that the driver is not driving in a straight line.
   c Cars will not let drivers operate the radio.
   d Cell phones will not operate in moving cars.
   e Cars will signal that the driver is starting to fall asleep.

8 Look over the reading again. In the chart, list things that are likely to
increase accidents in the first column. List things that are likely to improve
safety in the second column. The first one has been done for you.

LIKELY TO INCREASE ACCIDENTS	LIKELY TO IMPROVE SAFETY
Talking on a mobile phone or writing text messages while driving	Mobile phones that turn off when the car is moving

VOCABULARY STUDY: DEFINITIONS

Find words in Reading 3 that can complete the following definitions. If you
need help, use Key Vocabulary from the Readings on page 251.

1 _____ go across your body while you are driving. They protect
you in an accident. (n pl) Par. 3

2 A/An _____ is something that stops you from paying attention.
(n) Par. 4

3 If you know about something, you are _____ of it. (adj) Par. 4

4 _____ are people in a car, train, bus, or plane who are not driving. (*n pl*) Par. 4

5 _____ are short pieces of information for someone who is not with you. (*n pl*) Par. 6

6 _____ are people older than twelve but younger than twenty. (*n pl*) Par. 7

7 To _____ is to cut hair from the face or body. (*v*) Par. 10

8 _____ is something women put on their faces, especially their eyes and mouth, to make themselves look prettier. (*n*) Par.10

VOCABULARY STUDY: SYNONYMS

Read the sentences below. The words or phrases in parentheses mean the same or almost the same as the words in the list. For each sentence, replace the words in parentheses with a word from the list. Write it on the blank line. If necessary, review the words in Key Vocabulary from the Readings on page 251.

avoid	estimated	missed	text
basic	obeyed	conversation	injuries

1 The children (followed) _____ the teacher's instructions.

2 They had a long (talk) _____ about their plans for the future.

3 The government (guessed) _____ that about 200 people died in the fire.

4 The accident caused (physical harm) _____. The bike riders had broken legs and arms.

5 She tries to (stay away from) _____ food with a lot of fat and sugar.

6 She read the (written words) _____ three times, but she still did not understand it.

7 There are a few (simple) _____ things you can do to save energy.

8 I (did not receive) _____ your phone call, because I was not at home.

VOCABULARY REVIEW: ACADEMIC WORD LIST

The following are Academic Word List (AWL) words from all the readings in Unit 4. Complete the sentences below with these words. If necessary, review the AWL words in Key Vocabulary from the Readings on page 251.

text (*n*)	estimated (*v*)	issues (*n*)	contrast (*n*)	transportation (*n*)
location (*n*)	energy (*n*)	significantly (*adv*)	injury (*n*)	create (*v*)

1 Technology has improved _____ so that today people can go from one place to another quickly and easily.

2 The government must _____ more jobs so that more people can work.

3 We get _____ from oil, electricity, and the sun.

4 The store has moved to a new _____ on the other side of the city.

5 You can read the _____ of the president's speech online.

6 The child's health has improved _____. He is feeling much better this week.

7 There was a clear _____ between the dark water and the bright sun.

8 He _____ that it would cost about $1,000 to repair the car.

9 Air and water pollution are very important _____. We must find a way to decrease them.

10 Some of the soldiers died, and others had serious _____.

BEYOND THE READING

Research

Do some research on the city or town where you live. Find answers to the following questions:

- Are there laws that require seatbelts?
- Are there laws that require special seats for babies and children?
- Are there laws against talking on the phone while driving?
- Are there laws against reading or writing text messages while driving?

Discussion

Share your results with a partner or your classmates.

Writing

Which of these laws do you think is most important? Why? Write a short summary that gives the reasons for your opinion.

MAKING CONNECTIONS

The vocabulary in these exercises comes from all the readings in Unit 4. The exercises will help you see how writers make connections across sentences in a paragraph.

One way that writers make connections is to show a contrast. A contrast shows how one idea is different from another idea. Writers can use transition words or phrases such as *however, on the one hand, on the other hand, in contrast,* or *nevertheless* to make these connections. You learned these words and phrases in Skills and Strategies 8 on page 111.

EXERCISE 1

Read the following paragraphs. Highlight any transition words or phrases that signal contrast. Underline any words or phrases that signal additional information (see page 61) or facts and examples (see page 91). The first one has been done for you.

1   When visiting another country, driving a car is a good way to see the countryside. However, this may be dangerous, because driving in another country may be very different. For instance, in Canada and the United States, people drive on the right side of the road. In contrast, in England and Japan, people drive on the left.

2   In many countries all over the world, teenagers can start to drive at 18. However, in some countries, for example in New Zealand, they can get their driver's license at 15. In other locations, teenagers cannot drive by themselves for the first year of their license.

3   Many places have special rules for teenage drivers. For example, the rules may require teenage drivers to have an older driver in the car, or they may limit the number of passengers in the car. Teenagers may not like these rules. Nevertheless, these rules help to make the roads safe for all drivers.

4   Motorcycles are more energy efficient than cars. Research shows that motorcycles use half the fuel that cars use. On the other hand, they are also more dangerous. Eighty percent of motorcycle accidents result in injury or death. In contrast, only 20 percent of automobile accidents result in injury or death.

5   At one time, Los Angeles had a fast and efficient public transportation system. However, the city took away the streetcars and built more highways. Now, Los Angeles has the worst traffic in the United States. It also has very bad pollution.

EXERCISE 2

Make a clear paragraph by putting sentences A, B, and C into the best order after the numbered sentence. Look for pronouns and words or phrases that signal contrast or addition to help you. Write the letters in the correct order on the blank lines.

1 Companies have several choices about how to transport their products.
____ ____ ____

| A They are also cheaper because they need fewer workers to operate them. | B However, they are often not as convenient as trucks. | C For instance, trains use less energy than trucks. |

2 Bicycles with electric motors are becoming more popular. ____ ____ ____

| A This is because they go faster than other bicycles on the road and cannot stop as quickly. | B However, this has become a concern in some places. | C For example, in China they have caused a lot of injuries. |

3 People used to get good exercise when they rode their bicycles to work.
____ ____ ____

| A Now, however, more and more people ride bicycles with electric motors. | B However, the only exercise they get is starting the motor. | C These make it easier for people to get to work. |

4 Many parents encourage their children to obey all safety laws.
____ ____ ____

| A They also make them wear helmets when they ride their bicycles. | B For example, they make sure that their children wear seatbelts in the car. | C These actions will help children avoid injuries. |

5 Roundabouts are traffic circles where roads meet. ____ ____ ____

| A This is because some drivers don't know which direction to drive in. | B On the other hand, they reduce the number of injuries. | C They are sometimes confusing for drivers. |

Sleep

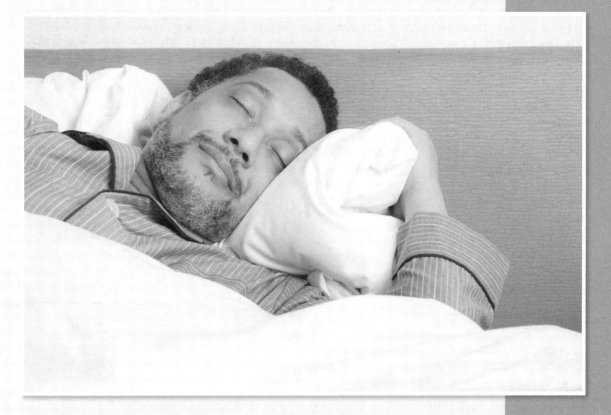

SKILLS AND STRATEGIES 9-10
- Finding the Meanings of Words (2)
- Finding Causes and Effects

READINGS
- The Importance of Sleep
- Getting Enough Sleep
- Your Body Clock

SKILLS AND STRATEGIES 9
FINDING THE MEANINGS OF WORDS (2)

In Skills and Strategies 1 on page 2, you learned that writers sometimes give definitions to explain words that readers may not know. Sometimes, however, writers do not give exact definitions. Instead, they give additional information, such as examples or contrasts. Examples and contrasts can help show the meaning of the word. You learned about some words and phrases that signal examples in Skills and Strategies 6 on page 80. You learned about some words and phrases that signal contrast in Skills and Strategies 8 on page 111. Good readers look for definitions as they read, but they also look for words and phrases that signal additional information. This helps them find the meanings of words.

EXAMPLES & EXPLANATIONS

Examples

Sleepwalking may be **genetic**. For example, a person who sleepwalks is likely to have a family member who also walks in his or her sleep.

I used to have **insomnia**, but now I have no difficulty sleeping at all.

Explanations

Sometimes writers give examples that show the meaning of a word. They sometimes introduce the examples with phrases, such as *for example*, *for instance*, or *such as*.

genetic = common among family members

Sometimes you can figure out a word because the writer gives a contrast or an opposite meaning. Here, the writer says that she had *insomnia* in the past. She signals a contrast with the word *but*, and says that now she has no difficulty sleeping.

insomnia = difficulty sleeping

STRATEGIES

These strategies will help you find the meanings of words while you read.

- When you read a word you do not know, do not stop reading. Continue to the end of the sentence that contains the difficult word, and then read the next sentence.
- Look for definitions of difficult words. See Finding the Meanings of Words (1) on page 2.
- Search for words and phrases that signal examples or contrasts. Use this information to guess the meaning of a word.

SKILL PRACTICE 1

Read the following sentences. What kind of additional information in each sentence can help you figure out the meaning of the words in **bold**? Is the information an example, a contrast, or a definition? Circle the type of information. Then underline the clues that helped you. The first one has been done for you.

1 A good **mattress** may be expensive, <u>but</u> a bad mattress is hard to sleep on and may give you a backache.

   a example (b) contrast c definition

2 **Snoring** can be very loud. For example, when someone in a family snores, it may wake up other people sleeping nearby.

   a example b contrast c definition

3 People often have **nightmares**. However, when they wake up, they often can't remember what scared them.

   a example b contrast c definition

4 Animals such as bears **hibernate**; that is, they go to sleep for the winter.

   a example b contrast c definition

5 Small, flat beds such as **futons** are very useful in small apartments.

   a example b contrast c definition

6 Some people take a **sleeping pill** at night, but many people have hot milk instead of medicine when they can't sleep.

   a example b contrast c definition

7 In the winter, some people use **electric blankets** (covers that you can turn on and off to heat your bed), but some people do not think they are safe.

   a example b contrast c definition

8 Although a lot of people avoid **caffeine** at night, I don't have any trouble sleeping when I have coffee after dinner.

   a example b contrast c definition

SKILL PRACTICE 2

Read the sentences in Skill Practice 1 again to figure out the meaning of each word in **bold**. Circle the correct meaning. The first one has been done for you.

1 A good **mattress** may be expensive, but a bad mattress is hard to sleep on and may give you a backache.

   a the thing that goes under your head when you sleep

   (b) the part of a bed that you put your whole body on when you sleep

2 **Snoring** can be very loud. For example, when someone in a family snores, it may wake up other people sleeping nearby.

   a walking while you sleep

   b making noise while you sleep

3 People often have **nightmares**. However, when they wake up, they often can't remember what scared them.

   a something that scares you while you sleep

   b something good that happens to you while you sleep

4 Animals such as bears **hibernate**; that is, they go to sleep for the winter.

   a go to sleep for the winter

   b go to a warmer area to live in the winter

5 Small, flat beds such as **futons** are very useful in small apartments.

   a small beds

   b small apartments

6 Some people take a **sleeping pill** at night, but many people have hot milk instead of medicine when they can't sleep.

   a medicine that helps you wake up in the morning

   b medicine that helps you sleep

7 In the winter, some people use **electric blankets** (covers that you can turn on and off to heat your bed), but some people do not think they are safe.

   a covers for your bed that have electric heating in them

   b covers you put under your head when you go to sleep

8 Although a lot of people avoid **caffeine** at night, I don't have any trouble sleeping when I have coffee after dinner.

   a a chemical in things such as coffee and tea that makes people feel more awake

   b a special strong coffee that people drink in very small cups after dinner

READING 1
THE IMPORTANCE OF SLEEP

GETTING INTO THE TOPIC

Discuss the following questions with a partner.

1 How many hours do you sleep every night?
2 Do you sleep more or less than you did when you were younger? Explain your answer.
3 How do you feel if you don't get enough sleep? Explain your answer.
4 Do you dream every night? Do you remember your dreams?

GETTING A FIRST IDEA ABOUT THE READING

Read the title, and look at the charts on pages 130 and 131 for Reading 1. What do you think this reading will be about? Write your answers below.

1 I think this reading will be about _____
_____.

2 Answer the following questions:
   a How long do adult humans sleep every night?
   b What are two animals that sleep more than adult humans?
   c What are two animals that sleep less than adult humans?
   d How does the amount humans sleep change as they grow older?
   e What do you think might be the reason for this change?

WHILE YOU READ

As you read, stop at the end of each sentence that contains words in **bold**. Then follow the instructions in the box in the margin.

The Importance of Sleep

For about one third of your life, you eyes will be closed. You will not move very much. You will breathe very slowly. You will be quiet. In other words, for about one third of your life, you will be asleep. 1

As you read, look for supporting details for this main idea. Number them.

Why do we sleep so much? What is the **purpose**? Scientists do not have a complete answer. They believe that sleep restores your energy and helps your brain to work better. If you do not sleep enough, you cannot concentrate on your work, and you feel tired all day. Without enough sleep, you are also more likely to get sick. 2

Look back in this sentence for a fixed phrase. Circle it.

Sleep is important for normal development. Children need a lot of sleep in order to grow up strong and **healthy**. They need more sleep than adults. During the first two weeks of life, babies sleep for about 16 hours every day. This changes as they grow and need less sleep. Teenagers need about nine hours of sleep every night. Most adults need about eight hours. After about the age of 70, most adults only sleep for about six hours every night. (See Figure 5.1.) 3

FIGURE 5.1 Number of Hours of Sleep We Need as We Grow

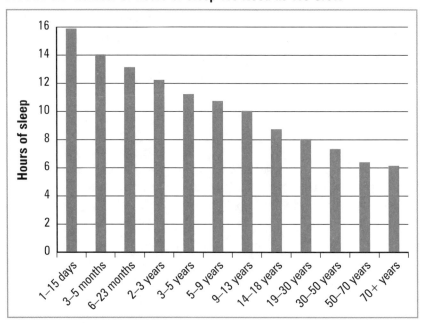

Source: www.faculty.washington.edu

As you read, find clues in this paragraph that signal the definition of *variation*. Circle the clues, and write the definition in the margin.

All animals sleep, but there is great **variation** in how much they sleep. (See Figure 5.2.) For example, some big snakes sleep for more than 18 hours a day. Sheep only sleep for about four 4

FIGURE 5.2 Hours of Sleep per Day

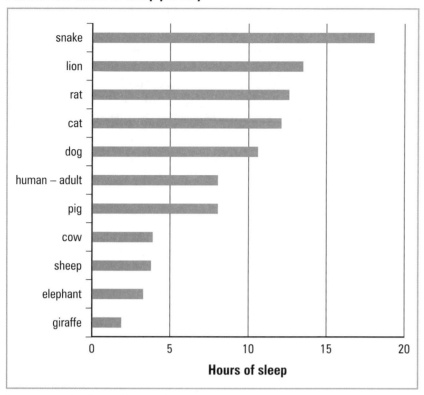

Source: www.faculty.washington.edu

hours, and giraffes sleep less than two hours a day! Pigs sleep for eight hours a day just like adult humans.

Adult humans usually sleep for a long period and then are awake for a long period. In contrast, most animals do not sleep for one long period. Instead, they sleep for shorter periods during the day and night. Human babies and animals have similar sleep patterns. They sleep for a few hours, and then they stay awake for a few **hours**.

Scientists are also learning more about how people sleep. They know there are five different stages of sleep. Brain activity changes during these stages. During the last stage of sleep, something strange happens. Many of the muscles in your body are **paralyzed**; in contrast, your brain becomes very active. Your eyes move rapidly, and you breathe more quickly, too. This stage is called Rapid Eye Movement (REM) sleep. About 20 percent of adult sleep is REM sleep. Adults usually go through about five periods of REM sleep every night.

REM sleep is when people have most of their dreams. If a person has one dream in each of these REM periods, that is about 2,000 dreams every year. Humans and many animals have dreams, but scientists are not sure of the purpose of

What is the main idea of paragraph 5? Write it in the margin.

Find a clue in this sentence that signals the definition of *paralyzed*. Circle the clue, and write the definition in the margin.

dreams. Some scientists believe dreams help people understand things that happen during the day. Other scientists think
dreams help us remember **things**.

There are still many things we do not understand about 8
sleep. However, one thing we do know is that all animals,
including humans, need to sleep. They need to sleep in order
to grow and to keep their brains and bodies active and healthy.
They need to sleep or they will get sick and die.

Look back in paragraph
7 for a collocation
with a verb and the
noun *dream*. Highlight
the collocation.

MAIN IDEA CHECK

Here are the main ideas of each paragraph in Reading 1. Match each paragraph
to its main idea. Write the number of the paragraph on the blank line.

Paragraphs 1–4

_____ A Scientists believe sleep may have several purposes.

_____ B While you sleep, your body is quiet.

_____ C Not all animals need the same amount of sleep.

_____ D Sleep is very important for healthy growth.

Paragraphs 5–8

_____ E The REM stage of sleep is when the brain is most active.

_____ F Dreams occur during REM sleep.

_____ G Sleep is necessary for all animals.

_____ H Some animals sleep for one long period every day; others sleep for
several shorter periods.

A CLOSER LOOK

Look back at Reading 1 to answer the following questions.

1 You sleep for about half of your life. True or False? (Par. 1)

2 Which of the following is *not* stated as a purpose of sleep? (Pars. 2 and 3)
   a Sleep restores our energy.
   b Sleep keeps us healthy.
   c Sleep helps us think better.
   d Sleep makes us more intelligent.
   e Sleep helps children grow up healthy.

3 Our need for sleep changes as we grow older. About how many hours do we need at each age? Fill in the chart below with the number of hours we need at each age. (Par. 3)

AGES	HOURS OF SLEEP
Babies	
Teenagers	
Adults	
People over 70 years old	

4 What is similar about the sleep patterns of human babies and many animals? (Par. 5)
   a They sleep for 16 hours a day.
   b They need less sleep as they grow older.
   c They sleep for short periods and then are awake for short periods.
   d They cannot concentrate if they do not sleep enough.

5 What happens during the REM stage of sleep? Circle four answers. (Pars. 6 and 7)
   a You breathe more quickly.
   b You save energy.
   c You dream.
   d Your body does not move.
   e Your eyes move.

6 Some scientists believe that dreams help people understand what happens to them during the day. True or False? (Par. 7)

VOCABULARY STUDY: DEFINITIONS

Find words in Reading 1 that can complete the following definitions. If you need help, use Key Vocabulary from the Readings on page 251.

1 To _____ something is to make it the way it was earlier. (v) Par. 2

2 Something that is usual and expected is _____. (adj) Par. 3

3 _____ are animals that are fully grown. For humans, this means 18 years or older. (n pl) Par. 3

4 _____ are the particular way that things occur. They occur in these same ways over and over. (n pl) Par. 5

5 _____ are specific periods during an activity. (n pl) Par. 6

6 Something that is very unusual is _____. (*adj*) Par. 6

7 _____ are the parts of the body that make you move. (*n pl*) Par. 6

8 Something that cannot move is _____. (*adj*) Par. 6

VOCABULARY STUDY: WORD FAMILIES

Read the words in the following chart. The words in **bold** are the parts of speech that appear in Reading 1. Find these words in the reading. If you need help, use Key Vocabulary from the Readings on page 251.

NOUN	VERB
breath	***breathe***
concentration	***concentrate***
development	*develop*
dream	***dream***
variation	*vary*

Choose the correct form of the words from the chart to complete the following sentences. Use the correct verb tenses and subject-verb agreement. Use the correct singular and plural noun forms.

1 When there is a lot of noise, it is difficult for me to _____ on my work.

2 The swimmer took a _____ every time his head came out of the water.

3 Most people have more than one _____ every night.

4 Children _____ at different rates. Some learn to speak before they walk, and others walk before they speak.

5 There was a lot of _____ in the test results. Some students did very well, but others received poor grades.

6 People often _____ at night about what happens to them during the day.

7 If there is a lot of air pollution, it is difficult to _____.

8 The student who won first prize said that _____ was an important part of his success in school.

9 Table manners are not the same everywhere. They _____ from culture to culture.

10 Healthy food and exercise are important for a child's _____.

BEYOND THE READING

Research
Do some research on sleep.
- Ask 10 people of different ages how many hours they usually sleep at night.
- Are their responses like the descriptions in paragraph 3 of the reading?
- How much sleep do you need? Does it match the descriptions in paragraph 3 of the reading?

Discussion
Share your research with a partner or your classmates.

Writing
Write a short summary comparing your class results with Figure 5.1 in the reading.

READING 2
GETTING ENOUGH SLEEP

GETTING INTO THE TOPIC

Read the title of Reading 2, and discuss the following questions with a partner.

1 Is it difficult for you to fall asleep at night?
2 Do you use a clock to wake up in the morning, or do you wake up without help?
3 Do you ever sleep during the day? Explain your answer.
4 Has anything bad ever happened to you when you didn't get enough sleep? Explain your answer.

GETTING A FIRST IDEA ABOUT THE READING

The following are the first sentences of the paragraphs in Reading 2. Read these sentences. Then, with a partner, discuss what you think the paragraphs will be about.

1 Sleep is important for our physical health. (Par. 1)
2 Sleep is necessary for memory and learning. (Par. 2)
3 Good decisions and good judgment also require sleep. (Par. 3)
4 Scientists have found that you respond more slowly if you have not had enough sleep. (Par. 4)
5 Although the importance of sleep is clear, many people do not get enough sleep. (Par. 5)
6 There are some things you can do if you do not get enough sleep during the night. (Par. 6)
7 Sleep is important for health and safety, so it is unfortunate that so many people do not get sufficient sleep. (Par. 7)

WHILE YOU READ

As you read, stop at the end of each sentence that contains words in **bold**. Then follow the instructions in the box in the margin.

Getting Enough Sleep

Sleep is important for our physical health. Without sleep, people would be too tired to work or play. However, sleep may be even more important for our mental health. Sleep helps our brains work when we are awake. It improves our ability to remember, learn, and make good decisions. It also helps us respond to things around us. If people don't get enough sleep, there can be serious **consequences**.

Sleep is necessary for memory and learning. People do not learn and remember as well when they are tired. One study compared two groups of students. The first group studied for a test for a few hours and then went to sleep for eight hours. The second group studied for most of the night and slept for only a few hours. The students in the first group did much better on the test the next day.

Good decisions and good judgment also require sleep. To make a good decision, it is useful to consider different sides of a problem or situation. Research shows that people who have not slept enough cannot do this very **well**. As a result, they sometimes make bad decisions. Sleepy people often do not realize that there is a problem with their behavior. They believe that they are acting and thinking normally.

Scientists have found that you respond more slowly if you have not had enough sleep. Many times every day, you respond to everything around you, such as a hot plate, a bright light, or a loud noise. It is often essential to respond quickly. Response time is especially important if you are driving or using a machine. For example, if a person walks into the street in front of your car, you must stop quickly. If you are sleepy, you may respond too slowly. Many car accidents occur because drivers are **tired**.

1

2

3

4

Look back in paragraph 1 for a collocation with a verb and the noun *decision*. Highlight the collocation.

Look back in this sentence for a fixed phrase. Circle it.

What is the main idea of paragraph 4? Write it in the margin.

A tired driver is a dangerous driver.

Although the importance of sleep is clear, many people do 5 not get enough sleep. Seventy-five percent of the people in a 2005 survey of adults in the United States said that they had sleep problems or insomnia. Many people cannot fall asleep easily, or they cannot stay asleep for very long. There are many reasons for this. Some people have health problems that prevent them from sleeping well. Other people eat or drink something, such as coffee, that keeps them awake. However, the most important reason for insomnia is stress. People often feel **stress**, for instance, when they work too hard or if they are worried about something.

Find a clue in this sentence that signals the definition of *stress*. Circle the clue, and highlight the definition.

A worker who has a lot of stress may also have insomnia.

Look back in paragraph 6 for a collocation with a verb and the noun *nap*. Highlight the collocation.

There are some things 6 you can do if you do not get enough sleep during the night. One solution is a nap – a short sleep during the day. A recent study showed that one third of all American adults take a nap every day. Many famous people in history liked to take naps. Albert Einstein, Winston Churchill, and Ronald Reagan often took naps. They believed that naps helped them work **better**.

Sleep is important for health and safety, so it is unfortunate 7 that so many people do not get sufficient sleep. If you cannot fall asleep or stay asleep, here are some ideas that may help you:

- Try to go to sleep and wake up at about the same time every day.
- Don't eat just before you go to bed.
- Don't drink alcohol or coffee before you go to bed.
- Don't work just before you go to bed.
- Do something to help you relax for at least 30 minutes before you go to bed. Read a book or listen to quiet music.
- Make sure your room is not too hot or too cold.
- Make sure your bed is comfortable.

MAIN IDEA CHECK

Here are the main ideas of each paragraph in Reading 2. Match each paragraph to its main idea. Write the number of the paragraph on the blank line.

Paragraphs 1–4

_____ A You need a good night's sleep to have good judgment.

_____ B Sleep influences response time.

_____ C You need a good night's sleep to have a healthy body and mind.

_____ D Sleep helps you to learn and remember.

Paragraphs 5–7

_____ E Many people do not sleep enough.

_____ F There are things you can do to help you fall asleep.

_____ G A nap can help if you do not sleep enough at night.

A CLOSER LOOK

Look back at Reading 2 to answer the following questions.

1 One study showed that students who study all night do well on tests. True or False? (Par. 2)

2 What happens to people's judgment if they do not sleep enough? Circle two answers (Par. 3)
   a People who do not sleep enough cannot think about different sides of a question or problem.
   b People who do not sleep enough often make decisions too quickly.
   c People who do not sleep enough do not know they are making bad decisions.
   d People who do not sleep enough sometimes get angry.

3 Why is response time important? Circle two answers. (Par. 4)
   a If you don't respond quickly, you will not get enough work done.
   b If you don't respond quickly in a dangerous situation, you could injure yourself.
   c If you don't respond quickly, you may forget important information.
   d If you don't respond quickly in a dangerous situation, you may injure someone else.

4 Some people cannot fall asleep because they have a lot of stress in their lives. True or False? (par. 5)

5 A _____ during the day can help you if you do not sleep enough during the night. (Par. 6)

6   Look at the list at the end of the reading. What are some ideas for people who cannot fall asleep at night? Circle three answers.

   a Eat something small just before you go to bed.
   b Relax for 30 minutes before you go to bed.
   c Run for 30 minutes just before you go to bed.
   d Make sure your room is warm.
   e Go to bed and wake up at about the same time every day.
   f Don't drink coffee at night.

VOCABULARY STUDY: DEFINITIONS

Find words in Reading 2 that can complete the following definitions. If you need help, use Key Vocabulary from the Readings on page 251.

1   _____ issues are related to thinking and to the brain. (*adj*) Par. 1

2   _____ are the results of a situation or activity. These results are often bad. (*n pl*) Par. 1

3   People who have good _____ can make good decisions. (*n*) Par. 3

4   To _____ something is to come to understand it, often quickly. (*v*) Par. 3

5   Something that is very, very important is _____. (*adj*) Par. 4

6   A/An _____ is a type of research that asks people for their ideas and opinions. (*n*) Par. 5

7   _____ is great concern and worry about a difficult situation. (*n*) Par 5

8   A/An _____ is a short sleep during the day. (*n*) Par. 6

VOCABULARY STUDY: WORDS IN CONTEXT

Complete the following sentences with words or phrases from the list below. If necessary, review the words in Key Vocabulary from the Readings on page 251.

sufficient	ability	comfortable	fell asleep
compared	at least	unfortunate	memory

1 Small babies do not have the _____ to speak or walk.

2 His family did not have _____ money to buy an expensive car, so they chose a smaller, less expensive one.

3 You must be _____ 18 years old to vote for the president.

4 The new student had an excellent _____. He never forgot anything.

5 It was _____ that there was very bad weather during the football game.

6 She was very tired, so she _____ soon after dinner.

7 She _____ the two photographs, but they looked exactly the same to her.

8 This chair is very _____. When I sit in it, I feel very relaxed.

VOCABULARY REVIEW: SAME OR DIFFERENT

The following pairs of sentences contain vocabulary from Readings 1 and 2 in this unit. Write *S* on the blank line if the two sentences have the same meaning. Write *D* if the meanings are different.

_____ 1 A nap and physical activity can reduce stress.

A short sleep and exercise can make you feel more relaxed and comfortable.

_____ 2 His muscles were paralyzed, so he could not move.

He was so tired that he could not move, so he fell asleep.

_____ 3 The survey compared the children's ability to remember things.

The research study asked questions to find out about the children's memory.

_____ 4 Variation in human development is normal.

Babies are in the first stage of development.

_____ 5 She did not have sufficient time to think hard and make the right decision.

She did not have enough time to concentrate and use good judgment.

BEYOND THE READING

Research

Do some research on sleep with your classmates. Find answers to the following questions:

- [ ] What do you do just before you go to bed?
- [ ] What do you do if you cannot fall asleep?
- [ ] What do you do if you wake up in the middle of the night?

Discussion

Share your research with a partner or your classmates.

Writing

Based on your classmates' responses, write a list of suggestions like the ones at the end of Reading 2. Include suggestions for the following:

- [ ] What to do if you want to fall asleep
- [ ] What to do if you wake up in the middle of the night and can't fall asleep again

SKILLS AND STRATEGIES 10
FINDING CAUSES AND EFFECTS

As you learned in Skills and Strategies 8 on page 111, writers use words or phrases to signal the relationship between ideas, such as a contrast. Writers can also use words or phrases to signal causes and effects. A *cause* explains why an *effect*, or a result, happens. Common words or phrases that signal causes and effects are *because, for this reason, so,* and *as a result.* Good readers notice these kinds of words or phrases. They help readers find causes and effects and understand what a writer is trying to say.

EXAMPLES & EXPLANATIONS

Example

[1]Although we think it is normal to sleep at night in our own separate rooms, this was not always normal. [2]In early human history, many people slept together in one place. [3]They did this **because** it was safer. [4]A large group could fight together against dangerous animals or enemies. [5]Some people had to stay awake to watch for danger. [6]**As a result**, some people slept at night and others slept in the daytime. [7]Now, people don't sleep in large groups, and most people sleep at night.

Explanation

The main idea in this reading is in sentence 1: *People did not always sleep the way we do now.*

Sentence 2 gives the first supporting detail: *In early human history, many people slept together in one place.*

Sentence 3 explains why. The word *because* introduces the reason: *It was safer.*

Sentence 4 explains why it was safer: *A large group could fight together.*

Sentence 5 gives another supporting detail: *Some people had to stay awake to watch for danger.*

In sentence 6, *as a result* introduces the effect: *Some people did not sleep at night.*

Sentence 7 is the conclusion.

THE LANGUAGE OF CAUSE AND EFFECT

Here are some common words and phrases that signal cause and effect.

WORDS AND PHRASES THAT SIGNAL CAUSE	WORDS AND PHRASES THAT SIGNAL EFFECT
because	*so*
since	*therefore*
one reason . . .	*because of this*
the causes of the . . .	*as a result*

STRATEGIES

These strategies will help you find causes and effects while you read.

- Look for words and phrases that signal causes and effects.
- When you see a cause or effect word, notice the meaning of the ideas before and after the word. Ask yourself: *Which idea is the cause? Which idea is the effect?*
- If the reading has a lot of causes and effects, it is a good idea to make a list of them as you read.

SKILL PRACTICE 1

Read the following paragraphs. Circle four words or phrases in each paragraph that signal causes and effects. Then answer the questions. The first one has been done for you.

1   Some people have trouble falling asleep. (One reason) may be the food that they eat at night. Some foods help you sleep because they create a chemical in your body called *serotonin*. Rice, pasta, and bread are good to eat at dinner, since they create serotonin, which will make you sleepy. On the other hand, foods such as ham, cheese, and chocolate create the opposite effect from serotonin. As a result, these foods will keep you awake at night.

a Why do some people have trouble falling asleep? <u>The food they eat.</u>
What words or phrases signaled this cause? <u>one reason</u>

b Why do some foods help you sleep? _____
What words or phrases signaled this effect? _____

c Why are rice, pasta, and bread good to eat at dinner? _____
What words or phrases signaled this effect? _____

d What happens if you have foods such as ham or cheese at night?

_____

What words or phrases signaled this effect? _____

2   Recent studies show that children are sleeping less than they used to. One of the causes is that young people often have cell phones or computers in their bedrooms. Instead of going to sleep, they get on the computer or on the phone. For this reason, doctors don't think it is a good idea for children to have computers, televisions, or phones in their bedrooms. Children who get less sleep are also more likely to gain weight than other children. This happens because too little sleep makes people hungrier. Children who don't get enough sleep are tired during the daytime, so they don't want to exercise.

a What is a reason that young people are sleeping less now?

_____

What words or phrases signaled this cause? _____

b Why do doctors think that children should not have computers, television, or phones in their bedrooms? _____

What words or phrases signaled this cause? _____

c Why do children who sleep less gain weight? _____

What words or phrases signaled this cause? _____

d What happens because children are tired when they don't get enough sleep?

_____

What words or phrases signaled this effect? _____

SKILL PRACTICE 2

Read the following paragraph. Underline the words that signal causes and effects. Then fill in the chart. Find two effects for the cause and two causes for the effect. Some examples have been done for you.

Where do young babies sleep? This depends on the culture. In most cultures, parents think that newborn babies cannot be alone, <u>since</u> they are so tiny. Therefore, the babies sleep with their mothers or in their parents' bed. In other cultures, mothers put their babies in separate beds and even separate rooms. Some mothers do this because they worry that they will roll over on their babies if they sleep in the same bed. Other mothers do this simply because it's a cultural custom.

CAUSES	EFFECTS
babies are tiny	_____ _____
_____ _____	separate beds

READING 3
YOUR BODY CLOCK

GETTING INTO THE TOPIC

Discuss the following questions with a partner.

1 When do you like to wake up?
2 When do you like to go to bed?
3 At what time of day do you have the most energy?
4 Have you always woken up and gone to bed at the same time? Have these times changed as you have grown older?

GETTING A FIRST IDEA ABOUT THE READING

Read the title, the section headings, and the first sentence of each paragraph of Reading 3. Then read the questions below. Write the number of the section (*I, II,* or *III*) next to the question or questions it will answer.

SECTION	QUESTIONS THAT EACH SECTION WILL ANSWER
	Does everyone have the same body clock?
	What is the body clock?
	Why do some people like to wake up early and some people like to stay up late?
	Why do blind people have problems with their body clock?
	What situations cause problems for the body clock?
	What jobs cause problems for the body clock?

WHILE YOU READ

As you read, stop at the end of each sentence that contains words in **bold**. Then follow the instructions in the box in the margin.

Your Body Clock

I. HOW THE BODY CLOCK WORKS

Your body has a clock. It is a tiny place in your brain that tells you when to sleep and when to be awake. This body clock responds to changes in light. Light signals you to wake up. Other things, like noise and stress, can also affect your body clock, but they cannot alter it very much. It is generally difficult to change your body clock.

Some situations can cause confusion for your body clock. If you travel a long distance across time zones, for example, from New York to Paris, your body clock loses six hours. You may arrive at night in Paris, when everyone is going to bed. However, your body clock thinks you are still in New York. It tells you that it is time for dinner. The next morning, the **alarm clock** rings. It wakes you up, but your body clock thinks it is the middle of the night. You probably feel exhausted. This confusion is called *jet lag*. Gradually, your body clock will change to Paris time, because it will begin to respond to the light and darkness in Paris. It usually takes several days for your body to adjust to a new time zone.

As you read, look for a definition of *alarm clock*. Write the definition in the margin.

II. PROBLEMS FOR THE BODY CLOCK

Blind people have problems with their body clocks, because they cannot see the light that tells their bodies to wake up. Without this light, many blind people have trouble with sleep. They have a sort of permanent jet lag.

Some people have jobs that cause problems for their body clocks. Electric light allows people to work at any time of day or night. People who work at night must be awake when it is dark outside. This is the time when their body clocks tell them to sleep. When they get home, it is bright, and their body clock tells them to stay awake. As a result, they may have trouble falling **asleep**.

Night jobs can sometimes be dangerous. People who work at night sometimes get sleepy, and then they make mistakes. Injuries and accidents in factories often occur at night because of this problem. On April 26, 1986, just after one o'clock in the morning, there was an accident in a nuclear power[1] plant in Chernobyl, Ukraine. It was the worst nuclear accident in history. Some scientists believe that the cause was a sleepy worker who made a mistake.

Look back in paragraph 4 for a word that signals cause and effect. Circle the word. Mark the cause with *C* and the effect with *E*.

---

1 *nuclear power*: energy from atoms

People who work at night may have problems with their body clocks.

III. DIFFERENT BODY CLOCKS

Most people sleep at night and stay awake during the day. However, not every body clock is the same. Some people like to wake up very early. They have a lot of physical and mental energy in the morning, but by evening, their energy is gone. They are sleepy, and they want to go to bed early. These people are "early birds." Other people do not like to get out of bed in the morning, but they have a lot of energy in the evening. Sometimes they stay awake until one or two o'clock in the morning. These people are "night owls." *Owls* are birds that are awake at **night**.

When night owls are married to early birds, they may have problems. An early bird may complain about his wife. For example, he may say that his wife goes to sleep too late, and she keeps him awake. A night owl may complain about her husband. She may say he is too noisy in the morning, and he disturbs her while she is still sleeping.

6

7

What is the main idea of paragraph 6? Write it in the margin.

Research shows that older people are usually early birds, and teenagers are usually night owls. Many teenagers cannot fall asleep until late at night. They are not very alert in the morning. In most countries, however, the school day begins early, between 7:00 and 8:30 in the morning. This means that many teenagers do not get enough sleep. They are not ready to learn when they get to school. For this reason, some schools now start later in the day.

Scientists have studied people with different body clocks. Many scientists believe that we cannot control our preferences. They think that this preference for morning or evening may be genetic, like eye color. In one study, scientists researched the **habits** of early birds and night owls. For example, they asked them how they felt and what they did at different times of the day. The chart below gives some typical answers that they gave.

As you read, find a clue that signals the definition of *habits*. Circle the clue, and write the definition in the margin.

Look for a fixed phrase under *Night Owls* in the chart. Circle it.

TABLE 5.1 **Early Birds and Night Owls**

	Early Birds	Night Owls
Do you use an alarm clock to wake up?	No	Yes
How do you feel in the morning?	I have a lot of energy. I talk a lot.	I don't talk very much, and I am often in a bad mood.
Do you sleep well most of the time?	Yes	No
Do you take naps?	Rarely	Sometimes
When do you like to exercise?	Morning	Evening

The body clock has a powerful effect on our daily activities and how we feel. Modern life, with airplane travel, night jobs, and electric lights, can cause problems for our body clocks. Most people would like to change their lives to fit their body clocks. However, most people have to adjust their body clocks to fit their jobs, their studies, and their family life.

MAIN IDEA CHECK

Here are the main ideas of each paragraph in Reading 3. Match each paragraph to its main idea. Write the number of the paragraph on the blank line.

Paragraphs 1–3

_____ A Many blind people have sleep problems.

_____ B Jet lag is the effect of confusion in your body clock.

_____ C Your body clock tells you when to sleep and when to be awake.

Paragraphs 4–6

_____ D People who work at night often have problems with their body clocks.

_____ E Different people have different sleep patterns.

_____ F People who work at night have more accidents than people who work during the day.

Paragraphs 7–10

_____ G The body clock has a lot of influence on what people do and how they feel.

_____ H Husbands and wives with different body clocks may have problems.

_____ I You probably cannot control your body clock.

_____ J Most teenagers are night owls.

A CLOSER LOOK

Look back at Reading 3 to answer the following questions.

1 Your body clock is located in a tiny place in your _____. (Par. 1)

2 How does the body clock adjust after jet lag? (Par. 2)
   a The body clock knows when your body changes to a new time zone.
   b The light in the new time zone signals the body clock.
   c An alarm clock in the new city tells the body clock to change.
   d The body clock responds to rapid travel across time zones.

3 _____ people cannot see and respond to light, so they sometimes have sleep problems. (Par. 3)

4 Why are night jobs sometimes dangerous? (Par. 5)
   a Machines often break during the night.
   b There is not as much light at night, so workers get sleepy.
   c Workers who are tired can make serious mistakes.
   d Injuries are more common at night.

5 Complete the chart below. Put a check (✓) next to the statements that are true for early birds. Put a check (✓) next to the statements that are true for night owls. (Par. 6)

STATEMENT	EARLY BIRD	NIGHT OWL
They wake up early.		
They have no energy at night.		
They like to stay up late.		
They don't like to wake up in the morning.		
They go to bed early.		

6 Night owls and early birds sometimes complain about each other.
True or False? (Par. 7)

7 Why do some schools start later in the day? (Par. 8)
   a It is too dark to start school early in the morning.
   b Teenage students are not ready to learn early in the morning.
   c It saves energy to start school later in the day.
   d Students have too much homework, so they have to work late at night.

8 According to Table 5.1, most night owls like to talk a lot in the morning.
True or False?

VOCABULARY STUDY: DEFINITIONS

Find words in Reading 3 that can complete the following definitions. If you need help, use Key Vocabulary from the Readings on page 251.

1 _____ is when a person doesn't understand what is happening or doesn't know what to do. (n) Par. 2

2 To _____ is to change a little bit to fit a new situation. (v) Par. 2

3 Someone who cannot see is _____. (adj) Par. 3

4 Something that goes on forever is _____. (adj) Par. 3

5 To _____ is to say that you don't like something. (v) Par. 7

6 If you are _____, you are awake and have enough energy to understand and learn. (adj) Par. 8

7 _____ are actions you do over and over again, often without really thinking about them. (n pl) Par. 9

8 A/An _____ is the way you feel at a certain time. (n) (Table 5.1)

VOCABULARY STUDY: SYNONYMS

Read the sentences below. The words or phrases in parentheses mean the same or almost the same as the words in the list. For each sentence, replace the words in parentheses with a word from the list. Write it on the blank line. If necessary, review the words in Key Vocabulary from the Readings on page 251.

exhausted	affect	typical	tiny
zone	plant	disturbs	alter

1 A large (factory) _____ outside of the city makes gas for cars and trucks.

2 After she ran 10 miles, she was (very tired) _____.

3 The news about the war will (influence) _____ the election.

4 Light (bothers) _____ her. It prevents her from sleeping.

5 She wrote the answer in (very small) _____ letters.

6 He tried to (change) _____ his answers after the test was over.

7 Their new home was in a different (area) _____, which was much safer than other parts of the city.

8 This is not (usual) _____ weather. It does not usually snow so late in the spring.

VOCABULARY REVIEW: ACADEMIC WORD LIST

The following are Academic Word List (AWL) words from all the readings in Unit 5. Complete the sentences below with these words. If necessary, review the AWL words in Key Vocabulary from the Readings on page 251.

adjust (v)	normal (adj)	concentrate (v)	restored (v)	sufficient (adj)
variation (n)	affects (v)	consequences (n)	mental (adj)	stress (n)

1 There is a lot of _____ in people's sleep patterns. Some people need more sleep than others.

2 She was worried about other things, so she could not _____ on her schoolwork.

3 The decisions that you make today may have important _____ for you in the future.

4 If you move to a different country, it may take some time to _____ to the new culture.

5 There is a lot of _____ in his new job. He works 12 hours a day, and he worries a lot.

6 Competition in the Olympic Games requires both physical and _____ energy.

7 It is _____ to be nervous before an important event. Most people feel this way.

8 Two weeks of vacation _____ her health and energy. She felt much better when she returned to her job.

9 The food we eat _____ how we feel and how we behave.

10 If you do not get _____ sleep, you may get sick. Adults should get about eight hours of sleep a night.

BEYOND THE READING

Research
Do a survey on early birds and night owls.
- Use the questions in Table 5.1 on page 149.
- Ask 10 people to answer your questions.
- Ask people of different ages.

Discussion
- Share your results with a partner or your classmates.
- Do your results match the results in the chart? In other words, are the people in your survey night owls or early birds? Or are they a mix of both?

Writing
Write a short summary of your survey research.

MAKING CONNECTIONS

The vocabulary in these exercises comes from all the readings in Unit 5. The exercises will help you see how writers make connections across sentences in a paragraph.

One way that writers make connections is to show causes and their effects. Writers can use words or phrases such as *because, because of this, for this reason, as a result,* or *therefore* to make these connections. You learned these words and phrases in Skills and Strategies 10 on page 143.

EXERCISE 1

Read the following paragraphs. Circle any words or phrases that signal cause and effect. Highlight each cause and mark it with a *C*. Underline each effect and mark it with an *E*. The first one has been done for you.

1   A lot of the research about sleep has concentrated on western cultures.
      Because of this, some people wonder if it is accurate. There are many
      variations in sleeping patterns around the world. For example, in some
      cultures, adults sleep twice a day. They sleep in the afternoon for a couple
      of hours and again at night for about six hours.

2   Thomas Edison invented the light bulb, but did he ever imagine the
      consequences? Before the invention of the light bulb, people went to sleep
      early because they did not have very much they could do after dark. As a
      result, they got plenty of sleep. After the development of electricity, people
      could stay awake easily and comfortably.

3   When people don't get enough sleep, they can't concentrate very well.
      Because of this, there are sometimes terrible accidents. For example, a huge
      ship ran into rocks in Alaska. The reason for this unfortunate accident was
      too little sleep.

4   Everyone knows that sleep is essential. It affects memory and mood.
      However, many people don't realize that it is also essential for life. In one
      study, researchers prevented rats from sleeping for five days. As a result of
      this, the rats died.

5   Sometimes people complain when they wake up. They say that they
      didn't sleep all night. It is possible they were asleep part of the night, but
      they thought they were awake the whole night. Because of this, they feel
      tired even when they get enough sleep.

EXERCISE 2

Make a clear paragraph by putting sentences A, B, and C into the best order after the numbered sentence. Look for pronouns and words or phrases that signal addition, contrast, or cause and effect to help you. Write the letters in the correct order on the blank lines.

1 Not sleeping can affect your work. ___ ___ ___

A	B	C
Because they are exhausted, they sometimes do not have good judgment.	For example, doctors in training at hospitals sometimes work for three days without sleep.	However, some jobs require people to work long hours with no time off.

2 Whales and dolphins have to think about breathing, because they do not have the ability to breathe automatically. ___ ___ ___

A	B	C
Therefore, they cannot go completely to sleep.	The other half stays awake.	Instead, they sleep with half of their brain.

3 The typical sleep pattern for most people in western cultures today is about eight hours of sleep during the night. ___ ___ ___

A	B	C
As a result of the invention of electric light, this sleep pattern began to change.	People used to go to sleep early in the evening, wake up for a few hours, and sleep again.	However, sleeping through the entire night is a recent habit.

4 Doctors understand that some babies die because of the way they sleep.
___ ___ ___

A	B	C
They fall asleep on their stomachs, and then they cannot breathe very well.	However, they are not strong enough to turn onto their backs.	Therefore, doctors now tell parents to put tiny babies on their backs to sleep.

5 Babies sometimes have a flat area on the back of their heads, because they spend a lot of time on their backs. ___ ___ ___

A	B	C
However, this is not a permanent change, so parents should not worry.	This happens because their heads are quite soft.	As a result, their heads can change shape when they are on the bed.

Music

SKILLS AND STRATEGIES 11-12

- Noticing Parts of Words (2)
- Organizing Notes in Time Lines

READINGS

- Music in Our Lives
- The Effect of Music on Behavior and Emotion
- The Business of Music

SKILLS AND STRATEGIES 11
NOTICING PARTS OF WORDS (2)

As you learned in Skills and Strategies 3 on page 34, one way to understand the meaning of a word is to notice the parts of the word, such as prefixes and suffixes. Sometimes, understanding the *root* of a word may also help you. A root is the basic part of a word. Many roots come from Greek or Latin, and you can often find the same root in several different words. For example, the root *port* means *to carry*. You see it in words such as *export* and *passport*. Roots don't usually give you the exact meaning of a word, but they can give you a clue to the meaning. Good readers notice roots. They use their knowledge of these roots as well as prefixes and suffixes to figure out a word's meaning.

EXAMPLES & EXPLANATIONS

Examples

She tried to listen to her grandfather's old radio, but the sound was in**aud**ible.

Explanations

A root can give you a clue to the meaning of a word. For example, the root *aud* means to hear.

Remember that the prefix *-in* means not. The suffix *-ible* means to be able to do something.

inaudible = not able to be heard

His music is **popular** in China, and the **population** of China is so large that his music sells a lot of copies.

Common roots can give you a clue about the meaning of a word, but they can't always tell you the specific meaning.

For example, the root *pop* means people. This is a clue that the words *popular* and *population* are related to people, even though they have different specific meanings.

popular = liked by many people
population = the number of people living in an area

Many people today use mobile phones instead of home or office **telephones**. One advantage of mobile phones is that you can listen to music on them.

Sometimes words have two roots in them, for example, *telephone*. The root *tele* means distant, and the root *phon* means sound.

telephone = a piece of equipment used to talk to someone in a distant place

THE LANGUAGE OF WORD ROOTS

Here are some common roots and their meanings.

ROOTS	MEANINGS	ROOTS	MEANINGS
aud	hearing	*port*	carry
bio	life	*tech*	skill
geo	earth	*tele*	distant
graph	write	*temp*	time
migra	move	*uni*	one
phon	sound	*vid, vis*	seeing
pop	people	*vit, viv*	live

STRATEGIES

These strategies will help you notice word roots. They may help you understand the meanings of words while you read.

- Study and remember the meanings of the roots in the chart.
- To learn more roots, find a dictionary or a source on the Internet that lists roots.
- Notice if a word you don't know has a familiar root. Ask yourself questions: *What other words have the same root as this word? What other words are related to this word?*
- Look at the whole sentence and the sentences around it. Notice how the meaning of the root connects to the other words and the general meaning of the sentence.

SKILL PRACTICE 1

Read the following sentences, and notice the different parts of the words in **bold**. Circle any roots you see in the words. The first one has been done for you.

1 Yo-Yo Ma is a famous musician. His parents were Chinese, but he was born in Paris. When he was a child, his family im**migra**ted to the United States.

2 The singers came from all over the country to make a CD together. They **united** to raise money for poor children.

3 A **technician** in the recording studio made a lot of changes to the recording. It sounds much better now.

4 Musicians with no **vision** usually learn to play by listening to music, because they can't see to read the musical notes.

5 I like the fast **tempo** of this music. However, it's very difficult to play.

6 I read the **biography** of Johann Sebastian Bach last year. He had an interesting life.

7 She always wanted to be a musician, but she studied **geology**, not music, in college.

8 In the 1960s, there was a **revival** of interest in music from the 1940s.

SKILL PRACTICE 2

Read the sentences in Skill Practice 1 again. Look at the roots you circled in each sentence. Then figure out the definitions for the words in **bold**. Write the definitions on the blank lines. The first one has been done for you.

1 Yo-Yo Ma is a famous musician. His parents were Chinese, but he was born in Paris. When he was a child, his family **immigrated** to the United States.

   immigrate = <u>move to a new country</u>

2 The singers came from all over the country to make a CD together. They **united** to raise money for poor children.

   unite = _____

3 A **technician** in the recording studio made a lot of changes to the recording. It sounds much better now.

   technician = _____

4 Musicians with no **vision** usually learn to play by listening to music, because they can't see to read the musical notes.

   vision = _____

5 I like the fast **tempo** of this music. However, it's very difficult to play.

   tempo = _____

6 I read the **biography** of Johann Sebastian Bach last year. He had an interesting life.

   biography = _____

7 She always wanted to be a musician, but she studied **geology**, not music, in college.

   geology = _____

8 In the 1960s, there was a **revival** of interest in music from the 1940s.

   revival = _____

READING 1
MUSIC IN OUR LIVES

GETTING INTO THE TOPIC

Discuss the following questions with a partner.

1 Do you like listening to music? What type of music do you listen to?
  Explain your answer.
2 Do you play a musical instrument, for example, the piano or guitar?
  Explain your answer.
3 What are some of the different ways that music comes into our daily lives?
  Make a list of the different ways.

GETTING A FIRST IDEA ABOUT THE READING

The following are the beginnings of the first one or two sentences of each
paragraph in Reading 1. Read them. Then, with a partner, discuss what you
think the paragraphs will be about.

1 There are only a few things that make human beings different from . . .
  (Par. 1)
2 Music has been a part of human history . . . (Par. 2)
3 Why is music important to humans? One possibility is . . . (Par. 3)
4 Another possibility is that music plays a role in brain . . . (Par. 4)
5 Music continues to help people today. Many doctors . . . (Par. 5)
6 Music can also help people who have problems with movement. After some
  brain injuries, people might need to . . . (Par. 6)
7 Music has always been part of . . . (Par. 7)

WHILE YOU READ

As you read, stop at the end of each sentence that contains words in **bold**.
Then follow the instructions in the box in the margin.

Music in Our Lives

There are only a few things that make human beings different from all other animals. Music is one of those things. Our connection with music begins early in life. Small babies respond to music. Mothers all over the world sing to their babies to comfort them and to help them sleep. Some animals, especially some birds, do respond to music. However, only humans are able to create music. All cultures create some kind of music. This music includes dances, songs, drums, or other musical instruments.

Music has been a part of human history for a very long time. Singing and dancing are the oldest forms of musical expression. They do not require any special equipment, such as **musical instruments**. Musical instruments are more recent, but they also have a long history. Flutes that are more than 35,000 years old were discovered in Germany in 2009. They were made from animal bones and teeth. Some simpler instruments, such as drums, which are even older, have also been found.

As you read, find clues in this paragraph that signal the definition of *musical instruments*. Circle the clues, and write the definition in the margin.

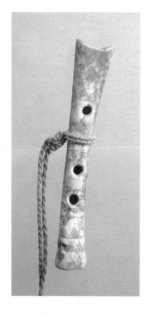 

A flute (left) and a drum (right) are very early musical instruments.

Why is music important to humans? One possibility is that music brings people together. Research shows that when people sing or dance together, their brains release special chemicals. These chemicals make them feel happy. They feel good about themselves and about their group. They trust the people in their group, and they want to stay with them. Long ago, this helped people survive because they were more successful in a group than alone.

Music can release chemicals in the brain that make people feel happy.

Another possibility is that music plays a role in brain **development**. Research shows that children who learn to play musical instruments can often solve problems more quickly and easily than children who do not. Scientists believe that learning to play music is different from learning about other things, like history or science. Scientists believe that learning to play music can change the way cells are connected in your brain. These new connections may improve how the brain works. It is possible that long ago, music helped people to think better and solve problems. This ability also helped people **survive**.

Music continues to help people today. Many doctors use music to help their patients. They use music to relieve pain and stress. Music is especially useful for patients with brain diseases or brain injuries. It can help people who have problems with speaking and memory. Patients who can no longer speak well may listen to familiar songs. When they hear familiar songs, they can recognize the words. Sometimes they can sing these familiar songs before they can speak again.

Music can also help people who have problems with movement. After some brain injuries, people might need to relearn to do simple things, like walking or tying their shoes. The rhythm in music can help them. When they follow the rhythm, physical movements become **easier**.

Music has always been part of the human experience. Scientific research shows that music can be important for the human body and brain. It can be helpful to many people – children, adults, and people with injuries. Scientists will continue to learn about the ways that music helps us and about its role in human history.

4

5

6

7

Look back in this sentence for a collocation with a verb and the noun *role*. Highlight the collocation.

Use your knowledge of word roots to guess the definition of *survive*. Write it in the margin.

Look back in paragraph 6 for a collocation with a verb and the noun *shoe*. Highlight the collocation.

MAIN IDEA CHECK

Here are the main ideas of each paragraph in Reading 1. Match each paragraph to its main idea. Write the number of the paragraph on the blank line.

Paragraphs 1–3

_____ A Music has a long history.

_____ B Music brings people together.

_____ C Only humans create music.

Paragraphs 4–7

_____ D Music helps us in many ways.

_____ E Doctors use music to help sick people.

_____ F Music helps brain development.

_____ G Music can help people with physical movement.

A CLOSER LOOK

Look back at Reading 1 to answer the following questions.

1 What are the two oldest forms of musical expression? (Par. 2)
   a Drums
   b Singing
   c Flutes
   d Dancing
   e Simple musical instruments

2 Flutes are the oldest musical instruments that people have found. True or False? (Par. 2)

3 Put the events (A–D) in the correct order in which they happen. Write the correct letter in each box. (Par. 3)

   A Chemicals in people's brains make them feel happy about themselves and their group.
   B When people make music together, their brains release chemicals.
   C People are more successful in groups, so they survive longer than people who live alone.
   D When people feel happy, they trust their group, and they want to stay together.

4 Music may help people to think better. True or False? (Par. 4)

5 How do doctors use music to treat patients? Circle three answers. (Par. 5)

 a To relieve stress
 b To help people learn to understand words again
 c To help people learn new songs
 d To relieve pain
 e To help people play music again

6 _____ is a characteristic of music that helps people with brain injuries learn to do simple things again. (Par. 6)

VOCABULARY STUDY: DEFINITIONS

Find words in Reading 1 that can complete the following definitions. If you need help, use Key Vocabulary from the Readings on page 251.

1 _____ is a set of tools or machines that you need for a special purpose. (*n*) Par. 2

2 To _____ something is to let it go. (*v*) Par. 3

3 _____ are basic substances. (*n pl*) Par. 3

4 A/An _____ is the use or function that something has. (*n*) Par. 4

5 _____ are the smallest units of living things. Skin, muscles, and your brain are all made of them. (*n pl*) Par. 4

6 _____ are people who go to a doctor or hospital because they are sick. (*n pl*) Par. 5

7 To _____ someone or something is to realize that you have seen or that you know the person or thing. (*v*) Par. 5

8 _____ is a regular pattern of sounds in music. (*n*) Par. 6

VOCABULARY STUDY: WORD FAMILIES

Read the words in the following chart. The words in **bold** are the parts of speech that appear in Reading 1. Find these words in the reading. If you need help, use Key Vocabulary from the Readings on page 251.

NOUN	VERB
comfort	**comfort**
expression	express
relief	**relieve**
survival	**survive**
trust	**trust**

Choose the correct form of the words from the chart to complete the following sentences. Use the correct verb tenses and subject-verb agreement. Use the correct singular and plural noun forms.

1 Long ago, people who lived in groups were more likely to _____ than people who lived alone.

2 _____ is an important part of the relationship between parents and children.

3 People _____ their creativity in different ways: in music, words, or painting.

4 She tried to _____ the small child who was crying.

5 The _____ of many plants and animals depends on human beings. Without our protection, they may die.

6 The medicine _____ her pain. She felt better after she took it.

7 When my son went away to college, his photograph was a great _____ to me.

8 Music is a major form of human _____.

9 The government officials did not _____ the traveler. They thought he was lying.

10 He felt great _____ after the doctor took the piece of glass out of his finger.

BEYOND THE READING

Research
Find at least two classmates or friends who sing or play a musical instrument. Find answers to the following questions:
- Do you sing or play an instrument? What instrument do you play?
- How long have you been doing this?
- How many hours a day or week do you practice?
- Why do you continue to sing or play?
- Do you think that music gives you advantages? For example, does it help you in your studies? Explain your answer.

Discussion
Share your research with a partner or your classmates.

Writing
Write a short summary of the reasons why people play music.

READING 2
THE EFFECT OF MUSIC ON BEHAVIOR AND EMOTION

GETTING INTO THE TOPIC

Discuss the following questions with a partner.

1 How does music affect your mood? Does it make you feel happy? Sad?
2 Do some songs make you think about an event or person in your past?
   Explain your answer.
3 When you listen to the music in advertisements for products, do you
   remember the advertisements later?
4 Do you want to buy the products in advertisements that have music?
   Explain your answer.

GETTING A FIRST IDEA ABOUT THE READING

Read the title and the first sentence of each paragraph in Reading 2. Then
put a paragraph number in the chart next to a topic that you think will be
discussed in that paragraph. Discuss your answers with a partner.

PARAGRAPH	TOPIC
	How music can change how people act
	How businesses use music
	The purpose of music in advertisements
	The effect of music on behavior, emotions, and judgment
	How music affects memory
	The influence of music on our feelings
	The effect of music on physical activity

WHILE YOU READ

As you read, stop at the end of each sentence that contains words in **bold**.
Then follow the instructions in the box in the margin.

The Effect of Music on Behavior and Emotion

Is there a song that makes you happy? Is there a song that makes you remember something or someone from your past? Music can have a powerful effect on you. When you listen to music, your brain releases chemicals that affect your emotions. Music can make you feel happy, sad, excited, or relaxed. This is why you may choose one kind of music for a party and another kind of music for a quiet dinner.

Music can affect people's behavior. One surprising example comes from the police. In several different countries, the police use music to reduce the number of crimes. In London, for example, the police worried about crimes in parks and at train stations. When they played quiet music in these places, there was a significant decrease in the number of crimes. This plan was very successful. As a result, the government now plays soft, quiet music in 40 train stations in **London**.

Look back in paragraph 2 for a word that signals cause and effect. Circle the word. Mark the cause with *C* and the effect with *E*.

Music in public places affects people's behavior.

Look back in paragraph 3 for a collocation with a verb and the noun *music*. Highlight the collocation.

The power of music can also have a physical effect. It can help athletes perform better. One scientist says music can act like medicine. Slow music can help athletes feel calm, and faster music makes them work harder. At a race in London, officials play special music to help the runners run **faster**.

Businesses use the power of music, too. Department stores and supermarkets often use music to try to influence how much money their customers spend. They choose music they think will make their customers feel happy. They want customers to feel good, stay longer, and spend more money. Restaurant owners use music in the same way. Some may choose soft, slow music. They believe the music makes people relax and spend more money. Other restaurant owners may choose something faster with a strong rhythm. One study showed that the rhythm in music can influence how fast people chew their food! If customers chew faster, they will finish more quickly. This lets the restaurant serve more customers.

As you read, underline the supporting details for this main idea in paragraphs 4 and 5.

Probably the most important use of music in business is in product advertisements. Most advertisements on the radio or on television include music. **There are several reasons why music is a part of effective advertisements.** First, music is a good way to get people's attention. Second, people enjoy music, so they may want to listen to the advertisement again. If they listen to it more than once, they will also hear the message about the product more than once. Perhaps they will want to buy the product.

As you read, look for words in paragraphs 5 and 6 that signal supporting details for this main idea. Circle the words. Then underline the details.

A final important factor is the effect of music on memory. Music can help people remember the words in a message. For example, songs can help children learn important lessons, such as the letters of the alphabet. The same thing happens in advertisements. Research shows that the repetition and rhythm in music help people remember words. Studies of advertisements have compared listeners' memories. One group of advertisements had just words; another group had words

Music can help people learn and remember.

and music. Listeners remembered the messages with words and music better than they remembered the messages with only words.

Music has a strong influence on our feelings, behavior, memories, and decisions. Governments have used the power of music to change people's behavior. Businesses use it to encourage people to relax, shop, and buy their products. If you understand the power of music, you can make it work for you.

MAIN IDEA CHECK

Here are the main ideas of each paragraph in Reading 2. Match each paragraph to its main idea. Write the number of the paragraph on the blank line.

Paragraphs 1–4

_____ A Music can change physical performance.

_____ B Music influences your emotions.

_____ C Music affects behavior.

_____ D Businesses use music to influence customers' behavior.

Paragraphs 5–7

_____ E Music can influence our feelings, behavior, and memory.

_____ F Music can improve memory.

_____ G Music has an important role in advertisements.

A CLOSER LOOK

Look back at Reading 2 to answer the following questions.

1 Why is there soft music in some London train stations? (Par. 2)
   a People prefer to hear soft music on the train.
   b Soft music may reduce the number of crimes.
   c The government paid for the music.
   d Soft music makes people happy.

2 Music can help some athletes run faster. (Par. 3) True or False?

3 How do some businesses use the power of music? Circle two answers (Par. 4)

   a They play slow music so customers will stay and eat more.

   b They play fast music so customers will eat quickly and leave.

   c They play soft music to reduce the number of crimes.

   d They play quiet music so customers will be quiet.

4 How does music make advertisements more effective? Circle three answers (Pars. 5 and 6)

   a It helps people remember the advertisements.

   b It helps people relax.

   c It makes people want to hear the advertisements again.

   d It gets people's attention.

5 Music can help young children to learn the _____. (Par. 6)

6 The _____ and _____ in music help people to remember the words in a song (Par. 6)

VOCABULARY STUDY: DEFINITIONS

Find words in Reading 2 that can complete the following definitions. If you need help, use Key Vocabulary from the Readings on page 251.

1 The _____ are officials who protect the public. They make sure that everyone obeys laws. (*n pl*) Par. 2

2 _____ are activities that break laws. (*n pl*) Par. 2

3 A/An _____ is a competition for runners. (*n*) Par. 3

4 _____ are places that sell many different kinds of things, such as clothing, dishes, and furniture. (*n pl*) Par. 4

5 _____ are large places that sell mostly food. (*n pl*) Par. 4

6 To _____ is to cut food with your teeth. (*v*) Par. 4

7 Something that works well and is successful is _____. (*adj*) Par. 5

8 The _____ is a set of letters that are used for all the words in a language. (*n*) Par. 6

VOCABULARY STUDY: WORDS IN CONTEXT

Complete the following sentences with words from the list below. If necessary, review the words in Key Vocabulary from the Readings on page 251.

perform	repetition	attention	excited
calm	lesson	athletes	owner

1 The children finished their reading _____ and then went out to play.

2 The little boy was very _____ when he saw the toy trains.

3 The students in our school always _____ well on examinations.

4 _____ can help you to remember words and facts. That is why we say things over and over again if we don't want to forget them.

5 The _____ of the store lived in the apartment above his business.

6 Hundreds of _____ competed in the race.

7 Everyone began screaming when the fire started, but one woman stayed _____ .

8 The children were very noisy, so the teacher turned the light on and off to get their _____ .

VOCABULARY REVIEW: SAME OR DIFFERENT

The following pairs of sentences contain vocabulary from Readings 1 and 2 in this unit. Write S on the blank line if the two sentences have the same meaning. Write D if the meanings are different.

_____ 1 If you see a crime, you should not get excited. You should call the police.
If you see someone break the law, you should stay calm and call the police.

_____ 2 The athletes survived the long race.
The runners performed badly at the competition.

_____ 3 The owner of the supermarket knew the customer when he saw her.
The man who owned the big store recognized the customer.

_____ 4 The patient did not believe that the equipment was safe.
The patient did not trust the machine. He thought it was dangerous.

_____ 5 In the morning, the children had a lesson about the alphabet.
The teacher used rhythm and music to teach the children their letters.

BEYOND THE READING

Research

Do some research on music and advertising. Ask several of your classmates to think of one product that uses music in its advertisement. Then ask them the following questions:

- What is the product?
- What do you remember about the music in its advertisement?
- Were there words as well as music? If so, do you remember the words?
- Did the advertisement make you want to buy the product? Explain your answer.

Discussion

Share your research with a partner or your classmates.

Writing

Based on your research, write a short summary on what you think makes a musical advertisement effective.

SKILLS AND STRATEGIES 12
ORGANIZING NOTES IN TIME LINES

Sometimes you need to understand a reading and remember the most important information for a test. Good readers take notes to help them study for tests. Sometimes a reading gives important information about when different events happened. The best way to understand these events is to organize your notes into a time line. A time line lists the events in the order in which they happened. To make a time line, look for dates, numbers, and words like *before*, *until*, and *then*. These will help you understand the *time sequence*, that is, the order in which things happened.

EXAMPLES & EXPLANATIONS

Example

[1]An Italian named Bartolemeo Cristofori invented the first piano **in the early 1700s.** [2] Few musicians knew about this musical instrument **until 1747**, when Johann Sebastian Bach wrote some music for the piano. [3]The first pianos had a soft sound and were very small, but **by 1860** the piano looked and sounded like modern pianos.

Explanation

The topic of this paragraph is the history of the piano. The time phrases *in the early 1700s*, *until 1747*, and *by 1860* give you information about when things happened.

There are two possible ways to make a time line of this paragraph.

1. You can write a list of dates like this:

    - early 1700s — Cristofori — first piano
    - 1747 — Bach wrote music for piano, people learned about it.
    - 1860 — Piano looked, sounded like modern pianos.

2. You can draw a line with the earliest event on the left and the most recent event on the right like this:

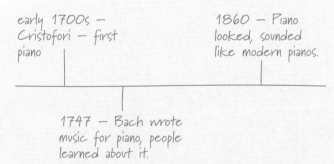

early 1700s — Cristofori — first piano

1860 — Piano looked, sounded like modern pianos.

1747 — Bach wrote music for piano, people learned about it.

Note that you don't have to use complete sentences in a time line. Just write the important words.

THE LANGUAGE OF TIME SEQUENCE

Here are some common words or phrases that signal time sequence.

in (year)	*before*	*until*	*later*
on (date)	*after*	*by*	*earlier*
	then	*since*	*now*

STRATEGIES

These strategies will help you understand when events in a reading happened.

- As you read a paragraph, look for words or phrases that signal when something happened.
- As you read, ask yourself questions: *When did this happen? Was it before or after other events in the reading?*
- Underline important dates, and number events to show the order.
- Take notes in a time line to understand and remember the sequence of events.

SKILL PRACTICE 1

Read the following paragraphs. Circle four words or phrases in each paragraph that signal when something happened. Then answer the questions. The first one has been done for you.

1   (In the early 1970s,) a German professor started work on a project to send music over telephone lines. This was the beginning of the development of MP3 music players. It took more than 20 years to develop the technology. In 1995, researchers gave the name MP3 to this technology. Three years later, the first MP3 portable music players became available in the United States and in South Korea.

a   When did the work begin that led to the development of MP3 music players? *in the early 1970s* _____

b   How many years did it take to develop the technology? _____

c   When did researchers first use the name MP3? _____

d   When did the first MP3 players become available? _____

2   Wolfgang Amadeus Mozart was born in 1756 in Salzburg, Austria. His
father was a well-known musician and violin teacher. Mozart started
writing music when he was only five years old. By 1764, he was writing
symphonies (long pieces of music for many instruments). Before he died in
1791, Mozart wrote almost 1,000 pieces of music.

a When was Mozart born? _____

b How old was he when he started writing music? _____

c When did he start to write symphonies? _____

d When did he die? _____

SKILL PRACTICE 2

Read the following paragraph. Circle the words or phrases that signal a time
sequence. Then make a time line in the space below the paragraph. You can
choose to make a list, with the earliest date and event first, or make a line,
with the earliest date and event on the left side of the line.

Rock music began in the United States. It started in Memphis, Tennessee,
in 1951, with the first "rock and roll" record, "Rocket 88." Some of the
early rock and roll singers were Chuck Berry and Elvis Presley. In the 1960s,
new styles of rock and roll music began with "soul music" from Detroit,
Michigan, and "surfing music" from California. Things changed in 1964 when
the Beatles came to the United States from England. This was the beginning
of the "British Invasion," when many rock bands came from the United
Kingdom. Now, rock is international. Musicians all over the world play it.

READING 3

THE BUSINESS OF MUSIC

GETTING INTO THE TOPIC

Discuss the following questions with a partner.

1 How do you listen to music? On your computer? On the radio?
   Another place?
2 Has the way that you listen to music changed in the last 10 years? Explain
   your answer.
3 When you buy music, do you buy one song at a time? Do you buy many
   songs by the same musician?
4 Do you like to share your favorite music with your friends? Explain
   your answer.

GETTING A FIRST IDEA ABOUT THE READING

Read the title, the section headings, and the first sentence of each paragraph
of Reading 3. Then read the questions below. Write the number of the section
(*I*, *II*, or *III*) next to the question or questions it will answer.

SECTION	QUESTIONS THAT EACH SECTION WILL ANSWER
	How did the Internet change the music business?
	How did people listen to music before CDs?
	What have been some recent changes in the music business?
	What are some new ways that the music business is making money today?
	When did people first begin to store music so they could listen to it any time they wanted to?
	What is the difference between music on CDs and music on the Internet?

WHILE YOU READ

As you read, stop at the end of each sentence that contains words in **bold**.
Then follow the instructions in the box in the margin.

The Business of Music

I. EARLY FORMS OF MUSIC TECHNOLOGY

Technology in the music business has changed a lot in the past 100 years. Long ago, you could only hear music **live**, that is, if other people were singing or playing an instrument in front of you. Then, in the early 1900s, it became possible to store music so that people could listen to it over and over again. They could listen to this music on the radio.

However, most people wanted to buy the music that they listened to on the radio. They wanted to be able to listen to it anytime they wanted. In the 1920s, technology made this possible. People could buy music on records. Your parents or grandparents probably bought their music on these records. In the 1970s, the music business began to produce music on special tapes. These tapes were much smaller than records. They were also less fragile. In other words, people did not break or scratch them as often as records. The popularity of tapes increased in 1979, when Sony began to sell the Walkman. With the Walkman, music was **portable** for the first time. Tapes continued to be the most common way to listen to music until the early 1990s.

Find a clue in this sentence that signals a definition of *live*. Circle the clue and highlight the definition.

Use your knowledge of word roots to guess the definition of *portable*. Write the definition in the margin.

A record

A cassette tape

During the 1990s, compact discs (CDs) became more popular. CDs are stronger than tapes, and the sound of the music is clearer. Sales of CDs increased through the 1990s. Although CDs are still a popular physical form of music, electronic forms of music have started to replace physical **forms**.

Review section I. Circle the dates, and underline what happened on those dates. Then make a time line of these events in your notebook.

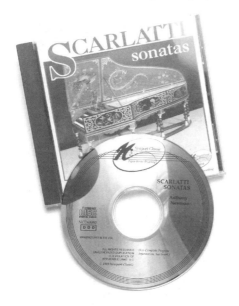

A compact disc

II. MUSIC ON THE INTERNET

In about 2000, CD sales began to fall, and the sale of music in electronic form on the Internet began to rise. With the Internet, people could listen to songs on their computers. They could also download them to a portable music player, such as an iPod. This change had two important consequences for the music business. First, with records, tapes, or CDs, customers had to buy an **album**, which is a whole collection of songs. The whole collection usually lasts about an hour. With the Internet, customers can buy only the songs they like. They don't have to buy songs they don't like.

Look in the rest of this sentence for a definition of *album*. Highlight the definition.

There is a second and more important consequence. Electronic forms of music are much easier to copy and share than physical forms. When listeners download electronic copies, they can share copies with all of their friends. The friends do not have to pay for their copies. It is very hard to prevent people from sharing their music. This is a challenge for musicians and music companies, because listeners do not pay for these **copies**.

Music companies have tried many ways to stop people from sharing their music. They have made technical changes in the electronic form of music. The changes make it harder for listeners to share their music. Music companies also want the

What is the main idea of paragraph 5? Write it in the margin.

government to punish people who share music. However, none of these efforts has been very effective. People can always find the music they want easily, and they often do not have to pay for it.

The Internet has also had some positive effects for musicians. In general, it is very difficult to be a successful musician. It is hard for most musicians to sell their songs. In 2008, there were 13 million songs for sale. Listeners bought only three million of them. However, the Internet makes it easier for musicians to bring their music to a large number of people quickly and easily. They can put it on an Internet site, where people can listen to it. 7

III. RECENT CHANGES IN THE MUSIC BUSINESS

The music business is changing again. Many customers have stopped downloading music because now they can find it in a new way. In the past, customers wanted to own their music. They wanted all of their songs on their own computer or music player. Now, customers can play music directly from many different Internet music sites. They can find the music they want and play it on their computer, mobile phones, or music players. They can play it anywhere they want and at anytime they want. They don't need to own it. 8

The music companies still want to make money, however. They are trying to do this in two new ways. First, they ask other companies to pay for advertisements on the Internet music sites. These companies hope that people will see their advertisements while they are listening to the music and then buy the products in the advertisements. Second, some Internet music sites require customers to pay for access. For example, a customer might pay $10 a month for access to any song in the world. 9

Music companies, musicians, and customers are still trying to find the best solutions for everyone. Music companies and musicians need money for their products. Customers want to listen to music anywhere and anytime. One thing is certain – the music business will continue to change with new **technology**. 10

Look back in paragraph 10 for a collocation with a verb and the noun *solution*. Highlight the collocation.

MAIN IDEA CHECK

Here are the main ideas of each paragraph in Reading 3. Match each paragraph to its main idea. Write the number of the paragraph on the blank line.

Paragraphs 1–3

_____ A Records and tapes were early forms of music that people could listen to anytime they wanted to.

_____ B At the end of the twentieth century, CDs became the most popular form of music.

_____ C About 100 years ago, it became possible to store music.

Paragraphs 4–7

_____ D At the beginning of the twenty-first century, people began to download their music from the Internet.

_____ E The Internet allows musicians to reach more people.

_____ F People share their music and sometimes do not pay for it.

_____ G The government has not been able to stop people from sharing music.

Paragraphs 8–10

_____ H Music companies are finding new ways to make money.

_____ I Today people have access to music, but they don't need to own it.

_____ J The music business will continue to change with technology.

A CLOSER LOOK

Look back at Reading 3 to answer the following questions.

1 In what ways are tapes better than records? Circle three answers. (Par. 2)
   a They are less fragile than records.
   b They are less expensive than records.
   c They are smaller than records.
   d They are portable.
   e They sound better than records.

2 In what ways are CDs better than tapes? Circle two answers. (Par. 3)
   a They are stronger than tapes.
   b They are less expensive than tapes.
   c They sound better than tapes.
   d They are more popular than tapes.

3 In about 2000, the sales of CDs began to increase. True or False? (Par. 4)

4 Before the Internet, listeners had to buy a whole _____ instead of just one or two songs. (Par. 4)

5 What are some consequences of music sales on the Internet? Circle three answers. (Pars. 4 and 5)

   a Customers can buy only the songs they want.

   b Musicians can reach more people easily.

   c Musicians must work more.

   d Customers can share their music easily.

   e Musicians can try new music.

6 The government has stopped listeners from sharing their music. True or False? (Par. 6)

7 Listeners bought fewer than 30 percent of the songs that were for sale in 2008. True or False? (Par. 7)

8 What are some new ways that music companies hope to make money? Circle two answers. (Par. 9)

   a Customers will pay for access to Internet music sites.

   b Customers will pay for whole collections of music.

   c Other companies will pay to put advertisements on Internet music sites.

   d Listeners will pay to share their music.

9 Put the different forms of music (A–E) in the correct order on the time line. Put the earliest form on the left of the line and the most recent form on the right of the line. Write the correct letters in the blank boxes.

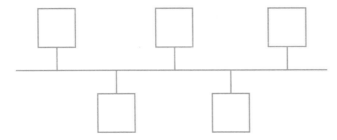

   A Tapes

   B Payment for access to Internet sites

   C Downloading from the Internet

   D Records

   E CDs

VOCABULARY STUDY: DEFINITIONS

Find words in Reading 3 that can complete the following definitions. If you need help, use Key Vocabulary from the Readings on page 251.

1 If you see or hear something _____, you see or hear it when it is happening. (*adj*) Par. 1

2 _____ are large, flat circles of plastic on which music is stored. (*n pl*) Par. 2

3 Something that is easy to carry is _____. (*adj*) Par. 2

4 If you _____ something, you start to use something else instead. (*v*) Par. 3

5 To _____ something (for example, a document, photo, or song) is to take it from the Internet and put it on your own computer. (*v*) Par. 4

6 A/An _____ is a very difficult situation or problem. (*n*) Par. 5

7 To _____ someone who has done something wrong, you may do something to them that they don't like. (*v*) Par. 6

8 _____ is the chance to use or have something. (*n*) Par. 9

VOCABULARY STUDY: SYNONYMS

Read the sentences below. The words or phrases in parentheses mean the same or almost the same as the words in the list. For each sentence, replace the words in parentheses with a word from the list. Write it on the blank line. If necessary, review the words in Key Vocabulary from the Readings on page 251.

method	compact	collection	positive
lasted	fragile	scratched	sites

1 You must be careful when you pick up the old teapot. It is very (breakable) _____.

2 She tried to solve the math problem without success, so she decided to try a new (way) _____.

3 There are many (places) _____ on the Internet where you can listen to music.

4 He had a (group) _____ of old photographs in his desk.

5 The new computer is (small) _____ and can fit into a small bag.

6 He had very (hopeful) _____ thoughts after the meeting ended.

7 The party (went on) _____ from 7:00 in the evening until 2:00 the next morning.

8 The sharp piece of glass (lightly cut) _____ his finger.

VOCABULARY REVIEW: ACADEMIC WORD LIST

The following are Academic Word List (AWL) words from all the readings in Unit 6. Complete the sentences below with these words. If necessary, review the AWL words in Key Vocabulary from the Readings on page 251.

challenge (*n*)	positive (*adj*)	chemicals (*n pl*)	survived (*v*)	access (*n*)
method (*n*)	released (*v*)	role (*n*)	equipment (*n*)	sites (*n*)

1 After the couple got married, they _____ two white birds into the air.

2 Climbing mountains requires a lot of special _____.

3 She realized that books on the Internet _____ were less expensive than books in stores.

4 She used a new _____ to make coffee. She had never made it this way before.

5 Children in many schools around the world do not have _____ to the Internet.

6 Exercise had a very _____ effect on his health. He became thinner and felt much better.

7 Math class was always a _____ for him. He found the subject very difficult.

8 Education plays an important _____ in getting a good job.

9 Most _____ in the water we drink are safe.

10 Only a few families in the village _____ the terrible fire. Most of the people there died.

BEYOND THE READING

Research
Interview five of your friends about how they get new music. Ask them if they get it for free online, pay for it online, buy it in stores, or some other way.

Discussion
Share your results with a partner or your classmates.

Writing
Write a short summary of your research. Describe the most popular ways to get new music.

MAKING CONNECTIONS

The vocabulary in these exercises comes from all the readings in Unit 6. The exercises will help you see how writers make connections across sentences in a paragraph.

One way that writers make connections is to show time sequence. Writers can use words or phrases such as *then*, *after that*, *before that*, or *since then* to make these connections. You also learned words and phrases of time sequence in Skills and Strategies 12 on page 174.

EXERCISE 1

Read the following sentences. Circle any words or phrases that signal time. Write *1* by the first event and *2* by the second event. The first one has been done for you.

1 The manager at the bus station started to play classical music (last summer). (Before that), the police reported a lot of crimes there.

2 In the early 1980s, CD players were very expensive. After a few years, the price dropped.

3 The rhythm of the music was slow at first. Then the music got much faster, and people started to dance.

4 In the 1950s, people could buy the first portable radios. Before that, people could only listen to large radios that were very heavy.

5 The Web site requires you to pay money. Then you can download the music or a movie.

6 She did not have access to music lessons as a child. Later, as an adult, she took piano lessons.

7 The calm expression of the music director made the young singers feel calm, too. Before that, they had been very nervous.

8 The director made them do a lot of repetitions of the same piece. Later, they performed the piece perfectly.

EXERCISE 2

Make a clear paragraph by putting sentences A, B, and C into the best order after the numbered sentence. Look for pronouns and words or phrases that signal time, addition, contrast, or cause and effect to help you. Write the letters in the correct order on the blank lines.

1 Two companies, Philips of the Netherlands and Sony of Japan, worked together to develop compact discs (CDs). ___ ___ ___

A	B	C
It held songs from ABBA, a Swedish rock group.	They produced the first CD in 1982.	Three years later, in 1985, a CD by Dire Straits was the first to sell one million copies.

2 A phonograph is a machine that uses a needle to play records. ___ ___ ___

A	B	C
At first, his company rented phonographs to businesses for a small amount of money.	Thomas Edison invented the first one in 1877.	After 10 years, Edison started to sell phonographs to people for home use.

3 The doctor decided to try music as a way to relieve headaches.

___ ___ ___

A	B	C
However, some said their headaches did not last as long when they played music.	Many of them said it was not effective.	Six months later, he asked his patients if the music relieved their headaches.

4 New equipment for playing music always gets people's attention.

___ ___ ___

A	B	C
However, when prices dropped, people replaced their old record players with CD players.	For example, people were very excited when CD players came out.	At first, these were very expensive.

5 The Rolling Stones rock band started to play together in 1962.

___ ___ ___

A	B	C
Over the next 40 years, they released more than 30 albums or CDs.	Ten of these were recordings from live concerts.	Who ever imagined in 1962 that this rock band would survive for almost 50 years?

Natural Disasters

SKILLS AND STRATEGIES 13
COLLOCATIONS (2)

As you learned in Skills and Strategies 5 on page 64, when two or more words often appear together, we call this a *collocation*. You learned that some collocations have a verb and a noun. Another type of collocation has an adjective and a noun. Good readers know these collocations. This helps them read more quickly.

EXAMPLES & EXPLANATIONS

Examples

The **heavy rain** caused floods.
Light snow fell all day in the mountains.

The **high temperatures** this afternoon will fall by nighttime.

Everyone stayed home today because of the **severe** winter **weather**.

Explanations

There are many collocations that we use to describe the weather. For example, we often use the adjectives *heavy* and *light* with the nouns *rain* and *snow*, such as **heavy rain**, **light rain**, **heavy snow**, or **light snow**.

We often use the adjectives *high* and *low* with the noun *temperature*.

Sometimes the adjective and noun are not next to each other. In this example, an additional adjective, *winter*, is in the collocation **severe weather**.

THE LANGUAGE OF COLLOCATION

Here are a few common collocations with adjectives and nouns.

ADJECTIVE + NOUN			
heavy / light	*high / low*	*severe*	*strong*
• *rain*	• *temperatures*	• *weather*	• *winds*
• *snow*	• *risk*	• *damage*	• *impact*
• *traffic*	• *pressure*	• *injuries*	• *chance*

STRATEGIES

These strategies will help you learn collocations.

- When you are reading, try to notice adjectives and nouns that often go together. These may be useful collocations. Be careful. Sometimes other words are between the adjective and noun. These words may not be part of the collocation.
- When you look up a word in a dictionary, notice words that go together with it.
- When you make a list of new vocabulary to study, write the collocations. Learn the words that go together, not just the single words.

SKILL PRACTICE 1

Read the following paragraphs. Choose words from the list above each paragraph to complete the collocations. Write the words on the blank lines. The first one has been done for you.

heavy	severe	high

1   In most of the world, there is some risk of ____severe____ weather. In
    the mountains, winter storms bring _____ snow. In other places,
                                          b
    storms bring too much rain. Perhaps the desert is the best place to live.
    There, you only have to worry about _____ temperatures.
                                             c

low	high	severe

2   Southern California has dry and sunny weather much of the year.
    However, there is a _____ risk of forest fires at certain times of
                          a
    the year, because it is very dry. These fires often cause _____
                                                                b
    damage. Signs at the entrance to a forest usually tell people whether the
    risk for fire is high or _____ .
                                c

low	heavy	strong

3   Air pressure affects the weather. High air pressure usually creates cool,
    dry weather and clear skies. On the other hand, _____ air
                                                      a
    pressure creates warm weather. With this type of pressure, there is a
    _____ chance of storms with _____ rain.
         b   c

SKILL PRACTICE 2

Read the following paragraphs. Highlight any adjective and noun collocations
you see. Then write the collocations on the blank lines next to their
meanings. The first one has been done for you.

1   The new bridge was beautiful. The builders used advanced technology to
     build it. The bridge was only two years old, so it was a complete surprise
     to everyone when it fell. A huge number of drivers now have to find other
     ways to get across the river. For the short term, the city will start running
     the old ferry boat across the river. However, it's important to replace the
     bridge as soon as possible.

     a a lot _____

     b something very unexpected _____

     c very modern, with the latest technology _____*advanced technology*_____

     d for now and in the near future _____

2   City officials are going to hold a public meeting to discuss building a new
     sea wall. The sea wall has strong support from people who live near the
     water. They think it will prevent severe flooding in a storm. Other people
     say that there is a very low risk of city flooding and that the new sea wall
     will be very expensive.

     a problems with water coming over the land _____

     b an event for people to talk to city leaders _____

     c many positive opinions _____

     d a small chance _____

3   It is difficult to get help to people after a natural disaster. At first, help
     usually goes to people in large urban areas. It takes much longer to get help
     to people in smaller rural areas. There may be no easy access to people if
     roads are blocked.

     a direct and fast way to get close to or to enter an area _____

     b places far away from a city or urban area _____

     c an event of nature that causes serious damage _____

     d cities _____

READING 1

THE DARK SIDE OF NATURE

GETTING INTO THE TOPIC

Read the title and look at the photographs on pages 192, 193, and 194. Then discuss the following questions with a partner.

1 What do you think the title of the reading means? What do you think the *dark side* is?
2 What do you think has happened in these photos?
3 What are the people doing? How do you think they feel?
4 Have you ever been in situations like these? Do you know someone who has been? Explain your answer.

GETTING A FIRST IDEA ABOUT THE READING

The following are the beginnings of the first one or two sentences of paragraphs 2–6 in Reading 1. Read them. Then, with a partner, discuss what you think the paragraphs will be about.

1 Violent storms bring heavy rain and strong winds. All of the rain can cause . . . (Par. 2)
2 When floods occur in the mountains, sometimes the water, along with rocks and earth, . . . (Par. 3)
3 Movement under the earth can also cause . . . (Par. 4)
4 The most severe damage is usually at the center of an earthquake, but . . . (Par. 5)
5 Eruptions from volcanoes also occur as the result of . . . (Par. 6)

WHILE YOU READ

As you read, stop at the end of each sentence that contains words in **bold**. Then follow the instructions in the box in the margin.

The Dark Side of Nature

Nature usually plays a positive role in our lives. Sometimes, however, nature can turn wild and dangerous. Some natural events can cause serious injuries, death, and significant damage. These events are called *natural disasters*. There are two main types of natural disasters. First, there are extreme weather events, such as violent storms. Second, some natural disasters are the result of movements under the earth. These movements can cause *earthquakes* or the eruption of *volcanoes*.

Violent storms bring heavy rain and strong winds. All of the rain can cause floods. The most serious violent storms begin over oceans. These are called *hurricanes*, *cyclones*, or *typhoons*. Their names depend on their locations. A hurricane is a massive storm in the Atlantic Ocean or the eastern Pacific Ocean. A cyclone is a storm that starts in the Indian Ocean or in the southwestern Pacific Ocean near Australia or Africa. A typhoon is a storm in the northwestern Pacific Ocean near Asia. In 2009, a typhoon hit Taiwan. Eighty inches (two meters) of rain fell in two days. Floods destroyed bridges and roads and caused **widespread damage**.

When floods occur in the mountains, sometimes the water, along with rocks and earth, moves down the side of a mountain. This is called a *mudslide*. Mudslides can destroy homes and injure people. In 1998, Hurricane Mitch resulted in about 10,000 deaths across the Caribbean. Many of the people died in the floods and mudslides when the water and mud washed their homes down the mountains.

Look back in paragraphs 1 and 2. Find seven collocations with adjectives and the following nouns: *damage*, *injury*, *rain*, *storm*, and *wind*. Highlight the collocations.

A mudslide washes through the streets after Hurricane Mitch.

Movement under the earth can also cause natural disasters. Massive earthquakes and volcano eruptions do not occur very often, but they can be deadly. In 2010, there was a major earthquake in Haiti. It killed more than 200,000 people, and it nearly destroyed or completely destroyed almost 300,000 buildings. A million people lost their **homes**.

Look back in paragraph 4 for a word that signals cause and effect. Circle the word. Mark the cause with *C* and the effect with *E*.

People examine the damage after an earthquake.

The most severe damage is usually at the center of an earthquake, but an earthquake can also cause disaster far away. For example, in 2004, there was a major earthquake in the Indian Ocean near Indonesia. No people live in the ocean, so the earthquake did not injure anyone or cause damage to any buildings. However, it caused a huge tsunami that hit 12 countries. A *tsunami* is a huge wall of water that hits the shore suddenly. This tsunami was 100 feet (30 meters) high. It destroyed many communities along the shore and killed about 230,000 people. More than one and a half million people had to leave their homes.

Eruptions from volcanoes also occur as the result of movements under the earth. These eruptions send smoke and lava[1] out of the mountain and into the air. In 1902, there was an eruption of a volcano in Martinique, an island in the Caribbean. It destroyed the town of St. Pierre and killed more than 30,000 people. Only two people in the town **survived**.

What is the main idea of paragraph 6? Write it in the margin.

---

[1] *lava*: hot liquid rock

A volcano erupts on Martinique in 1902.

7

Natural disasters occur when a community is vulnerable to natural events, such as violent weather and movements under the earth. Perhaps homes are on land that is very low, or they are near a river or a volcano. Perhaps the buildings are not very strong. These situations can make places vulnerable to storms, floods, or earthquakes. After disasters, communities often **rebuild** in ways that will help them to be less vulnerable to these events.

Circle the prefix in *rebuild*. Then write a definition for *rebuild* in the margin.

TABLE 7.1 **The 10 Worst Natural Disasters**

Event	Location	Year	Number of Deaths
Flood	China	1931	1,000,000–4,000,000
Flood	China	1887	900,000–2,000,000
Cyclone	Bangladesh	1970	500,000–1,000,000
Earthquake	China	1556	830,000
Cyclone	India	1839	300,000
Earthquake	Syria and Turkey	526	250,000
Earthquake	China	1976	242,000
Earthquake	China	1920	240,000
Tsunami	Indian Ocean	2004	230,000
Earthquake	Haiti	2010	230,000[2]

Source: About.com

[2] the number of deaths known at the time of publication

MAIN IDEA CHECK

Here are the main ideas of each paragraph in Reading 1. Match each paragraph to its main idea. Write the number of the paragraph on the blank line.

Paragraphs 1–3

_____ A Rain and wind from storms can cause a lot of damage.

_____ B There are two main types of natural disasters.

_____ C Strong storms in the mountains may cause mudslides.

Paragraphs 4–7

_____ D Movement under the earth can result in earthquakes.

_____ E The eruption of a volcano can be a major disaster.

_____ F Natural disasters usually are the most serious in vulnerable communities.

_____ G Earthquakes can cause tsunamis far away.

A CLOSER LOOK

Look back at Reading 1 to answer the following questions.

1 According to the whole reading, what kind of natural disaster is each of the following events related to? Write weather (W) or movement of the earth (ME) on the blank lines.

a _____ eruption of volcanoes

b _____ cyclones

c _____ earthquakes

d _____ floods

e _____ mudslides

f _____ tsunamis

2 Draw a line from the type of storm in the left column to the location where the storm occurs in the right column. Some storms occur in more than one location. (Par. 2)

STORM	LOCATION
Hurricanes Typhoons Cyclones	Eastern Pacific Ocean Indian Ocean Pacific Ocean near Australia or Africa Pacific Ocean near Asia Atlantic Ocean

3 More than half a million people died in the Haiti earthquake. True or False? (Par. 4)

4 Why was no one injured at the center of the 2004 earthquake? (Par. 5)

  a It was not a very strong earthquake.

  b It was in the middle of the ocean.

  c The communities were prepared.

  d All of the houses were very strong.

5 What factors may make a community vulnerable to a natural disaster? Circle three answers. (Par. 7)

  a It is too near something dangerous.

  b It has houses that are on very low land.

  c It has very bad weather.

  d It has houses that are not built very well.

6 Haiti's recent earthquake was one of history's 10 worst natural disasters. True or False? (Table 7.1)

7 According to the whole reading, which one of the following causes and effects is *not* true?

  a Major storms may cause floods.

  b Floods may cause mudslides.

  c Volcanoes may cause hurricanes.

  d Earthquakes may cause tsunamis.

VOCABULARY STUDY: DEFINITIONS

Find words in Reading 1 that can complete the following definitions. If you need help, use Key Vocabulary from the Readings on page 251.

1 Something that is the most serious and unusual is _____. (*adj*) Par. 1

2 Something that is sudden and powerful is _____. (*adj*) Par. 1

3 Something that is very large is _____. (*adj*) Par. 2

4 Something that happens in many places is _____. (*adj*) Par. 2

5 _____ is soil mixed with water. (*n*) Par. 3

6 Something that is very dangerous and is likely to kill people is _____. (*adj*) Par. 4

7 A/An _____ is a group of people who live in the same area. (*n*) Par. 7

8 It is easy to injure or damage something that is _____. (*adj*) Par. 7

VOCABULARY STUDY: WORD FAMILIES

Read the words in the following chart. The words in **bold** are the parts of speech that appear in Reading 1. Find these words in the reading. If you need help, use Key Vocabulary from the Readings on page 251.

NOUN	VERB
damage	*damage*
destruction	**destroy**
eruption	*erupt*
flood	*flood*
movement	*move*

Choose the correct form of the words from the chart to complete the following sentences. Use the correct verb tenses and subject-verb agreement. Use the correct singular and plural noun forms.

1 The storm _____ hundreds of homes. After the storm, there were only pieces of wood and metal on the ground.

2 The _____ of the volcano caused many injuries.

3 There was a sudden _____ in the trees, and then several birds flew into the sky.

4 The hurricane caused the river to _____. Many people who lived close to the river had water in their homes.

5 The disaster caused the complete _____ of the town. It took many years to rebuild it.

6 She looked for her keys everywhere. When she _____ a chair, she finally found them.

7 An accident caused serious _____ to his car.

8 Many people lost their homes in the massive _____ that followed the cyclone.

9 A large volcano _____ in Martinique in 1902. It killed a lot of people.

10 After the storm ended, the people in the town walked through the streets to look at the _____ to their community.

BEYOND THE READING

Research

Do some research on a recent natural disaster. Find answers to the
following questions:

- What happened? Describe it.
- Where did it happen?
- What caused it?
- Were people injured? How many? Did people die? How many?
- Was there any damage? Describe it.
- Who came to help after the disaster?

Discussion

Share your research with a partner or your classmates.

Writing

Write a short summary of your research.

READING 2
THE PREDICTION AND PREVENTION OF NATURAL DISASTERS

GETTING INTO THE TOPIC

Discuss the following questions with a partner.

1 Are you or your family prepared for a natural disaster? Explain your answer.
2 Does your country prepare for natural disasters? Explain your answer.
3 What did the government do the last time there was a natural disaster in your community?

GETTING A FIRST IDEA ABOUT THE READING

Read the first sentence of paragraphs 2–7 in Reading 2 and think about the title of the reading. Put a paragraph number (2–7) in the chart next to a topic that you think will be discussed in that paragraph. Discuss your answers with a partner.

PARAGRAPH	TOPIC
	Technology and prediction of natural disasters
	Disaster preparation
	Animals and earthquakes
	Education and disaster preparation
	Government warning systems
	Prediction of earthquakes

WHILE YOU READ

As you read, stop at the end of each sentence that contains words in **bold**. Then follow the instructions in the box in the margin.

The Prediction and Prevention of Natural Disasters

In 2008, there were 321 natural disasters all over the world. 1 They killed more than 235,000 people and caused $227 billion in damage. That was a very bad year, but there are disasters every year. In most years, about 65,000 people on average die in natural **disasters**. Many others lose their homes in the destruction. How can we prevent these terrible losses?

One way to prevent these losses is to predict natural 2 disasters. With new technology, scientists can now predict some events. Satellites show massive storms as they develop over the oceans. Special equipment shows when volcanoes are active. When there is an earthquake deep in the ocean, scientists can predict a **tsunami**.

Earthquakes are much more difficult to predict. One way 3 to predict earthquakes is very old. Some people believe that animals know when an earthquake is coming. For example, in Haicheng, China, in February 1975, many animals began to behave strangely. Government officials believed this was a warning. They believed an earthquake was coming. They ordered everyone to leave the city. A few days later, there was a strong earthquake. The next year, there was a stronger earthquake in another city in China. This time, however, animals did not behave strangely.

Most scientists believe that it is only possible to predict 4 where an earthquake is likely to happen. They do not believe that it is possible to predict the precise date and time that an earthquake will happen. Scientists know that before some earthquakes, there are often small movements, or tiny **tremors**, that shake the earth. It is possible that animals may feel these movements and begin to act strangely. However, because earthquakes do not always follow these tremors, and because animals do not always act strangely before earthquakes, scientists cannot use these events to predict earthquakes accurately.

Although we cannot predict most natural disasters, it is 5 **possible to prepare for them.** Many governments have warning systems. When a volcano or earthquake causes a mudslide, there is a loud warning sound. When a big storm or a tsunami is coming, the warning system can tell people to move away.

Look back in this sentence for a fixed phrase. Circle it.

Look back in paragraph 2 for a collocation with an adjective and the noun *storm*. Highlight the collocation.

Find a clue in this sentence that signals the definition of *tremors*. Circle the clue, and write the definition in the margin.

Underline the supporting details for this main idea in paragraphs 5 and 6.

This can save lives. Unfortunately, in many areas of the world, there are no warning systems. Scientists were able to predict the tsunami of 2004, but there was no warning system for thousands of people along the coast of the Indian Ocean.

The people who live in zones with frequent natural disasters 6 should also prepare for them. They should store extra food and water. They should make a plan to contact and find the people in their family. They should know where to find important news and information.

A warning system can move people to a safer place before a disaster occurs.

Education about natural disasters is crucial. Schools can 7 teach children what to do in a disaster and to understand the warning signs of a disaster. An eleven-year-old tourist named Tilly Smith was on a beach in Thailand with her family on December 26, 2004. The water had a lot of bubbles in it. Then the water went out very far. The beach was almost dry. Tilly remembered a school lesson about tsunamis, and she knew these were warning signs. She told her parents, and they told others. Many people were able to run to a safe place.

Natural disasters can cause terrible damage and loss of life. 8 We cannot prevent them. However, we can predict some kinds of disasters, and our ability to predict other kinds of disasters is improving. We can also prepare for disasters. If people and governments prepare carefully, we can reduce the consequences of natural **disasters**.

Look back in paragraph 8 to find a word that signals a contrast. Circle the word, and underline the two ideas the writer contrasts.

MAIN IDEA CHECK

Here are the main ideas of each paragraph in Reading 2. Match each paragraph to its main idea. Write the number of the paragraph on the blank line.

Paragraphs 1–4

_____ A Some people believe that animals know when an earthquake is coming.

_____ B Scientists cannot predict the exact day and time of an earthquake.

_____ C The prediction of natural disasters can prevent death and damage.

_____ D Natural disasters cause death and damage every year.

Paragraphs 5–8

_____ E It is possible to prepare for natural disasters.

_____ F Preparation can reduce damage and injuries in natural disasters.

_____ G People in vulnerable communities can plan for natural disasters.

_____ H Schools can teach children what to do if there is a natural disaster.

A CLOSER LOOK

Look back at Reading 2 to answer the following questions.

1 In 2008, there were 65,000 natural disasters all over the world.
True or False? (Par. 1)

2 What are successful methods of disaster prediction? Circle two answers. (Pars. 2 and 3)
   a Equipment can sense activity in volcanoes.
   b Satellites show storm activity.
   c Animals can predict natural disasters.
   d Schools can tell children when a disaster is coming.

3 A small movement under the earth is called a/an _____. (Par. 4)

4 Which of the following statements is true about earthquakes and tsunamis? Write _T_ on the blank lines before true statements. (Pars. 2–4)

   a _____ Scientists can predict the dates of earthquakes.

   b _____ Scientists can predict that a tsunami will follow an earthquake.

   c _____ Scientists can predict where earthquakes are likely to happen.

   d _____ Scientists can predict tremors in the earth.

5 How can governments and people prepare for natural disasters? Circle three answers. (Pars. 5 and 6)

  a People can store extra food and water.

  b Governments can use warning systems.

  c Governments can contact families.

  d People can move to a safer place.

6 A schoolgirl on vacation in Thailand probably saved the lives of her family and other tourists. True or False? (Par. 7)

VOCABULARY STUDY: DEFINITIONS

Find words in Reading 2 that can complete the following definitions. If you need help, use Key Vocabulary from the Readings on page 251.

1 A/An _____ is the usual number or amount. (*n*) Par. 1

2 Something that is very bad and very serious is _____. (*adj*) Par. 1

3 To _____ something is to say that it will happen in the future. (*v*) Par. 2

4 Something that is exact is _____. (*adj*) Par. 4

5 To _____ is to make movements from side to side. (*v*) Par. 4

6 A/An _____ is the shore between land and the ocean. (*n*) Par. 5

7 To _____ someone is to communicate with them. (*v*) Par. 6

8 Something that is very important and necessary is _____. (*adj*) Par. 7

VOCABULARY STUDY: WORDS IN CONTEXT

Complete the following sentences with words from the list below. If necessary, review the words in Key Vocabulary from the Readings on page 251.

prepares	tremors	accurately	warning
loss	bubbles	satellite	signs

1 There are often small _____ before a large earthquake.

2 The people in the town only had a few minutes of _____ before the tsunami came onto the shore.

3 She always _____ for examinations for a week. She reads all of her notes carefully.

4 The soap created lots of tiny _____ in the water.

5 A/An _____ above the earth sent information about weather back to officials on the ground.

6 It is important to report information _____ on government forms.

7 There was a significant _____ of jobs in the United States in the period between June and December.

8 Strong winds and dark clouds are often _____ that a storm is coming.

VOCABULARY REVIEW: SAME OR DIFFERENT

The following pairs of sentences contain vocabulary from Readings 1 and 2 in this unit. Write *S* on the blank line if the two sentences have the same meaning. Write *D* if the meanings are different.

_____ 1 The massive mudslide destroyed many of the buildings in the town.

The large mudslide seriously damaged many parts of the town.

_____ 2 The scientists looked for warning signs of a disaster.

The scientists tried to prevent extreme weather events.

_____ 3 It is difficult to predict earthquakes accurately.

It is a challenge to make a precise statement about when an earthquake will happen in the future.

_____ 4 The strong eruption of the earthquake had deadly consequences.

The volcano's violent eruption resulted in the loss of many lives.

_____ 5 Many communities are too vulnerable to weather events.

The communities on the coast tried to prepare for weather disasters.

BEYOND THE READING

Research

Do some research on disaster preparation in your community. Find answers to the following questions:

- What kinds of natural disasters are most likely to happen in your community?
- What should you do if there is a natural disaster?
- Where should you go?
- Whom should you contact?

Discussion

Share your research with a partner or your classmates.

Writing

Write a short summary of your research.

SKILLS AND STRATEGIES 14

ORGANIZING NOTES IN OUTLINES

As you learned in Skills and Strategies 12 on page 174, good readers take notes to help them study for a test. Time lines are one way to organize your notes. Another way is to make an outline. In an outline, you can organize your notes about the main ideas and supporting details. Organizing your notes in outlines can help you remember important information.

EXAMPLES & EXPLANATIONS

Example

The year 2008 was one of the worst in recent history for natural disasters. Two events caused almost all of the death and destruction. The first was Cyclone Nargis, in Myanmar, on May 3. Officials know that 84,000 people died in the cyclone, and 54,000 people disappeared. Another 2.5 million people lost their homes in the storm. Then, less than two weeks later, an earthquake in Sichuan, China, killed 70,000 people. Five million people lost their homes in the earthquake.

Explanation

As the student read this paragraph, she looked for the main idea of the paragraph.

The main idea in this paragraph is: *2008 was a very bad year for natural disasters*.

The student wrote the main idea in her outline (see below). Note that she didn't write a complete sentence. She wrote only the key words.

Then she found the two supporting details and put the important information and numbers into her outline.

Here is the complete simple outline that the student wrote in her notebook for this paragraph.

A. 2008 — bad year for natural disasters
   1. Cyclone Nargis — Myanmar
      a. 84,000 deaths
      b. 54,000 disappeared
      c. 2.5 million homeless
   2. Earthquake — Sichuan, China
      a. 70,000 deaths
      b. 5 million homeless
B. (Here the student wrote the main idea of the next paragraph and continued her outline.)

STRATEGIES

These strategies will help you organize your notes in an outline.

- As you read, look for the main ideas and supporting details. Make notes in the margins of the reading.
- When you make your outline, begin each section of your outline with the main idea of that section.
- Add the most important supporting details to your outline.
- Use a system of numbers and letters to show the difference between very important and less important details.
- Keep your outline simple. Don't write too much detail.

SKILL PRACTICE 1

Read the following paragraph. In this case, the student wrote notes in the margin of the page to help her write an outline. Use these notes to help you complete the student's outline below.

Earthquakes are impossible to predict, but it is possible to prevent loss of life in an earthquake. Most of the damage in an earthquake does not result from the earthquake itself. It results from falling buildings, roads, and bridges. Therefore, the most important way ① to prevent deaths from an earthquake is to build better roads and buildings. The second important thing to help prevent death and ② injury is to teach people what to do in an earthquake. A final action ③ that will help to save lives is to stop high-speed trains as soon as an earthquake happens.

poss. to prevent loss of life in earthquakes

A. Possible to prevent loss of life in earthquakes — three ways

  1. _____

  2. _____

  3. _____

Read the following paragraph. As you read, take notes in the margin. Find the main idea and number the supporting details. Then make an outline of the paragraph in the space below.

Most people think of a natural disaster as an event that happens very suddenly, with very little warning. This definition does not include drought, because a drought is a very long period of time with no rain. A drought does not happen very suddenly. However, droughts are certainly natural disasters. First, they affect large numbers of people in one region. In 1920, a drought in China killed 500,000 people and affected 20 million others. In the early 1980s, severe drought in a region of Africa killed millions of people. Second, droughts cause severe damage. In a drought, the land gets so dry that it often blows away. No crops can grow. People have to leave their farms to try to find food and work in other areas. Last, local officials are rarely able to take care of people's needs during a drought. Officials need assistance from outside. In all of these ways, a drought is a natural disaster.

READING 3
A NATURAL DISASTER FROM OUTER SPACE?

GETTING INTO THE TOPIC

Discuss the following questions with a partner.

1 Some people worry that objects from outer space will hit Earth. Do you think this will happen? Explain your answer.
2 Do you think this has happened in the past? Explain your answer.
3 What do you think would happen if an object from outer space hit Earth?

GETTING A FIRST IDEA ABOUT THE READING

Read the title, the section headings, and the first sentence of each paragraph of Reading 3. Then read the questions below. Write the number of the section (*I*, *II*, or *III*) next to the question or questions it will answer.

SECTION	QUESTIONS THAT EACH SECTION WILL ANSWER
	Have objects from outer space caused natural disasters in the past?
	Will any objects from outer space hit Earth in the future?
	Do objects fall from outer space?
	What can we do to prevent a natural disaster from outer space?
	How and why do objects fall to Earth from outer space?
	What happens when objects from outer space hit Earth?

WHILE YOU READ

As you read, stop at the end of each sentence that contains words in **bold**. Then follow the instructions in the box in the margin.

A Natural Disaster from Outer Space?

As you read, briefly note each paragraph's main ideas in the margin, and number the supporting details.

I. NEAR-EARTH OBJECTS

Have you ever seen a falling star? Do you wonder what would happen if an object from space hit Earth? Would it be a disaster? Most natural disasters start on Earth, but some start farther away. They start in outer space. *Near-Earth objects* (NEOs) from outer space, such as *asteroids* and *meteoroids*, sometimes hit Earth. These objects are made of rock or metal. They move in an orbit around the sun. They vary in size. Meteoroids can be as small as a few feet wide. Asteroids are bigger and can be almost 600 miles (1000 kilometers) wide.

Sometimes when the orbits of NEOs come near Earth, Earth's gravity pulls them toward us. Small meteoroids sometimes hit Earth's **atmosphere**, that is, the air and gas above Earth. However, when NEOs enter Earth's atmosphere, they start to burn. Most small NEOs burn up and disappear, so they never hit Earth. A few larger ones do not burn up completely, so they do hit Earth. What would happen if a large asteroid hit Earth? How real is the danger of a natural disaster from an asteroid?

Find a clue in this sentence that signals the definition of *atmosphere*. Circle the clue, and highlight the definition.

An NEO can cause damage if it hits Earth.

II. WHEN NEOS HIT EARTH

It is possible that asteroids have already caused natural disasters. NEOs may help explain a great mystery in Earth's history. About 250 million years ago, all of the plants and animals began to die. They disappeared from Earth forever. In other words, they became **extinct**. Ninety-six percent of all the animals in the sea and 70 percent of the animals on land at that time became extinct. Many scientists believe that one cause

Find a clue that signals the definition of *extinct*. Circle the clue, and highlight the definition.

may have been a giant asteroid that hit Earth. The impact of a very large asteroid creates a lot of dust and gas above the Earth. This cloud of dust and gas can block the light from the sun. Without the light from the sun, plants cannot live. Without plants, all the animals will also die.

About 65 million years ago, another asteroid hit Earth. It was almost six miles (10 kilometers) wide. In the 1980s, scientists found the site of the impact in Mexico. This impact created a hole that is 112 miles (179 kilometers) wide. Scientists have studied rocks and soil from that period, 65 million years ago. Their analysis suggests that the impact of this asteroid caused huge tsunamis. It also created dust and gas in the atmosphere that blocked the sunlight for years.

When giant asteroids hit the Earth, they can cause death and massive destruction. However, this destruction can lead to new life. When some plants and animals become extinct, other plants and animals begin to develop. For example, most scientists believe that dinosaurs developed after the first giant asteroid hit Earth. The second asteroid may be one of the reasons that dinosaurs later became extinct. Asteroids are a natural part of how life on Earth **changes**.

Look back in paragraph 5 for a collocation with an adjective and the noun *destruction*. Highlight the collocation.

Smaller NEOs hit Earth about every two or three hundred years. These can also cause major damage. The largest one in recent history was in Russia in 1908. It is called the Tunguska explosion. This explosion was many times more powerful than an atomic bomb.[1] Fortunately, it occurred in an area where no one lived. Scientists estimate that it burned 80 million trees across 830 square miles (2,150 square kilometers). This kind of explosion is big enough to destroy a major city.

In 1908, an NEO caused a powerful explosion in Russia.

---

[1] *atomic bomb*: a nuclear bomb that causes damage with a massive explosion and extreme heat

III. CAN WE PREPARE FOR AN NEO STRIKE?

Some people worry that another giant asteroid will hit Earth [7] in the future. This time, it may hit a large town or city. In 2002, a British scientist predicted that a large asteroid would hit Earth in 2019. Many other scientists immediately studied the NEO, and they disagreed. They do not think it will hit Earth. In their opinion, there is only one chance in a million that it will hit Earth. However, they predict it is more likely that another asteroid could hit Earth in 2880. They believe the chance is 1 in 300.

Our ability to predict these events is improving. We will [8] probably have a warning many years before a large asteroid hits. The U.S. government has a project to find and follow 90 percent of all NEOs that are at least one kilometer wide. What would happen if one of these NEOs began to move toward Earth? What could we do to prevent a natural disaster? If there is enough time, scientists and engineers could build a special machine to change the NEO's orbit. Another possibility is that they could stop the asteroid before it entered Earth's atmosphere. They could send a rocket to destroy it. Governments could also help people leave the area. They could store food and water. These would help people survive if dust and gas blocked the light from the sun for a long time.

Should people worry about asteroids? Probably not. A large [9] NEO that could cause a natural disaster only hits Earth once or twice in a million years. It is unlikely that an NEO will hit Earth soon. However, scientists will continue to keep track of the NEOs that could be a danger to us in the **future**.

Look back at your notes for main ideas and supporting details. Then make a simple outline of Section II in your notebook.

MAIN IDEA CHECK

Here are the main ideas of each paragraph in Reading 3. Match each paragraph to its main idea. Write the number of the paragraph on the blank line.

Paragraphs 1–2

_____ A NEOs could cause a natural disaster.

_____ B Most NEOs burn up in Earth's atmosphere.

Paragraphs 3–6

_____ C Some small NEOs have hit Earth recently.

_____ D The impact of an asteroid caused massive destruction 250 million years ago.

_____ E An asteroid hit Earth 65 million years ago and caused widespread damage.

_____ F Destruction can lead to new forms of life.

Paragraphs 7–9

_____ G Scientists don't think that a large NEO will hit Earth soon.

_____ H People should not worry about natural disasters from outer space.

_____ I Scientists may be able to prevent NEOs from hitting Earth.

A CLOSER LOOK

Look back at Reading 3 to answer the following questions.

1 Meteoroids are larger than asteroids. True or False? (Par. 1)

2 Why do NEOs sometimes hit Earth's atmosphere? (Par. 2)
   a Scientists are not sure why this happens.
   b They burn up so they do not hit Earth.
   c Gravity from Earth pulls them out of their orbit.
   d They are too large and heavy to stay in their orbit.

3 Put the events (A–E) in the correct order in which they happen. Write the correct letter in each box. (Par. 3–5)

[ ] → [ ] → [ ] → [ ] → [ ]

   A The explosion from the impact creates a lot of dust and gas in the air.
   B Plants and animals die.
   C Sunlight cannot reach Earth.
   D An asteroid hits Earth.
   E New and different plants and animals take the place of those that died.

4 If there is a very serious natural disaster from an NEO, many plants and animals may become _____. (Par. 3)

5 The impact of an asteroid can cause a tsunami. True or False? (Par. 4)

6 What were the consequences of the Tunguska explosion? (Par. 6)

  a Dust blocked the sun for 200 years.

  b A major city was destroyed.

  c It created an atomic bomb.

  d Eighty million trees burned down.

7 If an asteroid is coming toward earth, what can we do? Circle four answers. (Par. 8)

  a Scientists can try to destroy it.

  b People can prepare by storing food and water.

  c People can move to a safer place.

  d Scientists can try to change its orbit.

  e Governments can build a city under the ground.

8 According to most scientists, how often is a large asteroid likely to hit Earth? (Par. 9)

  a Once in two hundred years

  b Once or twice in a million years

  c Once in two million years

  d Probably never

VOCABULARY STUDY: DEFINITIONS

Find words in Reading 3 that can complete the following definitions. If you need help, use Key Vocabulary from the Readings on page 251.

1 _____ is the part of the universe that is farthest from Earth. (*n two words*) Par. 1

2 A/An _____ is the path that objects travel around the sun or a planet. (*n*) Par. 1

3 _____ is the force that pulls things to the ground. (*n*) Par. 2

4 A plant or animal that no longer exists anywhere in the world is _____. (*adj*) Par. 3

5 A/An _____, for example, oxygen, is something like air. It is not a solid or a liquid. (*n*) Par. 3

6 _____ are reptiles that once lived on earth. Many of them were very large. (*n pl*) Par. 5

7 A/An _____ is a planned piece of work. (*n*) Par. 8

8 A/An _____ is a man-made object that moves very fast through space. (*n*) Par. 8

VOCABULARY STUDY: SYNONYMS

Read the sentences below. The words or phrases in parentheses mean the same or almost the same as the words in the list. For each sentence, replace the words in parentheses with a word from the list. Write it on the blank line. If necessary, review the words in Key Vocabulary from the Readings on page 251.

mystery	impact	suggests	explosion
analysis	immediately	dust	blocked

1 My mother is very sick. I must take her to the hospital (right now)
   _____.

2 The (force) _____ of the crash injured many of the passengers in the car.

3 A large tree fell on the road and (stopped) _____ traffic.

4 The origin of the disease is still a/an (unknown thing) _____. Scientists and doctors do not understand it.

5 The study by the scientists (points to) _____ an important role of food in our health.

6 The air was full of (dry dirt) _____, so it was difficult to breathe.

7 The scientists did a/an (careful study) _____ of the NEOs that have hit Earth in the last 300 years.

8 The people on the street were afraid when they saw the fire and heard the loud (burst) _____ inside the factory.

VOCABULARY REVIEW: ACADEMIC WORD LIST

The following are Academic Word List (AWL) words from all the readings in Unit 7. Complete the sentences below with these words. If necessary, review the AWL words in Key Vocabulary from the Readings on page 251.

analysis (n)	crucial (adj)	community (n)	predicted (v)	contacts (v)
accurately (adv)	impact (n)	widespread (adj)	project (n)	precise (adj)

1 There was _____ unhappiness about the examination results. Everyone complained.

2 I cannot give you a/an _____ date for my visit, because I am not sure when I am coming to your town.

3 Everyone in the _____ helped the survivors of the flood with food, clothes, and money.

4 The government is working on a/an _____ to bring new business and jobs to the city.

5 The teacher always _____ the parents of the children who are having problems in school.

6 She wanted to make sure she had done everything _____, so she read her homework again to find any mistakes.

7 The weatherman on the television _____ a large snowstorm, but there was only a light rain.

8 The _____ of the meteoroid created a big hole in the ground.

9 The president is a very important person. He must make many _____ decisions every day.

10 A scientific _____ of the water showed that it contains harmful chemicals.

BEYOND THE READING

Research
Find out about NEOs in books and films. Ask some of your classmates the following questions:

- Have you ever seen a film or television show about an NEO that hit Earth? Have you ever read a book about an NEO? Describe the event in the film, television show, or book.
- Was the story based on any of the science that you read about in Reading 3?
- Why do you think people enjoy films and books about this topic?

Discussion
Share your results with a partner or your classmates.

Writing
Write a short summary of your discussions.

MAKING CONNECTIONS

The vocabulary in these exercises comes from all the readings in Unit 7. The exercises will help you see how writers make connections across sentences in a paragraph.

In Units 1–6, you learned that writers have several ways to make connections. To do this, they connect sentences using:

- pronouns to refer to previous things or ideas (See page 30.)
- words or phrases to signal addition (See pages 61 and 91.)
- words or phrases to signal contrast (See page 123.)
- words or phrases to signal causes and effects (See page 154.)
- words or phrases to signal time sequence (See page 185.)

EXERCISE 1

Read the following paragraphs. Highlight any pronouns, and underline what they refer to. Circle any words or phrases that signal addition, contrast, cause and effect, or time sequence. The first one has been done for you.

1   A tornado is a very strong and dangerous wind. It blows in a tight circle. If it contacts the ground, it can cause severe damage. For example, one tornado in 2010 in the southern region of the United States destroyed 700 houses.

2   Tornadoes occur all over the world. However, they occur most often in North America. Most of these occur in the central part of the United States. For this reason, people call this area "Tornado Alley."

3   At one time, scientists were not able to predict when or where tornadoes would occur. Now, however, satellite images help them predict tornadoes. These images also can show when a tornado is nearby.

4   Emergency officials suggest the following steps to prepare for a tornado. First, decide which room in your building will give you the most protection. Next, buy flashlights and some emergency supplies. Finally, when you hear a tornado warning, move away from windows to the safest area of your building.

5   After a tornado hits, officials immediately go from street to street to help injured people. They try to contact all the residents in the area. Later, they survey the damage and try to figure out the losses and the precise costs of the damage.

EXERCISE 2

Make a clear paragraph by putting sentences A, B, and C into the best order
after the numbered sentence. Look for pronouns and words or phrases that
signal addition, contrast, cause and effect, or time sequence to help you. Write
the letters in the correct order on the blank lines.

1 Natural disasters cause widespread destruction. ___ ___ ___

| A   And finally, there is often a harmful impact on the environment that can last a long time. | B   In addition, there is damage to buildings, roads, and highways. | C   Death and injuries are the most significant loss. |

2 There was, of course, no warning of the earthquake. ___ ___ ___

| A   Next, the building began to shake. | B   First, everyone felt slight tremors. | C   The whole event seemed to last forever, but it only lasted for 15 seconds. |

3 In one part of the city, a fire destroyed an entire street. ___ ___ ___

| A   This happened because a gas line broke. | B   It took a long time to control the fire, but no one died. | C   The gas caused a huge explosion and started a fire. |

4 Rockets lift the weather satellite into outer space. ___ ___ ___

| A   They can even watch the storms move around the world. | B   When it is in orbit, it starts to send photos back to earth. | C   Weather officials use these to predict storms. |

5 Before the hurricane, the road went along the coast. ___ ___ ___

| A   Because of this, city officials do not want to rebuild the road. | B   People who live nearby, however, want the city to start rebuilding it immediately. | C   Now, after the hurricane, there is no sign of it. |

Leisure

SKILLS AND STRATEGIES 15
PHRASES (2)

As you learned in Skills and Strategies 7 on page 94, some words always go together to form a fixed phrase. You must learn the meaning of these phrases as a unit, not as individual words. Another group of words that you must learn as a unit is *phrasal verbs*. Phrasal verbs are a combination of a verb plus one or more prepositions. For example, *take off* and *check in* are phrasal verbs. Good readers notice phrasal verbs and learn them. If you can find phrasal verbs in a reading, it can help you understand a reading better and read more quickly.

EXAMPLES & EXPLANATIONS

Examples	Explanations
They **set out** with plans to travel for a month, but they **ran out of** money in only two weeks.	A phrasal verb often has a different meaning from the individual words. *set out* = begin a trip *run out of* = not have any more of something
We will **pick** the rental car **up** in Paris and **drop** it **off** in Marseilles.	Some phrasal verbs are *separable*. In other words, the object of these verbs can come between, or separate, the two parts of the phrasal verb. In this example, *the car* and *it* are the objects of *pick up* and *drop off*. *pick the car up* (or *pick up the car*) = go to get the car However, when the object of a separable phrasal verb is a pronoun, the pronoun must always come between the verb and the preposition. *drop it off* = deliver something (You cannot say, "drop off it.")
The teenager couldn't go to the party because she had to **look after** her little brother.	Some phrasal verbs are *inseparable*. In other words, the object of these verbs must always go after the whole phrasal verb. In this example, *her little brother* is the object. *look after her little brother* = watch and make sure that nothing bad happens to her little brother
She **put** some cookies **out** on the table for the children to eat after they return home. They tried to **put** the fire **out**, but it was too big.	As with other vocabulary words, phrasal verbs may have more than one meaning. *put out* = make something available *put out (a fire)* = stop

THE LANGUAGE OF PHRASAL VERBS

Here are some common phrasal verbs and their meanings.

PHRASAL VERBS	MEANINGS
check in	register (for example, at a hotel)
cut back (on)	reduce
drop off (separable)	deliver; leave someone
figure out (separable)	understand; find; solve
grow up	become an adult
look after	take care of
pick up (separable)	go to get; collect; take into a vehicle
put away (separable)	save
put out (separable)	make something available
put out (separable)	stop (for example, a fire or a cigarette)
run out (of)	use up; not have any more
set out (on)	start on a trip
show up	appear
take off	leave

STRATEGIES

These strategies will help you identify and learn phrasal verbs.

- When you read, look for words that often go together.
- When you make a list of new vocabulary to study, write words that go together, not just the single words.
- When you look up a verb in a dictionary, notice if the dictionary lists a special meaning for the verb when it combines with a preposition.
- Notice whether phrasal verbs are separable or inseparable.

SKILL PRACTICE 1

Read the following paragraphs. Fill in the blank lines with phrasal verbs from the list above each paragraph. If you need help, use the Language of Phrasal Verbs chart above. The first one has been done for you.

figure out	grow up	look after	pick up

1   Parents are very busy when their children are young. They do not have a
     lot of free time, because they have to ___*look after*___ their children. They
     have to _____ their children at the end of the school day and
            b
     take them to different activities. In no time, the children _____
                                                                            c
     and leave home. When parents have no children at home, this is called "an
     empty nest." Parents often have to _____ new ways to spend
                                                  d
     their time.

cut back on	put away	run out of	show up

2   Usually, when people work, they _____ money for retirement.
                                              a
     They dream about the time when they won't have to _____ for
                                                                  b
     work every day. Many people hope to travel at that time. However, as
     people live longer lives, they worry about whether they might
     _____ money in retirement. Therefore, they often decide to
            c
     _____ their expenses.
            d

SKILL PRACTICE 2

Read the following paragraph. Highlight any phrasal verbs you see. Then write
the phrasal verbs on the blank lines next to their meanings. The first one has
been done for you.

   The couple planned a trip to get away for a short vacation. They took off
on Friday immediately after work. Unfortunately, at the hotel, they found out
that the hotel mixed up the dates of their reservation. Therefore, the couple
went back home. They were very unhappy that their plans for a wonderful
vacation did not work out.

a succeed _____

b confused _____

c left *took off* _____

d discovered _____

e returned _____

f leave or escape _____

READING 1
WORK AND LEISURE

GETTING INTO THE TOPIC

Read the definition below. Then discuss the following questions with
a partner.

- **leisure** *n* the time when you are free from work, school, and other
  responsibilities and can relax

1 Do you think people have more leisure now, or did they have more in the
   past? Explain your answer.
2 In what parts of the world do you think people have the most leisure?
3 Do you think leisure is important for people? Explain your answer.

GETTING A FIRST IDEA ABOUT THE READING

Read the title and the first sentences in each paragraph, and look at the chart
on page 226 in Reading 1. What do you think this reading will be about? What
topics do you think will be in the reading? Write your answers below.

1 I think this reading will be about _____

_____ .

2 Circle the topics that you think might be in the reading.
   a Work and leisure around the world
   b The connection between work and leisure
   c Leisure activities
   d Reasons why people don't like to work
   e The history of leisure
   f The best places to go in your leisure time

WHILE YOU READ

As you read, stop at the end of each sentence that contains words in **bold**.
Then follow the instructions in the box in the margin.

Work and Leisure

Look back in this sentence for a phrasal verb. Highlight it.

People often complain that they work too hard. They complain that they don't have enough time for leisure. Leisure is what you do when you are not working, studying, or looking after your home and family (for example, cooking and **cleaning**). It is what you do when you relax and enjoy yourself. Today, we have leisure time at the end of the workday or school day or on weekends. 1

The amount of time we have for leisure has changed throughout history. In the past, most people worked on the land, so their work depended on the weather and the seasons. For example, in Europe and North America, people did most of the work during the late spring, summer, and early fall. They did not do as much work during the winter. 2

The amount of time that people have for leisure changes when their work changes. For instance, in Europe and North America, during the late eighteenth century and early nineteenth century, many people left their farms. They went to work in factories in towns and cities. Their work in factories was very hard, and both the workday and workweek became longer. Many people worked for 16 hours a day, six days a week. Their only leisure time was on Sunday. 3

As you read this paragraph, look for words that signal cause and effect. Circle the words. Mark the causes with *C* and the effects with *E*.

In the middle of the nineteenth century, **factory work began to change in two ways**. First, the machines in the factories became faster and more efficient, so that workers did not need to work as much. They had more free time. Second, the factories began to pay their workers more money. As a result, workers had more money to spend. 4

Look back in this sentence for a phrasal verb. Highlight it.

With more time and money, workers had more opportunity for leisure activities. People who worked in or near cities in the second half of the nineteenth century had many new choices about how to spend their time and money. The world was changing rapidly. Transportation was continuing to improve, so people could get around more **easily**. Trains and streetcars could take people into the city for entertainment. In the cities, there were new public parks and gardens. Workers took their families to the city for games, picnics, and concerts. The first movies and professional baseball games appeared at this time. They were both very popular. There were also trains to take people to the beach or other places outside the city for a day of leisure. 5

In the nineteenth century, many people had more time for leisure.

The workday and workweek continued to get shorter. By the beginning of the twentieth century, the eight-hour workday and the five-day workweek became typical in most western countries. Other parts of the world have followed a similar path. When people move from farms to cities to work in factories, work hours increase. Then, as a country's economy develops, work hours go **down**.

The workweek continues to get shorter, especially in Australia and Western Europe. France has the shortest workweek – 35 hours. Most workers in Eastern Europe and North America still have a 40-hour workweek. In other parts of the world, however, people continue to work much longer. South Koreans work an average of 45 hours every week. People in India and Singapore work an average of 46 hours every week. According to a 2009 study of 80 cities, workers in Cairo have the longest hours and the least leisure time (see Figure 8.1). In general, work hours have decreased and leisure time has increased in the twentieth and twenty-first **centuries**.

6

7

Review paragraphs 3–6. Circle the dates, and underline what happened on those dates. Then make a time line of the events in your notebook.

Look back in paragraph 7 to find a word that signals a contrast. Circle the word, and underline the two ideas the writer contrasts.

FIGURE 8.1 **Number of Work Hours Per Year**

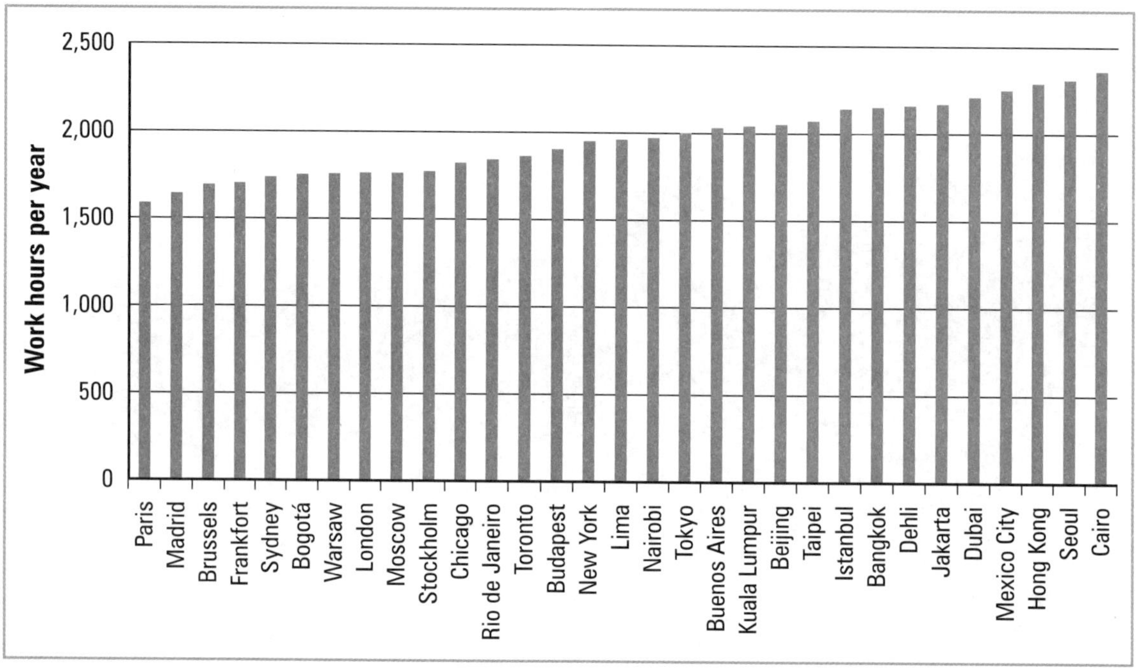

Source: UBS Prices and Earnings, 2009

MAIN IDEA CHECK

Here are the main ideas of each paragraph in Reading 1. Match each paragraph to its main idea. Write the number of the paragraph on the blank line.

Paragraphs 1–4

_____ A The amount of time we have for leisure has changed through the years.

_____ B Leisure is the time you have to relax.

_____ C Factory work changed in the mid-nineteenth century.

_____ D When people moved from farm work to factory work, their leisure time decreased.

Paragraphs 5–7

_____ E At the end of the nineteenth century, workers had more time and money for leisure.

_____ F The workweek is getting shorter in many countries, but it is still long in others.

_____ G Work hours decrease as a country's economy grows.

A CLOSER LOOK

Look back at Reading 1 to answer the following questions.

1 In the past, the amount of work often depended on the following factors. Circle two answers. (Par. 2)

  a Seasons

  b Location

  c Factories

  d Weather

2 When people moved from farms to factories, their leisure time decreased. True or False? (Par. 3)

3 In the middle of the nineteenth century, machines in factories became _____ and more _____. (Par. 4)

4 What did workers do in their leisure time in the nineteenth century? Circle three answers. (Par. 5)

  a They went to the beach.

  b They went to parks.

  c They listened to music.

  d They listened to the radio.

  e They played music.

5 Put the events (A–D) in the correct order in which they happened. Write the correct letter in each box. (Par. 6)

  A Work hours decreased.

  B People moved from farms to factories.

  C Factories became more efficient.

  D Work hours increased.

6 According to Figure 8.1, people in Western Europe generally work for fewer hours than people in North America. True or False?

VOCABULARY STUDY: DEFINITIONS

Find words in Reading 1 that can complete the following definitions. If you need help, use Key Vocabulary from the Readings on page 251.

1 _____ are places where things are made by machines. (*n pl*) Par. 3

2 A/An _____ is a chance to do or get something. (*n*) Par. 5

3 Something that is open and available to everyone is _____. (adj) Par. 5

4 _____ are meals that you eat outside, often in parks. (n pl) Par. 5

5 _____ are performances of live music. (n pl) Par. 5

6 A/An _____ is the area of land next to a sea or a lake. (n) Par. 5

7 Two things that are almost the same are _____. (adj) Par. 6

8 The _____ is the system in which a country makes and uses things and money. (n) Par. 6

VOCABULARY STUDY: WORD FAMILIES

Read the words in the following chart. The words in **bold** are the parts of speech that appear in Reading 1. Find these words in the reading. If you need help, use Key Vocabulary from the Readings on page 251.

NOUN	VERB
appearance	**appear**
enjoyment	**enjoy**
entertainment	entertain
improvement	**improve**
relaxation	**relax**

Choose the correct form of the words from the chart to complete the following sentences. Use the correct verb tenses and subject-verb agreement. Use the correct singular and plural noun forms.

1 I _____ many different leisure activities, but listening to music is my favorite one.

2 For many people who have stressful jobs, exercise is an important form of _____. They feel better after they exercise.

3 After she stopped smoking, her health began to _____.

4 Films, concerts, and games are all forms of _____.

5 The tourists watched the performance with great _____.

6 The sun _____ for a few minutes and then went behind the clouds.

7 The children _____ their parents with their musical performance.

8 The _____ of the president surprised all of the people who were waiting at the train station.

9 His parents were very happy with the _____ in his grades in math and science.

10 Everyone in the office hopes there will be time to _____ after they finish the project. They have all been working very hard.

BEYOND THE READING

Research

Do some research on work hours in your country or another country that interests you. Find answers to the following questions:
- How long is the average workday?
- How long is the average workweek?

Discussion

Share your research with a partner or your classmates.

Writing

Use your class's results to create a chart like the one below. Use answers to one of the questions above to create your chart. Then write a few sentences about the information in the chart.

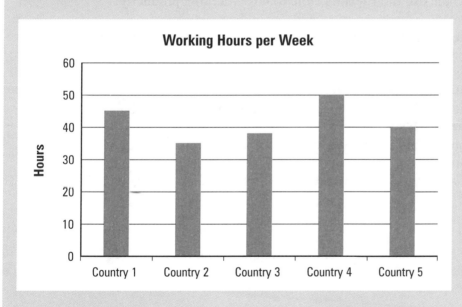

Working Hours per Week

READING 2
LEISURE ACTIVITIES

GETTING INTO THE TOPIC
Discuss the following questions with a partner.

1 How do you spend your leisure time?
2 Do you prefer to spend your leisure time by yourself or with other people? Explain your answer.
3 Do you enjoy sports or games of competition? Which ones?
4 Do you spend some of your leisure time on the Internet? Explain your answer.

GETTING A FIRST IDEA ABOUT THE READING
The following are the first one or two sentences of paragraphs 2–7 in Reading 2. Read these sentences. Then, with a partner, discuss what you think these paragraphs will be about.

1 Today, many people use their leisure time to do something productive. (Par. 2)
2 For some people, the most important thing about leisure time is to spend it with other people. (Par. 3)
3 Some of these games are very traditional. However, in some countries, the younger generation likes to make up new games. (Par. 4)
4 Leisure activities, such as games, create a community, that is, a group of people who share interests. (Par. 5)
5 Communication on the Internet is a very popular leisure activity for millions of people. (Par. 6)
6 Social network sites are global communities, and they are growing. (Par. 7)

WHILE YOU READ
As you read, stop at the end of each sentence that contains words in **bold**. Then follow the instructions in the box in the margin.

Leisure Activities

Most people today have more time for leisure than people had in the past. What are they doing with this time? Some people just want to relax. They watch television, read, or listen to music. Others want to be more active and productive with their leisure time. They want to learn something new or to develop a new skill. Other people want to participate in activities with people who have similar **interests**.

Today, many people use their leisure time to do something productive. Perhaps because they work only with their minds all day, they want to do something with their hands. They want to do something very different from their office jobs or schoolwork. Some enjoy working in a garden. Others like to build or fix things in their leisure time. For example, they may want to work with wood, build furniture, or paint. Others learn how to cook foods from other countries.

For some people, the most important thing about leisure time is to spend it with other people. This is especially true for those people who like to play sports. All over the world, soccer, basketball, tennis, and other **sports** bring people together. Other games of competition also bring people together. Card games, such as poker, are popular in the United States. Dominos are popular in Latin America and the Caribbean. Many people in Asian countries, especially in China, enjoy mahjong.

1

Look back in paragraph 1 for a collocation with a verb and the noun *television*. Highlight the collocation.

2

3

Find clues that signal the definition of *sports*. Circle the clues, and write the definition in the margin.

People all over the world enjoy playing games.

Look back in this sentence for a phrasal verb. Highlight it.

Some of these games are very traditional. However, in 4 some countries, the younger generation likes to make up new **games**. In Japan, for example, there is a new popular game called *cosplay*. Cosplay comes from the words *costume* and *play*. In cosplay, people dress in costumes. They want to look like their favorite characters from comic books, movies, or video games. In Japan, people dress as their favorite anime[1] characters. In western countries, cosplay is also beginning to be popular. There, people dress up as characters from *Star Trek* or comic books.

Cosplay is popular in Japan.

As you read this paragraph, look for words that signal supporting details of this main idea. Circle the words. Then, underline the details.

Leisure activities, such as games, create a community, that 5 is, a group of people who share interests. **Technology makes it possible to create a community even if people are far apart.** The best example of this is online games. People all over the world play online games such as *Final Fantasy* and *World of Warcraft*. Others participate in virtual online communities, such as *Second Life*. In these virtual communities, people can pretend to be someone else. They can choose to be a different person or even an animal or a plant.

Look back in this sentence for a phrasal verb. Highlight it.

Communication on the Internet is a very popular leisure 6 activity for millions of people. They keep up with old friends and meet new friends on social network sites such as Facebook, MySpace, Twitter, Orkut, Mixi, Cyworld, and **Xiaonei**. These are online communities where people can share news, information, pictures, and videos.

Social network sites are global communities, and they are 7 growing. In 2009, Facebook had more than 100 million members all over the world. The users spent almost twice as much time on social network sites in 2009 than in 2006. One year later, the number reached 500 million, with over 100 million

---

1 *anime*: a form of animation in films and television that began in Japan

in the United States. The popularity of this form of leisure will continue to grow because more people are using the Internet, especially in countries like China. One young man in China recently told a newspaper, "I spend most of my leisure time on the Internet."

People spend their leisure time in many different ways. 8 Some people want to learn. Others just want to have fun. Some prefer to spend their time alone. Others want to spend their leisure time with other people. The most important recent development in leisure activities is in technology. More and more people depend on technology for their leisure activities today.

MAIN IDEA CHECK

Here are the main ideas of each paragraph in Reading 2. Match each paragraph to its main idea. Write the number of the paragraph on the blank line.

Paragraphs 1–4

_____ A Some people want to work with their hands during their leisure time.

_____ B Sports and other games are popular leisure activities.

_____ C People make different choices about how to spend their leisure time.

_____ D Some people like to dress as their favorite characters in their leisure time.

Paragraphs 5–8

_____ E Social network sites are becoming more popular.

_____ F There are many different choices for leisure activities.

_____ G Many people spend leisure time on social network sites.

_____ H Playing games online is a popular leisure activity.

A CLOSER LOOK

Look back at Reading 2 to answer the following questions.

1 Why do some people like to do leisure activities that require them to use their hands? Circle three answers. (Par. 2)
  a They want to do something different from their daily jobs.
  b They want to get some exercise.
  c They work with their minds most of the day.
  d They want to be productive in their leisure time.

2 Why do people like leisure activities such as sports and games? (Par. 3)
   a They get to spend time with other people.
   b They like to learn new things.
   c They like to meet people from different countries.
   d They like to use technology.

3 The word *cosplay* is a combination of the words _____ and
   _____. (Par. 4)

4 How does technology expand leisure opportunities? Circle three answers.
   (Pars. 5 and 6)
   a It allows people to communicate when they are far away.
   b It helps create virtual communities.
   c It increases competition.
   d It allows people all over the world to play games online together.
   e It increases the time for leisure.

5 In some virtual communities, people can pretend to be plants or animals.
   True or False? (Par. 5)

6 In 2010, about how many Facebook members did not live in the United
   States? (Par. 7)
   a About 100 million
   b About 200 million
   c About 400 million
   d About 500 million

7 Fill in the chart to show the features of leisure activities according to
   Reading 2. Put a check (✔) in the appropriate boxes.

LEISURE ACTIVITY	FEATURE			
	Is it productive?	Does it require other people?	Is there competition?	Does it use technology?
Building furniture				
Basketball				
Mahjong				
Cosplay				
Online games				
Social networks				

VOCABULARY STUDY: DEFINITIONS

Find words in Reading 2 that can complete the following definitions. If you need help, use Key Vocabulary from the Readings on page 251.

1 A/An _____ is the ability to do something well, because you have practiced it. (*n*) Par. 1

2 To _____ something means to repair it. (*v*) Par. 2

3 _____ includes tables, chairs, beds, and desks. (*n*) Par. 2

4 To _____ something is to invent something new, such as a game or story. (*phrasal v*) Par. 4

5 A/An _____ is a special kind of clothing from a time in history, a country, or a story. (*n*) Par. 4

6 _____ are sets of stories with drawings and very few words. (*n pl two words*) Par. 4

7 _____ is the act of sharing information, ideas, and feelings with other people. (*n*) Par. 6

8 _____ means two times. (*adv*) Par. 7

VOCABULARY STUDY: WORDS IN CONTEXT

Complete the following sentences with words or phrases from the list below. If necessary, review the words in Key Vocabulary from the Readings on page 251.

apart	productive	character	keep up
network	pretended	virtual	participated

1 My brother always wants to do something _____ with his free time. He likes to paint the house or fix things, but I prefer to relax and read a book.

2 I _____ with my best friend from school. We send each other e-mail messages every week.

3 Orkut is the most popular social _____ site in Brazil, but Mixi is the most popular one in Japan.

4 He _____ to know the answer, but he really did not know it.

5 The students and teachers both _____ in the school basketball game.

6 The two brothers live far _____, but they talk on the phone every Sunday.

7 She knows that the _____ worlds on the Internet are not real, but she likes to visit them.

8 His favorite _____ from the movies is the Terminator.

VOCABULARY REVIEW: SAME OR DIFFERENT

The following pairs of sentences contain vocabulary from Readings 1 and 2 in this unit. Write *S* on the blank line if the two sentences have the same meaning. Write *D* if the meanings are different.

_____ 1 Many people use social network sites to keep up with their friends.

Many friends use sites on the Internet to communicate with each other.

_____ 2 The furniture from this factory is similar to furniture from the nineteenth century.

This factory makes tables, chairs, and other furniture that looks like furniture from 200 years ago.

_____ 3 They wore costumes to the picnic at the beach.

They pretended to be characters from their favorite comic book.

_____ 4 Many people like to relax and enjoy concerts in their leisure time.

Many people like to listen to live music for entertainment.

_____ 5 There were many opportunities to use our skills.

We participated in games like football and basketball.

BEYOND THE READING

Research

Do some research on how your friends spend their leisure time. Ask at least three of your classmates the following questions:

- How do you spend most of your leisure time?
- Do you prefer to spend it alone or with other people?
- Do your leisure activities use technology, such as music players, cameras, computers, or the Internet?

Discussion

Share your research with a partner or your classmates. Use the chart in Question 7 of A Closer Look on page 234 to organize your research. Add your classmates' leisure activities to the chart, and fill in the features.

Writing

Write a short summary of the features of the leisure activities in your class research.

SKILLS AND STRATEGIES 16
READING QUICKLY

As you have learned in previous Skills and Strategies, good readers look
for topics, main ideas, and supporting details as they read. This helps them
understand what the reading is about. Good readers also learn to read quickly.
They use an important strategy as they read. They don't read every single
word. They let their eyes find and focus on the most important words in a
sentence – usually the nouns, verbs, adjectives, and adverbs. When you do
this, you read more quickly, and you usually can still understand the most
important ideas in the reading.

EXAMPLES & EXPLANATIONS

Examples

Most people in the United States say
that reading is their favorite leisure time
activity. However, reading is not the most
common way that people actually spend
their time. For example, one study asked
people, "How did you spend your free time
last night?" The number of people who
spent the evening reading was half the
number who spent the evening watching
television. In this case, people's actions
tell a different story than their words.
They would like to spend more time
reading, but they actually spend more
time watching television.

Most people in the United States say
that reading is their favorite leisure time
activity. However, reading is not the most
common way that people actually spend
their time. For example, one study asked
people, "How did you spend your free time
last night?" The number of people who
spent the evening reading was half the
number who spent the evening watching
television. In this case, people's actions
tell a different story than their words.
They would like to spend more time
reading, but they actually spend more
time watching television.

Explanations

Try reading only the "important" words in this paragraph.
Time yourself. Then answer the two questions.

Start time: _____

End time: _____

Total time: _____

• Which leisure activity do Americans say is their favorite?

• Which leisure activity do Americans actually do most?

Probably you could answer these questions. In other
words, you could get the most important ideas of
the paragraph.

Now read the paragraph again. Read every word. Put your
finger under each word as you read. Time yourself.

Start time: _____

End time: _____

Total time: _____

You probably read more slowly but understood the same
amount as before.

STRATEGIES

These strategies can help you read more quickly.

- Look quickly at paragraphs to identify the topic, main ideas, and supporting details.
- As you read, let your eyes focus on the "important" words in a sentence, not every single word.
- Do not use a pencil or finger under the words as you read. This slows you down.
- Do not speak the words as you read. This will also slow you down.
- Time yourself sometimes as you read. Try to read fast. Reading more quickly can then become a habit.

SKILL PRACTICE 1

Read each paragraph below as quickly as you can. Try to focus only on the most important words as you read. After you read a paragraph, look at the three possible main idea choices for the paragraph. Circle the best choice.

1   There is a big difference between the way people would like to spend their leisure time and the way they actually spend it. For example, in a research study, cleaning the house was not on the list of favorite ways to spend leisure time. However, it was number eight on a list of how people actually spent their time. This shows that people do not always have a choice about how they spend their leisure time.

Main idea:

a Cleaning the house is a favorite activity of many people.
b People often have to do things in their leisure time that are not favorite activities.
c People tell researchers things that are not true about the way they spend leisure time.

2   Teenage girls and boys like to spend their leisure time in different ways. In a research study, 43 percent of the teenage girls said that their favorite way to spend an evening was to hang out with friends and family. In contrast, only 26 percent of the teenage boys said this was their favorite way to spend an evening. Fifteen percent of the teenage boys said they would like to play video games. However, no girls gave this answer. There is clearly a difference in the activities that teenage girls and boys like to do in their leisure time.

Main idea:

a There are differences in the ways that teenage girls and boys like to spend their leisure time.

b Teenage girls don't like to play video games.

c Teenage boys and girls like to do a lot of things.

SKILL PRACTICE 2

Read the paragraph below. Time yourself. Try to read the paragraph in 45 seconds (a rate of about 150 words a minute). As you read, focus on the most important words in each sentence only. Then look at the three possible main idea choices for the paragraph. Circle the best choice.

Research shows that teenagers spend a lot of time in front of a computer or television screen. Researchers in Canada did a study of 1,300 teenagers. They wanted to know how much time the teens spent watching television or looking at a computer. They called this "screen time." On average, the teens' screen time was 20 hours a week. The screen time of some of the teenagers in the group was much higher. For example, 30 percent of the teens spent about 40 hours a week at a television or computer. Seven percent of the teens spent more than 50 hours a week doing these things. Most of the screen time was at the television.

Main idea:

a Teenagers spend a lot of time watching television.

b Teenagers spend a lot of time in front of a television or a computer.

c Researchers studied a group of teenagers in Canada.

READING 3
VACATIONS

GETTING INTO THE TOPIC

GETTING INTO THE TOPIC

Discuss the following questions with a partner.

1 What do you usually do on your vacations?
2 Do you travel to different places? Explain your answer.
3 Is this different from what your parents did on their vacations when they were your age? Explain your answer.
4 If you could do anything or go anywhere, what would you do on your vacation?

GETTING A FIRST IDEA ABOUT THE READING

Read the title, the section headings, and the first sentence of each paragraph of Reading 3. Then read the questions below. Write the number of the section (*I, II,* or *III*) next to the question or questions it will answer.

SECTION	QUESTIONS THAT EACH SECTION WILL ANSWER
	Do some companies try to stop their workers from taking vacations?
	How do most people choose to spend their vacations?
	Why do some people keep working on their vacations?
	What are some less traditional choices for vacations?
	What is the history of vacations?
	Do some vacations require special knowledge?

WHILE YOU READ

As you read, stop at the end of each sentence that contains words in **bold**. Then follow the instructions in the box in the margin.

Vacations

I. TRADITIONAL VACATIONS

Vacations are a fairly new idea. Until the twentieth century, most people worked every day except on Sundays and religious holidays. Even students had to work when they were not in school. Today, many people have more time for leisure activities in the evenings and on weekends. They also have time for vacations, that is, days when they do not have to go to school or to their jobs.

People choose different ways to spend their vacations. Some people stay home and relax or visit people in their family. However, more and more, people choose to travel on their vacations. For example, they may go camping in the mountains or go swimming at a beach. Some people want to explore somewhere new and exciting. They want to visit another country. In 2007, London was the most popular city for tourists, followed by Hong Kong, Bangkok, Singapore, Paris, and New York. France was the most popular country for tourists, followed by the United States, Spain, China, and Italy. Tourists want to visit famous attractions like the Statue of Liberty, the Great Wall, and famous museums like the **Louvre**.

II. OTHER VACATION CHOICES

Some people want less traditional vacations. They want to do something physical and active on vacation. Some of them want vacations that are more than just active. They want an *extreme* vacation. An extreme vacation has activities that are physically difficult and also risky. Some extreme vacation activities are more than risky. They are dangerous. Examples of extreme vacation activities are skiing in high mountains and exploring caves. Some people like to do dangerous things because they think danger is exciting.

Traditional and extreme vacations are not the only choices. Some people choose volunteer vacations. On volunteer vacations, people do things to help

Some people enjoy extreme leisure activities, like exploring caves.

Time yourself as you read Reading 3. Then go back and read it again. This time, practice reading quickly. Read in word groups. See if your reading speed improves.

Look back in paragraph 2 for a collocation with a verb and the noun *vacation*. Highlight the collocation.

other people, animals, or the environment. For example, they may teach children or build houses in developing countries. Some people want to work with scientists on a project. For example, they may help injured birds or plant trees in a **forest**.

Most of these volunteer vacations do not require special 5 knowledge. However, there are also volunteer vacations for people who want to continue to work during their vacations. They find great satisfaction in their work. They do not want to relax during their vacations. They do not want to go to a beach or the mountains on their vacations. Every year, for instance, hundreds of dentists and doctors leave their offices and work in other places during their vacations. They go to places where people need their help.

Most people do not want to work on their vacations. They 6 just want to relax, but they do not want their vacation activities to harm the environment. Unfortunately, this has happened, especially in popular tourist locations where there are lots of big hotels and shopping malls. For example, some people worry that too many tourists have damaged the environment in places like Hawaii. As a result of these concerns, many people choose "green" vacations. On green vacations, people can enjoy the natural beauty of the places they visit, but they will not damage the environment. On green vacations, tourists can learn about nature. They watch birds or other wild animals. They can also find out information about the culture of the people who live **there**. If they visit wild and fragile places, "green" tourists stay in small, simple places that do not use a lot of resources, like water and energy.

Look back in paragraph 4 for a collocation with an adjective and the noun *countries*. Highlight the collocation.

Look back in this sentence for a phrasal verb. Highlight it.

On green vacations, people enjoy nature and protect the environment.

III. THE DISAPPEARING VACATION

Most workers now have more time for vacations, and they have more options about how to use their vacation time. However, a study of workers in 11 countries shows that not all workers take their vacations. Many workers just continue to work. They do not use all of the vacation days that they have earned on their **job** (see Figure 8.2).

Even when some people do take a vacation, they often continue to work during their vacation. They answer their e-mail, or they call their office to check on their work. They do this because they are afraid something important might happen during their vacation. They do not want to miss anything. They cannot completely relax and enjoy their leisure time. Many workers say that it is too stressful to take a long vacation. When they return to work, they have to do all the work that they did not do when they were on vacation. This means they have to work even **harder**.

Some people are also afraid their bosses will think they are not good workers if they take a long vacation. However, research shows that most workers feel better after they return from a vacation. They return to the office with new ideas and lots of energy. Workers who spend time away from the office and relax are better workers. Some companies, like Hewlett Packard and Price Waterhouse, understand this. They require

7

Look back in paragraph 7 for a collocation with a verb and the noun *vacation*. Highlight the collocation.

8

Look back in paragraph 8 for a word that signals cause and effect. Circle the word. Mark the cause with *C* and the effect with *E*.

9

FIGURE 8.2 **Number of Vacation Days per Country – 2009**

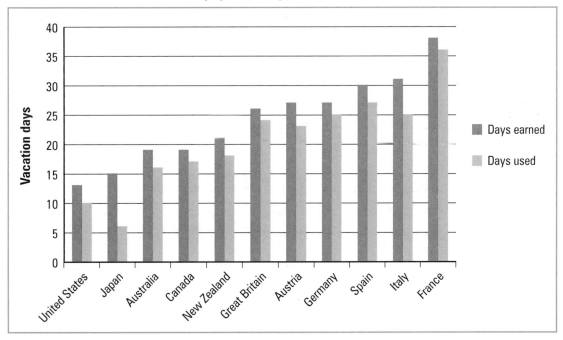

Source: Expedia.com

their employees to take a vacation. Workers may not check their e-mail or mobile phones while they are away. Some hotels help them do this with new, special programs. The guests give up their computers and mobile phones while they are at the hotel. They cannot contact their work.

There are many different kinds of vacations: traditional, 10 extreme, volunteer, and green, among others. It does not matter what kind of vacation people choose, as long as they take their vacation. They should not put it off. They should relax and forget about their work or their studies for a while. They might feel better when they return to work or school, and they may be more productive.

MAIN IDEA CHECK

Here are the main ideas of each paragraph in Reading 3. Match each paragraph to its main idea. Write the number of the paragraph on the blank line.

Paragraphs 1–2

_____ A Many people choose traditional vacations.

_____ B Today, people have more time for vacations than in the past.

Paragraphs 3–6

_____ C Green vacations are a good choice for people who do not want to harm the environment.

_____ D Some people use their knowledge to help other people on their vacations.

_____ E Some people enjoy dangerous activities on their vacations.

_____ F Some people want to help others on their vacations.

Paragraphs 7–10

_____ G People who take a vacation are better workers when they return.

_____ H It is important to take a vacation, but it doesn't matter what kind.

_____ I Some people believe that a vacation will make their work harder when they return.

_____ J Many workers do not use all their vacation time.

A CLOSER LOOK

Look back at Reading 3 to answer the following questions.

1 What are some examples of traditional vacations? Circle two answers. (Par. 2)
   a Going swimming at the beach.
   b Exploring caves
   c Visiting famous attractions
   d Planting trees

2 Paris was the most popular city for tourists in 2007. True or False? (Par. 2)

3 What are some examples of extreme vacation activities? Circle two answers. (Par. 3)
   a Climbing the Great Wall
   b Exploring caves
   c Skiing in high mountains
   d Camping in the mountains

4 Extreme vacation activities are physically _____ and
_____. (Par. 3)

5 What are some things that people do on volunteer vacations? Circle three answers. (Pars. 4 and 5)
   a They help sick people.
   b They help scientists.
   c They explore the environment.
   d They plant trees.
   e They meet people.

6 People who are worried about the environment may choose a/an
_____ vacation. (Par. 6)

7 Why do some people continue working on vacation? Circle two answers. (Par. 8)
   a They think they will miss something important.
   b They think vacations are stressful.
   c They think they will feel better.
   d They are afraid they will have a lot more work when they return to their jobs.

8 Workers who take a vacation are often more productive than workers who do not. True or False? (Par. 9)

9 How do hotels help workers who need a vacation? (Par. 9)

   a They provide e-mail access to guests.

   b They contact their bosses.

   c They take away their mobile phones and computers.

   d They provide green vacations.

VOCABULARY STUDY: DEFINITIONS

Find words in Reading 3 that can complete the following definitions. If you need help, use Key Vocabulary from the Readings on page 251.

1 If you go _____ on vacation, you sleep and eat outside. (*n*) Par. 2

2 _____ are places that a lot of people want to visit. (*n pl*) Par. 2

3 A/An _____ is a person who does work without payment. (*n*) Par. 4

4 The _____ is the natural world all around us. (*n*) Par. 4

5 _____ are places where there are many stores in one location. (*n pl*) Par. 6

6 Something that helps protect nature is _____. (*adj*) Par. 6

7 To _____ something is to stop using it. (*phrasal v*) Par. 9

8 To _____ something is to wait until later to do it. (*phrasal v*) Par. 10

VOCABULARY STUDY: SYNONYMS

Read the sentences below. The words in parentheses mean the same or almost the same as the words in the list. For each sentence, replace the words in parentheses with a word from the list. Write it on the blank line. If necessary, review the words in Key Vocabulary from the Readings on page 251.

risky	options	program	satisfaction
earns	employees	simple	boss

1 The (head) _____ of the company told the workers that the factory was closing.

2 The tourist office in Paris offers a (plan) _____ for people who have only a few days to visit all of the city's attractions.

3 Many businesses are hiring more (workers) _____ this year.

4 The trip through the mountains was (very dangerous) _____. Two of the travelers fell and had serious injuries.

5 Her work with children gives her a lot of (pleasure) _____.

6   She (makes) _____ $20 an hour.

7   Travelers today have many (choices) _____ for places to visit.

8   The house was very (plain) _____ and did not have
    much furniture.

VOCABULARY REVIEW: ACADEMIC WORD LIST

The following are Academic Word List (AWL) words from all the readings in
Unit 8. Complete the sentences below with these words. If necessary, review
the AWL words in Key Vocabulary from the Readings on page 251.

participate (v)	virtual (adj)	environment (n)	communication (n)	network (n)
volunteers (n)	options (n)	relax (v)	economy (n)	similar (adj)

1   We can do many things to protect the _____. For example, we
    can save water and energy.

2   There are many different social _____ sites on the Internet.
    The most popular one in the world is Facebook.

3   When the _____ is growing, there are more jobs, and people
    spend more money.

4   My friend and I have _____ coats, so I took hers by mistake.

5   Hundreds of _____ went to Haiti to help victims of
    the earthquake.

6   It is important to _____ sometimes. It is not healthy to work
    hard all the time.

7   The English program offers several different _____. Students
    can take classes during the day, at night, or on weekends.

8   Many young people spend a lot of time in _____ communities
    on the Internet.

9   Today there are many different forms of _____, including
    telephones, e-mail, and text messages.

10 All of the different political groups have agreed to _____ in the
    new government.

BEYOND THE READING

Research

Do a survey of your classmates about how they like to spend their vacations. Ask three of them the following questions:

- What do you like to do most on a vacation? Go to the beach? Go to a new city? Explore nature? Explain your answer.
- If you could do anything on your next vacation, what would it be? Explain your answer.

Discussion

Share your results with a partner or your classmates.

- What do most of your classmates like to do on their vacations?
- What would most of them like to do if they could choose?

Writing

Write a short description of what you like to do on your vacations.

MAKING CONNECTIONS

The vocabulary in these exercises comes from all the readings in Unit 8. The exercises will help you see how writers make connections across sentences in a paragraph.

In Units 1–6, you learned that writers have several ways to make connections. To do this, they connect sentences using:

- pronouns to refer to previous things or ideas (See page 30.)
- words or phrases to signal addition (See pages 61 and 91.)
- words or phrases to signal contrast (See page 123.)
- words or phrases to signal causes and effects (See page 154.)
- words or phrases to signal time sequence (See page 185.)

EXERCISE 1

Read the following paragraphs. Highlight any pronouns, and underline what they refer to. Circle any words or phrases that signal addition, contrast, cause and effect, or time sequence. The first one has been done for you.

1   As people change their ideas about vacations, <u>new types of travel companies</u> start up. They offer tourists opportunities to participate in many different types of activities on their vacation trips. (For example,) "wilderness" travel companies take people to spend time in rainforests or mountains.

2   Many hotels are trying to be green. They hope to have a smaller impact on the environment than in the past. For example, many hotels give guests an option to use their towels twice before washing them.

3   The first home video game, Pong, appeared in 1972. People played it on their television sets. Then, when personal computers became popular, companies started to develop new games for computers. Now, home video games are very common. The Nintendo Wii, for example, is in 70 million homes.

4   Many people just want to relax on their vacations. Therefore, they choose vacations where they can stay home and visit local attractions. In contrast, other people give up their comfortable homes and go camping outdoors.

5   What is the healthiest way to spend leisure time? Most experts say that it is important to be active. In addition, communication with friends and family is also important. For these two reasons, a walk in the park together is a great way to spend free time.

EXERCISE 2

Make a clear paragraph by putting sentences A, B, and C into the best order after the numbered sentence. Look for pronouns and words or phrases that signal addition, contrast, cause and effect, or time sequence to help you. Write the letters in the correct order on the blank lines.

1 As employees, many people spend all day on the computer. ___ ___ ___

| **A** For example, you can play card games without a partner or participate in virtual games. | **B** Therefore, it is surprising that they also spend a lot of their leisure time on the computer. | **C** However, at home, people use their computers for entertainment more than for work. |

2 The first games appeared on computers many years ago. ___ ___ ___

| **A** At that time, many people only had computers at work. | **B** When their boss came in, they pretended to be working, but they really were not very productive. | **C** Because of this, employees sometimes played computer games at work. |

3 People who were downtown last weekend got some unexpected entertainment. ___ ___ ___

| **A** They were dressed as their favorite comic book characters. | **B** It was an unusual sight, because people do not usually walk around in public in costumes. | **C** They were able to see thousands of people dressed in costumes. |

4 Volunteer vacations are becoming more and more popular. ___ ___ ___

| **A** The volunteers learn about different cultures, and the community gets economic help. | **B** They may build new schools, for example, or help communities start new businesses. | **C** On these vacations, people go to different communities in the world that need help. |

5 Many people take vacations in travel trailers. ___ ___ ___

| **A** They enjoy driving to see things in the daytime. | **B** Then, at night, they spend the night in the trailer. | **C** This simple way to travel is popular in many countries. |

APPENDIX 1

KEY VOCABULARY FROM THE READINGS

Words that are part of the Academic Word List are noted with an Ⓐ in this appendix.

UNIT 1, READING 1: BORDERS ON THE LAND, IN THE OCEAN, AND IN THE AIR

careful *adj* giving a lot of attention to what you are doing so that you do not have an accident, make a mistake, or damage anything • *The official took a* **careful** *look at my passport.* **care** *n* serious attention to something so that you do not have an accident, make a mistake, or damage anything • *Take* **care** *when you pack to make sure you don't forget anything.*

check *v* to take a careful look at • *The police officer* **checked** *the man's identification card.*

control *v* to have the ability to make someone or something do what you want • *The government* **controls** *the border.*

dangerous *adj* able to harm or hurt someone • *It is* **dangerous** *to drive a car too fast.* **danger** *n* something that may harm you • *Police officers are always aware of possible* **danger** *when they do their jobs.*

feature Ⓐ *n* an important part of something • *The map shows* **features** *such as mountains very clearly.*

national *adj* relating to the whole of a country • *They played the South Korean* **national** *song at the Olympics because the gold medal winner was South Korean.* **nation** *n* a country or the people living in a country • *The whole* **nation** *joined in the feeling of excitement before the big football game.*

official *n* someone who has an important position in an organization such as the government • *Government* **officials** *watch who comes into the country.* **official** *adj* approved by the government or by someone in authority • *The* **official** *language of the country is Spanish, but many people speak English.*

permission *n* when you allow someone to do something • *You need* **permission** *to enter the building.*

physical Ⓐ *adj* relating to real things that you can see and touch • *The* **physical** *border is the river between the two countries.*

resource Ⓐ *n* a valuable thing that belongs to a person, group, or country • *Water is an important natural* **resource**.

safe *adj* not dangerous or likely to cause harm • *Is it* **safe** *to travel in that country?* **safety** *n* the condition of not being near danger or near harm • *The book had important information about* **safety** *when you travel.*

shore *n* the land at the edge of an ocean, lake, or large river • *The border of the country is a few miles from its* **shore**.

straight *adj* not curved or bent • *They walked in a* **straight** *line from the table to the door.*

UNIT 1, READING 2: WALLS AS BORDERS

agree *v* to have the same opinion or idea • *The two governments* **agree** *on many things.*

attempt *v* to try to do something, especially something difficult • *The man* **attempted** *to cross the border without a passport, but the officials stopped him.*

divide *v* to separate into more than one part • *The officials* **divided** *everyone into two groups, one for tourists and the other for citizens.*

electronic *adj* using computers or parts of computers • *The* **electronic** *door only opens after you type in your identification numbers.*

enemy *n* a person or army you don't like • *The country fought against its* **enemies**.

entrance *n* a door or opening • *We walked through the* **entrance** *of the building.*

fence *n* a wall made of metal or wood • *There is a **fence** around the building. We can't go in.*

guard *n* a person who watches or protects a person or place • *The **guard** asked me for my identification and then let me go inside the building.*

invasion *n* the arrival of enemies • *The government was worried about an **invasion** on its northern border.*

major Ⓐ *adj* more important or more serious than other things or people of a similar type • *The **major** problem is the length of the border. It's very long.*

prevent *v* to stop something from happening or to stop someone from doing something • *The official **prevented** her from entering the country.*

purpose *n* a reason for doing something • *The official asked, "What's the **purpose** of your visit?"*

recent *adj* happening or starting a short time ago • *Look at the Internet for news about **recent** changes at the border.*

search *v* to try to find someone or something • *Guards are **searching** for the man who entered the country without stopping at the border.*

separate *adj* not together, independent or apart from • *They used to be part of the same country, but now the two governments are **separate**.*

suddenly *adv* very quickly and without warning • *The change happened very **suddenly**. They didn't tell us about it before it happened.*

UNIT 1, READING 3: BORDER CONTROL

advantage *n* something that is good about a situation and that helps you • *When Mei Ling visits the United States with her friends, she has an **advantage**. She speaks excellent English.*

citizen *n* someone who was born in a particular country or who lives in a particular country and has special rights to live and work there • *He was born in Turkey, but has become a German **citizen** after living there for many years.*

depend on *v* to be influenced by something or change because of something • *The amount of time it takes to cross the border **depends on** the number of people who are crossing.*

disappear *v* to stop appearing, to go away • *After he crossed the border, he **disappeared**. No one saw him, and no one knows where he went.*

document Ⓐ *n* a piece of paper with official information on it • *When I got my passport, I had to show several **documents**.*

examine *v* to look at someone or something very carefully • *At the border, the official **examined** our passports.*

fake *adj* not real, but made to look real • *He was arrested for having a **fake** passport.*

identification Ⓐ *n* an official document that proves who you are • *A driver's license is the most common type of **identification**.*

require Ⓐ *v* to need or demand something • *The law **requires** all drivers to pass a driving test before getting a license.*

store *v* to keep information on a computer • *With computers, it is easier to **store** and find information.*

tape Ⓐ *n* a thin piece of plastic which has glue on one side and is used for sticking things together • *The **tape** held the note on the paper.*

technology Ⓐ *n* knowledge, equipment, and methods that are used in science and industry • *New **technology** makes it easier to see who enters or leaves a country.*

tourist *n* someone who visits a place for pleasure and does not live there • *The **tourists** needed visas to enter the country.*

trick *v* to make someone believe something that is not true and to do something that the person does not want to do, often as a part of a plan • *The young men tried to **trick** the guard by using fake documents.*

twin *n* one of two children who are born to the same mother at the same time • *They are **twins**, but they do not look exactly alike.*

unique Ⓐ *adj* different from everyone and everything else • *No one has exactly the same face. Each face is **unique**.*

WHERE DOES YOUR NAME COME FROM?

common *adj* frequent and usual • *My name is not* ***common***, *so I always have to spell it for people.*

culture Ⓐ *n* the way of life, including customs and beliefs, of a particular group of people • *Each* ***culture*** *has different traditions for naming children.* **cultural** Ⓐ *adj* relating to the habits, traditions, and beliefs of a society • *There are a lot of* ***cultural*** *differences between people from different countries.*

embarrassing *adj* making you uncomfortable in front of other people • *She had a beautiful name, but her initials spelled an* ***embarrassing*** *word.*

generally *adv* usually • *In the United States, parents* ***generally*** *choose names for their babies before they are born.*

invent *v* to create something new • *No one has my name because my parents* ***invented*** *it. They wanted a unique name for me.*

leader *n* a person who controls a group or country • *He was a wonderful speaker, but he wasn't a great* ***leader***. *He tried to do too many things by himself.*

lucky *adj* having good things happen to you • *The number seven is a* ***lucky*** *number in many countries.* **luck** *n* good and bad things caused by chance and not by your own actions • *Some people think that you will have good* ***luck*** *in life if you are born on a Sunday.*

origin *n* the beginning or cause of something; the way something began • *We have had that name in our family for a very long time, but I don't know its* ***origin***. **original** *adj* existing since the beginning, or being the earliest form of something • *The family's* ***original*** *name was Zabinsky, but they changed it to Sabin.*

popular *adj* liked by many people • *Michael is a very* ***popular*** *name for boys in the United States.* **popularity** *n* when something is liked by many people • *At one time everyone listened to the singer's music, but over time her* ***popularity*** *decreased.*

professional Ⓐ *n* a person who uses special knowledge and training in a job • *I have no training in computers. I'm not a* ***professional***.

religious *adj* relating to a system of beliefs in a god or gods • *He is a* ***religious*** *leader.* **religion** *n* the belief in a god or gods, or a particular system of belief in a god or gods • *The beliefs of the Buddhist* ***religion*** *are very different from the beliefs of the Hindu* ***religion***.

select Ⓐ *v* to choose someone or something • *It's difficult to* ***select*** *a child's name because there are so many choices.*

share *v* to have the same thing as another person • *The girls in the family* ***shared*** *the same first name, Maria.*

CHANGING NAMES

conflict Ⓐ *n* a serious disagreement between people or groups • *The* ***conflict*** *started because the two groups had different ideas.*

couple Ⓐ *n* two people, usually a husband and a wife • *After they got married, the* ***couple*** *lived in a small apartment.*

discrimination Ⓐ *n* when people are treated badly because of their sex, race, or religion • *When the manager offered the job to a man instead of a woman, the woman thought this was because of* ***discrimination***.

ethnic Ⓐ *adj* relating to the same race or cultural group • *The city has a lot of* ***ethnic*** *groups, so it has a lot of different types of restaurants.*

hunter *n* a person who finds animals and kills them for food • *The* ***hunters*** *walked through the woods very quietly and stopped when they saw the animal.*

identity Ⓐ *n* who someone is • *The* ***identity*** *of the man in the photo is not clear, and there is no name on the photo.*

immigrant Ⓐ *n* a person who comes from one country to live in another country • *Some* ***immigrants*** *change their names when they move to another country.*

natural *adj* expected and usual • *It's* ***natural*** *for a child to want a special name.*

ordinary *adj* not special, different, or unusual in any way • *In Latin America, Jesus is an* ***ordinary*** *name, but it is not common in Britain or Canada.*

period Ⓐ *n* a fixed time during the life of a person or in history • *Names change according to the values of the **period**. For example, at one time many girls were named Patience and Grace.*

prefer *v* to like someone or something more than another person or thing • *Some people **prefer** to use a nickname with family and friends, but they use their real name at school or work.*

pronounce *v* to say a word or letter in a specific way • *The name Matt is easy to **pronounce**.*

reveal Ⓐ *v* to give someone a piece of information that is surprising or that was previously secret • *The names Garcia and Patel **reveal** different family backgrounds: one is probably Spanish and the other is probably Indian.*

serious *adj* thinking carefully about everything and not laughing a lot • *When she was a little girl, her name was Susu. When she became an adult, she changed her name to Susan because it sounded more **serious**.*

talent *n* a natural ability to do something well • *Some nicknames are given because of a person's **talent**. For example, a good card player might have the name Ace.*

tradition Ⓐ *n* a belief or custom that has existed for a long time • *Their **tradition** is to name the oldest son after his father.*

UNIT 2, READING 3: NAMES IN BUSINESS

advertisement *n* a picture, song, or other information that may make people buy something • *Most companies spend a lot of money on television **advertisements**.*

advice *n* an idea or opinion someone gives you to help you make a decision • *The company needed **advice** about what to name its product.*

consider *v* to spend time thinking about a decision • *It is important to **consider** how a product name will sound in a different language.*

crash *n* an accident in which a car or a plane hits something • *After the plane **crash**, the airline changed its name.*

emotion *n* a strong feeling such as love or anger, or strong feelings in general • *A good name may be connected to a positive **emotion** such as happiness.*

factor Ⓐ *n* a fact or situation that influences a result • *The main **factor** in the company's decision was the cost of changing everything to the new name.*

hire *v* to give someone a job • *The company **hired** a translator to give advice on product names.*

influence *v* to change what people think or do • *A good name may **influence** a shopper's decision to buy a product.*

modern *adj* using the most recent ideas, design, and technology • *A name such as Tech Shop sounds more **modern** than Record Store.*

product *n* something that companies make and sell • *The company sold its **products** in twelve different countries.*

related to *adj* to be connected to, or to be about someone or something • *The word tech or tek in a name shows that it is **related to** technology.*

research Ⓐ *v* to find information about something • *The company **researched** what names sounded best to people.*

response Ⓐ *n* an answer or reaction to something that has been said or done • *People had a negative **response** to the new name, so the company stopped using it.*

successful *adj* getting the results you want • *A good name may make a product more **successful** because people will notice or try it.*

technical Ⓐ *adj* relating to the knowledge, machines, or methods used in science and industry • *The name Product 409 sounds more **technical** than Bubble Cleaner.*

victory *n* when you win a race or a game • *The company used the V sign for **victory** to show that the company was a winner.*

available 🅐 *adj* able to be used or found • *Fresh fruits and vegetables are **available** in the summer.*

crop *n* a plant that is grown in large amounts on a farm • *The farmer planted his **crop** in April when the weather got warmer.*

explore *v* to travel to a new place in order to learn about it • *It is interesting to walk around different areas and **explore** when you go to a new city.* **exploration** *n* when people travel to a new place in order to learn about it • *We discovered an interesting new restaurant during our **exploration** of the city.*

familiar *adj* something you have often seen or heard before • *After traveling to other countries, it feels good to eat **familiar** food when you are back home again.*

flavor *n* the taste of a particular type of food or drink • *Chocolate is a very popular ice cream **flavor**.*

increase *n* when the number, size, or amount of something gets bigger • *There was an **increase** in the price of oranges because the weather was very bad last month.* **increase** *v* to get bigger or to make something bigger in size or amount • *The restaurant **increased** its prices, which made customers unhappy.*

occur 🅐 *v* to happen • *When bad weather **occurs**, the price of food usually goes up because the farmers lose some of their crops.* **occurrence 🅐** *n* something that happens • *Reading the newspaper at breakfast is a regular **occurrence** for many people all over the country.*

plant *n* a living thing that grows in the soil or water and has leaves and roots • *The **plants** died because they didn't get enough water.* **plant** *v* to put seeds or plants in the ground so that they will grow • *People usually **plant** flowers in the spring and summer.*

population *n* the number of people living in a particular area • *The **population** in China is the largest in the world.* **populate** *v* live in; be the inhabitants of • *The great, great grandchildren of the first explorers **populated** the island.*

raise *v* to take care of growing children, plants, or animals • *Farmers **raise** flowers in that area of the country. They don't raise vegetables.*

rare *adj* unusual and hard to find • *The fruit was expensive because it was very **rare**.*

soil *n* the top part of the earth where plants can grow • *The **soil** near the river is very good for farming.*

valuable *adj* worth a lot of money • *The land was very **valuable**, so it sold for a lot of money.*

consumption 🅐 *n* eating or using something • ***Consumption** of sugar in the United States is very high.*

continent *n* one of the seven main areas of land on the Earth, such as Asia, Africa, or Europe • *Apples are common now in North America, but at one time there were no apples on that **continent**.*

convenient *adj* easy to use, helpful • *Fast-food restaurants are very **convenient**.*

effect *n* a result; an impact • *Eating too much fat and sugar can have a bad **effect** on people's health.*

expand 🅐 *v* to increase in size or amount • *The fast-food restaurant **expanded** to Asia in 2009 when it opened a store in Seoul, South Korea.*

gain weight *v* to become heavier and bigger • *Eating cheese and ice cream every day will make you **gain weight**.*

global 🅐 *adj* relating to the whole world • *A lot of fast-food restaurants are now **global**; they are all over the world.*

health *n* the condition of your body • *Eating a lot of sugar is not good for your **health**. It can lead to a disease called diabetes.*

instead of *prep* in the place of someone or something else • *In Asia, most fast-food restaurants serve rice **instead of** potatoes.*

likely *adj* will probably happen • *Fast food is more **likely** to have a lot of fat in it than food at a regular restaurant.*

offer *v* to give or provide something • *The new restaurant **offers** a variety of seafood at a low price.*

percentage ⓐ *n* an amount of something, often stated as a number out of 100 • *Today, people eat a higher **percentage** of meals at fast-food restaurants than they used to.*

satisfy *v* to please someone by giving them what they want or need • *Restaurants that can **satisfy** their customers are successful.*

serve *v* to give someone food or drink, especially guests or customers in a restaurant • *The restaurant **serves** dinner from 5:00 p.m. until 10:00 p.m.*

worry *v* to feel uncertain or nervous; to think about problems or unpleasant things that might happen in a way that makes you feel nervous • *Government officials **worry** about the number of people who are not healthy because they weigh too much.*

yogurt *n* a kind of food made from milk, often sweetened because it has a sour taste • ***Yogurt** is a very popular food because it is healthy and also very easy to eat.*

UNIT 3, READING 3: TABLE MANNERS

appreciation ⓐ *n* value; when you understand and enjoy something or someone • *She sent a thank-you letter to show her **appreciation** for the dinner.*

behavior *n* the way a person acts or responds • *His **behavior** is surprising. He acts more like a nine-year-old than a fifteen-year-old.*

error ⓐ *n* a mistake, especially one that can cause problems • *The teacher marked the **errors** on the students' papers, but the students had to figure out how to correct them.*

final ⓐ *adj* last in a series or coming at the end of something • *Cost is the **final** reason that I don't go to that restaurant. It's too expensive.*

germ *n* a very small living thing that causes disease • *Wash your hands to get rid of **germs**.*

hide *v* to put something in a place where no one can see it • *I could not eat the meat, so I **hid** it in my napkin.*

host *n* someone who organizes a party and invites the guests • *I called the **host** to get directions to his house before the party.*

impolite *adj* not polite; rude • *It is **impolite** in some cultures to finish all the food on your plate. You should leave some food to show that you got enough to eat.*

lean *v* to bend your body forward, back, or to the side • *At the restaurant, he **leaned** forward and talked in a quiet voice so that no one at the other tables could hear him.*

noodle *n* a thin piece of pasta (made from flour, eggs, and water) • ***Noodles** are important in both Italian and Chinese cooking.*

observe *v* to watch someone or something carefully • *If you don't know what to do, **observe** other people.*

offend *v* to make someone upset or angry • *He **offended** everyone when he yelled in the restaurant.*

order *n* a strong request or demand • *The restaurant manager gave an **order** to the waitresses to make sure that they picked up the food while it was still hot.*

protection *n* keeping someone or something safe and away from danger • *The fence gives the home **protection** from people walking along the road.*

spread *v* to move across a bigger area and have a stronger effect • *The illness **spread** quickly through the city.*

visible ⓐ *adj* able to be seen • *People felt safer at the table when everyone's hands were **visible** above the table.*

competition *n* when a company or a person is trying to win something or be more successful than someone else • *Car makers now have more* **competition** *from motorcycle makers.* **compete** *v* to try to be more successful than someone or something else; to take part in a race or competition • *The store* **competed** *for customers by cutting its prices.*

crowded *adj* very full of people or things • *The roads are much more* **crowded** *in the afternoons than they are in the middle of the night.*

efficient *adj* working quickly and effectively in an organized way without waste • *The public transportation system in Tokyo is very* **efficient**.

encourage *v* to make someone more likely to do something • *High gas prices* **encourage** *people to ride bicycles instead of driving cars.* **encouragement** *n* when you give someone the confidence or interest to do something • *Some companies offer their workers free bus passes as* **encouragement** *to ride the bus.*

energy Ⓐ *n* the power from something like oil or electricity, which makes things work • *Large cars and trucks use a lot of* **energy**.

location Ⓐ *n* a specific place • *Public transportation is best in* **locations** *such as New York and Tokyo.*

narrow *adj* not wide; measuring a small distance from one side to the other • *The streets in the old part of the city are very* **narrow**.

operate *v* to make a machine do what it is designed to do • *You have to have training and a special driver's license to be able to* **operate** *a truck.* **operation** *n* the process of doing something or the way something works • *When you buy a motorcycle, you get a book that explains its* **operation**.

pollution *n* damage caused to water, air, or land by harmful substances or waste • *A lot of* **pollution** *in the cities is caused by cars sitting in traffic.* **pollute** *v* to make water, air, or soil dirty or harmful • *New cars do not* **pollute** *the air as much as older cars used to, because new cars have cleaner engines.*

system *n* a set of connected things or pieces of equipment that work together • *The subway* **system** *in Paris is called the Metro.*

transportation Ⓐ *n* a vehicle or system of vehicles, such as buses and trains, for getting from one place to another • *Millions of people use public* **transportation** *in New York. They ride the subway, trains, and buses.* **transport** Ⓐ *v* to move people or goods from one place to another • *Trains are the cheapest way to* **transport** *things from Montreal to Toronto.*

tunnel *n* a long road or passage under the ground or through a mountain • *Buses usually travel on city streets, but the subway is under the ground in a* **tunnel**.

wide *adj* not narrow; measuring a long distance or longer than usual from one side to the other • *It's easy to drive on modern streets because they are* **wide** *enough for trucks and buses.*

UNIT 4, READING 2: BICYCLES AS TRANSPORTATION

concern *n* a feeling of worry about something, or the thing that is worrying you • *Safety is a big* **concern** *of bicycle riders because drivers cannot always see them well, especially at night.*

contrast Ⓐ *n* something that shows that someone or something is different from someone or something else; an obvious difference between two people or things • *The traffic on a Sunday morning is very light in* **contrast** *to traffic in the mornings on weekdays.*

create Ⓐ *v* to make something happen or exist; to make something new • *The city* **created** *a special road for bicycles along the side of the highway.*

decrease *v* to become less; to go down • *The number of cars on the road* **decreased** *after gas prices went up.*

exercise *n* physical activity that you do to make your body strong and healthy • *Riding a bicycle is great* **exercise**. *It helps to keep people healthy.*

helmet *n* a strong, hard hat that protects your head • *In many locations,* **helmets** *are required for all motorcycle and bicycle riders.*

issue Ⓐ *n* an important subject or problem that people are discussing • *In some places, people can talk on cell phones as they drive. This is a public safety* **issue** *that the police are worried about.*

path *n* a small road, usually for walking, biking, or riding a horse. • *You have to park your car on the road and walk along the **path** to her house.*

pick up *v* to get something • *They **picked up** a rental car at the airport to use during their visit.*

production *n* the process of making or growing something to be sold • *Most bicycle **production** is in China, but the bicycles are sold in many countries.*

reduce *v* to make something smaller or less, especially in price, amount, or size • *If more people ride bicycles, this will **reduce** pollution.*

rise *v* to increase in level; to go up • *The number of bicycle riders is **rising**. It increased by 15 percent last year.*

significantly ⒜ *adv* in an important or noticeable way • *The number of bicycles on the road increased **significantly** when gas prices went up.*

solution *n* an answer to a problem • *Perhaps bicycle use is the **solution** to traffic problems everywhere.*

traffic *n* all the cars, trucks, and buses on a road • *There is a lot of **traffic** in the mornings and afternoons when people go to work or back home.*

trip *n* a journey in which you visit a place for a short time • *I had to make two **trips** into the city yesterday because I forgot my wallet in the morning.*

UNIT 4, READING 3: THE DANGERS OF DRIVING

avoid *v* to stay away from a person, place, or situation • *It is hard to **avoid** driving at the busiest times of the day when you have a job.*

aware ⒜ *adj* knowing about something. • *Be **aware** of other drivers on the road in case they do something dangerous.*

basic *adj* simple, most important • *You can't drive a big truck with a **basic** license. You need a special truck license.*

conversation *n* a talk between two or more people, usually an informal one • *It's difficult to pay attention to the road when you are having a **conversation** with someone.*

distraction *n* something that stops you from paying attention. • *Children in the backseat can be a big **distraction** to the driver, especially when the children are noisy.*

estimate ⒜ *v* to guess the cost, size, or value of something • *The government **estimated** that it would cost about $11.2 million to build the road.*

injury ⒜ *n* the physical harm or damage done to a person or animal • *She had a lot of **injuries** after the accident, so it took a long time for her to feel better.*

makeup *n* something that a woman puts on her face to make herself look prettier • *Putting on **makeup** while you are driving a car seems very dangerous to me.*

message *n* information or an idea that someone is trying to communicate • *Do not write or read a text **message** while you are driving!*

miss *v* to not be present at an activity or event • *I'm sorry that I **missed** your call. I was on the subway.*

obey *v* to do what you are told to do by a person, rule, or instruction • *If you **obey** the laws and drive carefully, the police won't stop your car.*

passenger *n* a person in a car, train, bus, or plane who is not driving • *There were too many **passengers** in the little car.*

seatbelt *n* a narrow piece of strong material that you put across your body when traveling in a car or a plane to stop you moving forward when the car or plane reduces speed suddenly • *Everyone needs to wear a **seatbelt** in the car.*

shave *v* to cut hair off your face or body • *He **shaves** every weekday, but not on weekends.*

teenager *n* someone who is between 13 and 19 years old • *Some **teenagers** are not good drivers, and they have a lot of accidents.*

text ⒜ *n* written words • *She sent a **text** message from the bus stop to say that she was late for school.*

UNIT 5, READING 1: THE IMPORTANCE OF SLEEP

adult Ⓐ *n* an animal that is fully grown; a human who is eighteen years or older • *Adults do not need as much sleep as children.*

breathe *v* to take air in and out of your body • *People breathe more slowly when they are sleeping.* **breath** *n* the air that comes in and out of your body • *Swimmers take a deep breath before they dive into the water.*

concentrate Ⓐ *v* to think very carefully about something you are doing • *You can concentrate better when you get enough sleep.* **concentration** Ⓐ *n* the ability to think carefully about something you are doing • *Concentration during the test was difficult because people were making a lot of noise outside the classroom.*

development *n* when someone or something grows or changes and becomes more advanced • *Doctors can see if a baby's development is slower than normal.* **develop** *v* to grow or change and become more advanced • *Babies develop very quickly in their first year of life.*

dream *n* a series of events and images that happen in your mind while you are sleeping • *When you sleep, you have dreams. However, you usually can't remember your dreams when you wake up.* **dream** *v* to experience events and images in your mind while you are sleeping • *People often dream that they are falling. However, they wake up before they fall all the way to the ground.*

muscle *n* the part of the body that makes you move • *The day after she ran in a race, all of her muscles were very sore.*

normal Ⓐ *adj* usual and expected • *Eight hours of sleep is normal for most people.*

paralyzed *adj* not able to move all or part of your body • *When you are in a deep sleep, your muscles are paralyzed.*

pattern *n* the particular way that something occurs; something that occurs in the same way over and over • *The sleep pattern of babies is different from the sleep pattern of older children.*

restore Ⓐ *v* to make something the way it was earlier • *After a race, runners sometimes use special drinks to restore their energy.*

stage *n* a specific period during an activity • *When you sleep, you go through five different stages.*

strange *adj* very unusual • *Sometimes when people are sick, they have very strange dreams.*

variation Ⓐ *n* something that is slightly different from the usual form • *There is a lot of variation in sleep patterns among animals.* **vary** Ⓐ *v* to be different from something else of the same type • *The prices of beds vary from store to store. This makes it hard to decide which one to buy.*

UNIT 5, READING 2: GETTING ENOUGH SLEEP

ability *n* the physical or mental skill or qualities that you need to do something • *The ability to remember changes as we grow older.*

at least *adv* as much as, or more than, a number or amount • *Most adults need at least eight hours of sleep each night.*

comfortable *adj* relaxed and having no pain • *It is important to have a comfortable place to sleep.*

compare *v* to examine the ways in which two people or things are different or similar • *A study compared the sleep patterns of two different groups of people.*

consequence Ⓐ *n* the result (often bad result) of a situation or activity • *Falling asleep in class is a possible consequence of not getting enough sleep the night before.*

essential *adj* very, very important • *Getting enough sleep is essential to human health.*

fall asleep *v* to begin to sleep • *Some people think that a glass of milk helps them to fall asleep quickly.*

judgment *n* the ability to make decisions • *People who do not get enough sleep often have poor judgment.*

memory *n* the ability to remember • *Getting too little sleep can have a bad effect on your memory.*

mental Ⓐ *adj* related to thinking and to the brain • *Sleep is important for mental and physical health.*

nap *n* a short period of sleep during the day • *Every day he took a nap on the bus on the way home from work.*

realize *v* to come to understand it, often quickly • *She finally began to **realize** that her lack of sleep was causing her a lot of problems.*

stress Ⓐ *n* great concern and worry about a difficult situation • *The **stress** about taking an exam the next day can make it difficult to fall asleep at night.*

sufficient Ⓐ *adj* as much as is necessary • *It is difficult for students to get **sufficient** sleep when they have exams.*

survey Ⓐ *n* a type of research that asks people for their ideas and opinions • *Sleep researchers often do **surveys** to find out about sleep patterns.*

unfortunate *adj* used to show that you wish something was not true or had not happened • *It is **unfortunate** that the garbage truck makes noise outside her window so early in the morning.*

UNIT 5, READING 3: YOUR BODY CLOCK

adjust Ⓐ *v* to change something a little so that it works better in a new situation • *When you travel to a different time zone, your body has to **adjust** to the new time.*

affect Ⓐ *v* to cause something to change • *Noise can **affect** your body clock.*

alert *adj* awake and having enough energy to understand and learn • *Most teenagers are not **alert** in the morning.*

alter Ⓐ *v* to make something change • *They had to **alter** their travel plans because they were so tired on the first day in the different time zone.*

blind *adj* not able to see • ***Blind** people may not wake up easily in the mornings because they can't see the sunlight.*

complain *v* to say that you don't like something • *The people next door called us to **complain** about the loud music at our party.*

confusion *n* when a person doesn't understand what is happening or doesn't know what to do • *The school wanted to hold classes in the afternoon and early evening. However, there was a lot of **confusion**, and some students went to class in the morning instead.*

disturb *v* to interrupt what someone is doing by making noise or annoying them • *The loud noises on the busy street outside **disturb** the parents every night, but the baby sleeps well.*

exhausted *adj* very tired • *When you don't get enough sleep, you will feel **exhausted** the next day.*

habit *n* an action you do over and over again, often without really thinking about it • *She had the **habit** of waking up early in the morning and then taking a short nap in the afternoon.*

mood *n* the way you feel at a certain time • *If you don't get enough sleep, it may affect your **mood**.*

permanent *adj* going on forever • *This work schedule is **permanent**, so you'll have to get used to working late at night.*

plant *n* a large factory • *People on the night shift in a **plant** often work all through the night.*

tiny *adj* very small • ***Tiny** babies sleep a lot. As they get older, they sleep less.*

typical *adj* having all the qualities you expect a particular person, group, object, or place to have • *What is your **typical** schedule for waking up and going to sleep?*

zone *n* an area where a particular thing happens • *He was exhausted because he wasn't used to the new time **zone**.*

cell *n* the smallest unit of living things; skin, muscles, and your brain are all made of these • *Some people think music may change the **cells** in the brains of babies and young children.*

chemical **Ⓐ** *n* a basic substance • *Your brain releases **chemicals** during certain activities that may make you feel happy or sad.*

comfort *v* to make someone feel better when they are worried or sad • *A familiar song may **comfort** you if you are not feeling well.* **comfort** *n* when you feel better after being worried or sad • *Letters from friends give people **comfort** when a friend or relative dies.*

equipment **Ⓐ** *n* a set of tools or machines that you need for a special purpose • *When rock bands travel around the world to give concerts, they need to have a lot of **equipment** at each place they play.*

expression *n* showing how you feel using words, music, or actions • *Music, art, and books are all forms of **expression** by the people who created them.* **express** *v* to show what you think or how you feel using words or actions • *Sending flowers is a way to **express** feelings that are difficult to say in words.*

patient *n* a person who goes to a doctor or hospital because he or she is sick • *Doctors try to help their **patients** feel better.*

recognize *v* to realize that you have seen or that you know the person or thing • *We all **recognize** songs even though we don't know the name of the song or all the words in the song.*

release **Ⓐ** *v* to let something go • *Our brains **release** chemicals when we exercise or when we hear music.*

relieve *v* to make pain or a bad feeling less • *Soft music may **relieve** the pain of a headache.* **relief** *n* the good feeling that you have when something unpleasant stops or does not happen • *The music was terrible and very loud. It was a big **relief** when it stopped.*

rhythm *n* a regular pattern of sounds in music • *Everyone likes to dance to fast music because it usually has a great **rhythm**.*

role **Ⓐ** *n* the use or function that something has • *The university's music program played a big **role** in the student's decision to study there.*

survive **Ⓐ** *v* to continue to exist after being in a difficult or dangerous situation • *The man's knowledge of how to live in the woods helped him **survive** when he got lost.* **survival** **Ⓐ** *n* when someone or something continues to live or exist, especially after a difficult or dangerous situation • *Food and water are necessary for **survival**. Without them, people will die.*

trust *n* the belief that someone is good and honest and will not harm you • *The two friends felt a lot of **trust** for each other because they did so much together.* **trust** *v* to believe that someone is good and honest and will not harm you • *The parents **trusted** their son. They knew he was a serious student and a good person.*

alphabet *n* a set of letters that are used for all the words in a language • *The English **alphabet** goes from A to Z.*

athlete *n* someone who is very good at a sport and who competes with others in organized events • *Before the game began, all the **athletes** and the people watching sang their country's national song.*

attention *n* when you watch, listen to, or think about something carefully or with interest • *Listening to music helps some people pay **attention** better when they're working.*

calm *adj* relaxed and not worried, frightened, or excited • *Quiet music can make you feel **calm**.*

chew *v* to cut food with your teeth • *Research showed that people **chew** their food at the same speed as the music they hear in restaurants.*

crime *n* an activity that breaks a law • *Copying music from the Internet without paying for it is a **crime**.*

department store *n* a place that sells many different kinds of things, such as clothing, dishes, and furniture • *The **department store** was famous for its piano player who played music for the shoppers.*

effective *adj* working well; successful • *Researchers found that playing music in public places is an **effective** way to reduce crime.*

excited *adj* feeling very happy and positive • *She wasn't nervous before she played in the concert. Instead, she was **excited**.*

lesson *n* a period of time when a teacher teaches people • *He took piano **lessons** when he was young, but he didn't play the piano when he was an adult.*

owner *n* someone who has something that legally belongs to him or her • *Before he started the coffee shop, he was the **owner** of a music store. As a result, he loved playing music at his coffee shop.*

perform *v* to entertain people by acting, singing, or dancing • *Most people are nervous when they **perform** in public.*

police *n* officials who protect the public and make sure that everyone obeys laws • *The **police** arrived in time to stop the crime from happening.*

race *n* a competition for runners • *The athletes lined up and waited for the **race** to begin.*

repetition *n* when something is repeated • *Practicing music requires a lot of **repetition**.*

supermarket *n* a large place that sells mostly food • *Some **supermarkets** play music because they hope it will make shoppers buy more groceries.*

UNIT 6, READING 3: THE BUSINESS OF MUSIC

access Ⓐ *n* the chance to use or have something • *On the Internet, you can have **access** to a lot of music. However, you have to pay to download it.*

challenge Ⓐ *n* a very difficult situation or problem • *Music companies face a **challenge** today because people can copy music so easily and not pay for it.*

collection *n* a group of objects of the same type that have been collected by one person or in one place • *He loves jazz, so he has a very large **collection** of jazz CDs.*

compact *adj* small and including many things in a small space • ***Compact** discs hold a lot of music, but digital music players such as the iPod hold a lot more.*

download *v* to take something (for example, a document, photo, or song) from the Internet and put it on your own computer • *When you **download** music from the site, you pay for each song.*

fragile *adj* easily broken, damaged, or destroyed • *Records were more **fragile** than compact discs, so people often bought new ones when the music on the records wasn't clear any more.*

last *v* to continue to happen, exist, or be useful • *A recorded song usually **lasts** for a couple of minutes.*

live *adj* seen or heard at the time when something is happening • *Music companies often change the sound of **live** music when they put it together as a recording.*

method Ⓐ *n* a way of doing something, often one that involves a system or plan • *Downloading is a **method** of getting music from the Internet onto a music player.*

portable *adj* easy to carry • *Before the Sony Walkman music player, music was not **portable**.*

positive Ⓐ *adj* showing without any doubt that something is true • *People immediately had a **positive** feeling about compact discs when they first appeared because the sound was very clear.*

punish *v* to do something to someone that they won't like because they have done something wrong • *Sometimes the government catches people who copy music without paying for it and **punishes** them by making them pay a lot of money.*

record *n* a flat circle of plastic on which music is stored • *In the 1990s, compact discs replaced **records** as the best way to play music.*

replace *v* to start to use something instead of the thing or person that is being used now • *Music players such as the iPod **replaced** CDs as the best way to buy music in about 2000.*

scratch *v* to make a slight cut or long, thin mark with a sharp object • *When you **scratch** a record, it sounds terrible or repeats the same sound every time you play it.*

site Ⓐ *n* an area on the Internet where you can find information about a particular subject or organization • *Music **sites** provide songs that you can buy and download.*

community Ⓐ *n* a group of people who live in the same area • *The whole* **community** *came together to rebuild the town after the flood.*

damage *n* harm or injury • *There was a lot of* **damage** *from the hurricane, and a few people got hurt. However, no one died.* **damage** *v* to harm or break something • *The tree fell on top of a car and* **damaged** *it.*

deadly *adj* very dangerous and likely to kill people • *A* **deadly** *storm came through the area, and three people died.*

destroy *v* to damage something so badly that it does not exist or cannot be used • *The tornado* **destroyed** *the house completely, but it didn't touch the garage.* **destruction** *n* when something is destroyed • *Officials arrived to look at the* **destruction** *from the storm. Then they had a meeting to figure out what to do.*

eruption *n* an event when a volcano suddenly throws out smoke, fire, and melted rocks. • *The* **eruption** *of the volcano caused a huge mudslide.* **erupt** *v* to suddenly throw out smoke, fire, and melted rocks • *The volcano* **erupted** *with no warning.*

extreme *adj* more than expected or more than usual • *The weather forecast calls for some* **extreme** *weather this weekend with high winds and a lot of rain.*

flood *n* when a lot of water covers an area that is usually dry, especially when a river becomes too full • *The* **flood** *caused a great deal of damage in the neighborhood near the river.* **flood** *v* to cover a place with water; to fill or enter a place large numbers or amounts • *The river* **floods** *every spring.*

massive *adj* very large • *A* **massive** *hurricane hit the coast and caused damage to many communities.*

movement *n* a change of position or place • *The* **movement** *of the earth in an earthquake depends on how deep the earthquake is.* **move** *v* to change place or position • *The building* **moved** *back and forth in the earthquake. However, there wasn't any damage.*

mud *n* soil or earth mixed with water • *The* **mud** *came all the way down the river after the volcano erupted.*

violent *adj* sudden and powerful • *The* **violent** *movement of the earth caused a lot of damage.*

vulnerable *adj* able to be hurt or influenced easily • *Areas along the coast are* **vulnerable** *to severe storms called hurricanes, cyclones, or typhoons.*

widespread Ⓐ *adj* happening in many places • *The huge storm caused* **widespread** *flooding in the area.*

accurately Ⓐ *adv* correctly or exactly • *It is very difficult to predict the weather* **accurately**.

average *n* the usual number or amount • *There were more hurricanes this year than on* **average**.

bubble *n* a ball of air or gas with liquid around it • *Before a tsunami, there are a lot of* **bubbles** *in the water on the beach.*

coast *n* the shore between land and the ocean • *Severe weather that starts in the ocean often hits the* **coast**.

contact Ⓐ *v* to communicate with someone • *After a natural disaster, it is difficult to* **contact** *friends and relatives.*

crucial Ⓐ *adj* very important and necessary • *A plan for a response to an emergency is* **crucial** *for every community.*

loss *n* a thing or a number of related things that are lost, destroyed, or killed • *A lot of houses and buildings fell down, but there was no* **loss** *of life.*

precise Ⓐ *adj* exact • *It is impossible to know the* **precise** *number of people who died in the disaster.*

predict Ⓐ *v* to say that something will happen in the future • *New technology is helping scientists to* **predict** *severe weather.*

prepare *v* to get someone or something ready for something that will happen in the future • *People can* **prepare** *for a hurricane. They can cover the windows in their houses and move away from dangerous areas.*

satellite *n* a piece of equipment that is sent into space around the earth to receive and send signals or to collect information • ***Satellites*** *help people predict where storms will cause problems.*

shake *v* to move something in one direction and then the other direction many times • *Everything in the house started to **shake** when the earthquake began.*

sign *n* something that shows that something is happening • *The bubbles in the water are a **sign** of a tsunami.*

terrible *adj* very bad and very serious • *The storm caused **terrible** damage to the coast.*

tremor *n* an uncontrolled shaking; a slight earthquake • *After a big earthquake, there are often smaller **tremors**.*

warning *n* something that tells or shows you that something bad may happen • *There was no **warning** before the earthquake.*

UNIT 7, READING 3: A NATURAL DISASTER FROM OUTER SPACE?

analysis Ⓐ *n* a careful study • *A scientific **analysis** showed that a disaster was not very likely to happen in that area.*

block *v* to stop or prevent anyone or anything from moving from one place to another • *The dust from the volcano explosion **blocked** the sunlight.*

dinosaur *n* a reptile that once lived on earth • *No one knows exactly why **dinosaurs** became extinct.*

dust *n* dry dirt • *What would happen if **dust** blocked the sun for a long time?*

explosion *n* a burst with a loud noise when something such as a bomb explodes • *An asteroid can cause a huge **explosion** if it hits the earth.*

extinct *adj* no longer existing anywhere in the world (describing plants or animals) • *Dinosaurs are **extinct**.*

gas *n* something like air that is not a solid or a liquid, for example, oxygen • *An asteroid explosion sent a lot of **gas** into the atmosphere.*

gravity *n* the force that pulls things to the ground • *Earth has **gravity** that pulls asteroids towards it.*

immediately *adv* right away • *Scientists **immediately** began to study the asteroid that someone thought might hit the earth.*

impact Ⓐ *n* the force or action of one object hitting another object • *The **impact** of the explosion caused severe damage.*

mystery *n* an unknown thing that people do not understand • *No one really knows the answer to the **mystery** of why there are no dinosaurs on Earth any more.*

orbit *n* the path that objects travel around the sun or a planet • *The earth travels in an **orbit** around the sun.*

outer space *n* the part of the universe that is farthest from Earth • *A near-Earth object is something that is in **outer space** and comes in an orbit near the Earth.*

project Ⓐ *n* a carefully planned piece of work that has a particular purpose • *Several governments are working on a **project** to identify all the near-Earth objects.*

rocket *n* a man-made object that moves very fast through space • ***Rockets*** *go into space to put satellites into orbit.*

suggest *v* to point to • *Research **suggests** there is a way to solve this problem.*

appear *v* to become noticeable or to be present • *The first televisions **appeared** in homes in the 1930s.* **appearance** *n* when you arrive somewhere or can be seen somewhere • *His **appearance** at the party surprised everyone. He usually doesn't go to parties.*

beach *n* the area of land next to the sea or a lake • *They stayed at a hotel near the **beach**, so they went swimming every day.*

concert *n* a performance of live music • *Many people go to **concerts** outdoors in the summer.*

economy ⓐ *n* the system in which a country makes and uses things and money • *The **economy** is not growing as fast as it was a few years ago, so it is more difficult to get a job today.*

enjoy *v* to get pleasure from something • *The young children **enjoy** swimming at the beach.* **enjoyment** *n* the pleasure you get from something • *The singer's music brought **enjoyment** to millions of people.*

entertainment *n* shows, films, television, or other performances or activities that people enjoy • *As people get older, their favorite **entertainment** is often watching other people, especially at parks or shopping centers.* **entertain** *v* to keep someone interested and help them to have an enjoyable time • *Electronic games are a good way to **entertain** children on long trips.*

factory *n* a place where things are made by machines • *The shoe **factory** employed 60 people.*

improve *v* to get better or to make something better • *Speech classes help people **improve** their ability to speak in public.* **improvement** *n* when something gets better or when you make it better • *Everyone noticed the **improvement** in air quality after the plant closed.*

opportunity *n* a chance to do or get something • *The students had an **opportunity** to travel during the summer.*

picnic *n* a meal that you eat outside, often in a park • *It rained yesterday, so we did not have our **picnic**.*

public *adj* open and available to everyone • *There are **public** parks in almost every city and town in France.*

relax ⓐ *v* to become less active and more calm and happy • *Listening to music helps many people **relax**.* **relaxation** ⓐ *n* when you become less active and feel more calm and happy • *Travel is a form of **relaxation** for some people. For others, it is work.*

similar ⓐ *adj* almost the same • *The two hotels are **similar** in price, but one is closer to the center of the city.*

apart *adj* living or staying in a different place from other people • *The twins live far **apart** from each other, so they can only see each other once a year.*

character *n* a person in a film, play, or story • *My favorite **character** in the movie was the old man.*

comic book *n* a set of stories with drawings and very few words • *People used to read **comic books** only when they were children, but today many adults read them, too.*

communication ⓐ *n* sharing information, ideas, and feelings with other people • *A social network on the Internet is a new form of **communication**.*

costume *n* a special kind of clothing from a time in history, a country, or a story • *The characters in the play wore **costumes** from the late 1920s.*

fix *v* to repair something • *It was not possible to **fix** the car because it had so much damage from the crash.*

furniture *n* things such as tables, chairs, beds, and desks • *Very few people make their own **furniture** today, but it is possible to take classes to learn how to do it.*

keep up *v* to stay informed • *Social networks make it easier to **keep up** with friends who are far away.*

make up *v* to invent or create • *When young people are bored, they sometimes **make up** new games to play.*

network ⓐ *n* a group of people who know each other or who work together • *Facebook is a very well-known social **network** that many people participate in.*

participate ⓐ *v* to be involved with other people in an activity • *A lot of people from the school **participated** in a discussion about plans for the new building.*

pretend *v* to behave as if something is true when it is not • *It is easy to **pretend** to be someone else on the Internet.*

productive *adj* producing a good or useful result • *Some people get bored if they are not **productive** on vacations.*

skill *n* the ability to do something well because you have practiced it • *During her vacation, she took a class to improve her tennis **skills**.*

twice *adv* two times • *After they finished college, the two friends only saw each other **twice**. However, they kept up with each other through e-mail.*

virtual ⓐ *adj* using computer images and sounds that make you think a pretend situation is real • *Some people participate in **virtual** communities on the Internet.*

UNIT 8, READING 3: VACATIONS

attraction *n* a place that a lot of people want to visit • *The Taj Mahal is a famous **attraction** in India that many tourists visit.*

boss *n* the head of a company • *The employees asked their **boss** for an extra week of vacation.*

camping *n* sleeping and eating outside on vacation • *I don't think anyone enjoys **camping** in the rain.*

earn *v* to get money for doing work • *Teenagers usually don't **earn** very much money in their jobs.*

employee *n* a worker • *The factory did not need as many **employees** because fewer people were spending money on the company's products.*

environment ⓐ *n* the natural world all around us • *Eco-tourism is popular with people who are interested in saving the **environment**.*

give up *v* to stop using something • *You have to **give up** all the comforts of home when you go camping.*

green *adj* helping to protect nature • *Hotels try to be **green** by asking guests to use their towels more than once and to recycle glass, plastic, and paper.*

mall *n* a large, covered shopping area • *The largest **mall** in the United States is in King of Prussia, Pennsylvania.*

option ⓐ *n* a choice • *The travel company offered a lot of **options** for ways to visit Europe, but the most popular one was a group tour.*

program *n* a plan • *The hotel started a new **program** for visitors to do volunteer work in the community on their vacation.*

put off *v* to wait until later to do something • *If you **put off** making your plane reservations, you will probably have to pay more for your ticket.*

risky *adj* very dangerous • *Some people like to go rock climbing, but I think it's too **risky**.*

satisfaction *n* pleasure • *Volunteer work gives people **satisfaction** when they are able to help other people.*

simple *adj* plain • *The hotel offered **simple** meals, but they were delicious.*

volunteer ⓐ *n* a person who does work without payment • *Many **volunteers** came to help rebuild the city after the earthquake.*

APPENDIX 2
INDEX TO KEY VOCABULARY

Words that are part of the Academic Word List are noted with an Ⓐ in this appendix.

instead of, **3.2**
invasion, **1.2**
invent, **2.1**
issue Ⓐ, **4.2**

judgment, **5.2**

keep up, **8.2**

last, **6.3**
leader, **2.1**
lean, **3.3**
lesson, **6.2**
likely, **3.2**
live, **6.3**
location Ⓐ, **4.1**
loss, **7.2**
luck, **2.1**
lucky, **2.1**

major Ⓐ, **1.2**
make up, **8.2**
makeup, **4.3**
mall, **8.3**
massive, **7.1**
memory, **5.2**
mental Ⓐ, **5.2**
message, **4.3**
method Ⓐ, **6.3**
miss, **4.3**
modern, **2.3**
mood, **5.3**
move, **7.1**
movement, **7.1**
mud, **7.1**
muscle, **5.1**
mystery, **7.3**

nap, **5.2**
narrow, **4.1**
nation, **1.1**
national, **1.1**
natural, **2.2**
network Ⓐ, **8.2**
noodle, **3.3**
normal Ⓐ, **5.1**

obey, **4.3**
observe, **3.3**
occur Ⓐ, **3.1**
occurrence Ⓐ, **3.1**
offend, **3.3**
offer, **3.2**
official, **1.1**
operate, **4.1**
operation, **4.1**

opportunity, **8.1**
option Ⓐ, **8.3**
orbit, **7.3**
order, **3.3**
ordinary, **2.2**
origin, **2.1**
original, **2.1**
outer space, **7.3**
owner, **6.2**

paralyzed, **5.1**
participate Ⓐ, **8.2**
passenger, **4.3**
path, **4.2**
patient, **6.1**
pattern, **5.1**
percentage Ⓐ, **3.2**
perform, **6.2**
period Ⓐ, **2.2**
permanent, **5.3**
permission, **1.1**
physical Ⓐ, **1.1**
pick up, **4.2**
picnic, **8.1**
plant, **3.1, 5.3**
police, **6.2**
pollute, **4.1**
pollution, **4.1**
popular, **2.1**
popularity, **2.1**
populate, **3.1**
population, **3.1**
portable, **6.3**
positive Ⓐ, **6.3**
precise Ⓐ, **7.2**
predict Ⓐ, **7.2**
prefer, **2.2**
prepare, **7.2**
pretend, **8.2**
prevent, **1.2**
product, **2.3**
production, **4.2**
productive, **8.2**
professional Ⓐ, **2.1**
program, **8.3**
project Ⓐ, **7.3**
pronounce, **2.2**
protection, **3.3**
public, **8.1**
punish, **6.3**
purpose, **1.2**
put off, **8.3**

race, **6.2**
raise, **3.1**
rare, **3.1**

realize, **5.2**
recent, **1.2**
recognize, **6.1**
record, **6.3**
reduce, **4.2**
related to, **2.3**
relax Ⓐ, **8.1**
relaxation Ⓐ, **8.1**
release Ⓐ, **6.1**
relief, **6.1**
relieve, **6.1**
religion, **2.1**
religious, **2.1**
repetition, **6.2**
replace, **6.3**
require Ⓐ, **1.3**
research (v) Ⓐ, **2.3**
resource Ⓐ, **1.1**
response Ⓐ, **2.3**
restore Ⓐ, **5.1**
reveal Ⓐ, **2.2**
rhythm, **6.1**
rise, **4.2**
risky, **8.3**
rocket, **7.3**
role Ⓐ, **6.1**

safe, **1.1**
safety, **1.1**
satellite, **7.2**
satisfaction, **8.3**
satisfy, **3.2**
scratch, **6.3**
search, **1.2**
seatbelt, **4.3**
select Ⓐ, **2.1**
separate, **1.2**
serious, **2.2**
serve, **3.2**
shake, **7.2**
share, **2.1**
shave, **4.3**
shore, **1.1**
sign, **7.2**
significantly Ⓐ, **4.2**
similar Ⓐ, **8.1**
simple, **8.3**
site Ⓐ, **6.3**
skill, **8.2**
soil, **3.1**
solution, **4.2**
spread, **3.3**
stage, **5.1**
store, **1.3**
straight, **1.1**
strange, **5.1**

stress Ⓐ, **5.2**
successful, **2.3**
suddenly, **1.2**
sufficient Ⓐ, **5.2**
suggest, **7.3**
supermarket, **6.2**
survey Ⓐ, **5.2**
survival Ⓐ, **6.1**
survive Ⓐ, **6.1**
system, **4.1**

talent, **2.2**
tape Ⓐ, **1.3**
technical Ⓐ, **2.3**
technology Ⓐ, **1.3**
teenager, **4.3**
terrible, **7.2**
text Ⓐ, **4.3**
tiny, **5.3**
tourist, **1.3**
tradition Ⓐ, **2.2**
traffic, **4.2**
transport Ⓐ, **4.1**
transportation Ⓐ, **4.1**
tremor, **7.2**
trick, **1.3**
trip, **4.2**
trust, **6.1**
tunnel, **4.1**
twice, **8.2**
twin, **1.3**
typical, **5.3**

unfortunate, **5.2**
unique Ⓐ, **1.3**

valuable, **3.1**
variation Ⓐ, **5.1**
vary Ⓐ, **5.1**
victory, **2.3**
violent, **7.1**
virtual Ⓐ, **8.2**
visible Ⓐ, **3.3**
volunteer Ⓐ, **8.3**
vulnerable, **7.1**

warning, **7.2**
wide, **4.1**
widespread Ⓐ, **7.1**
worry, **3.2**

yogurt, **3.2**

zone, **5.3**

REFERENCES

The following materials were consulted during the development of *Making Connections Low Intermediate*.

UNIT 1, READING 1

African Voices, *Smithsonian Institution*. http://www.mnh.si.edu/Africanvoices/ax/fs/primary_fs.html? history+colonialism+pass_holder.
Territorial waters, *Britannica Concise Encyclopedia*. http://www.answers.com/topic/territorial-waters.
United Nations, Convention on the Law of the Sea, http://www.un.org/Depts/los/convention_ agreements/texts/unclos/closindx.htm.

UNIT 1, READING 2

BBC News. 2009. The Great Wall of China even longer. April 20. http://news.bbc.co.uk/2/hi/8008108. stm.
Berlin Wall, Newseum. http://www.newseum.org/berlinwall/.
Berlin Wall Online, http://www.dailysoft.com/berlinwall/history/index.htm.
Frontiers of the Roman Empire, World Heritage, *UNESCO*, http://whc.unesco.org/en/list/430.

UNIT 1, SKILLS AND STRATEGIES 2

Basic Information sheet about SARS. (2005) *Centers for Disease Control*. May 3. http://www.cdc.gov/ ncidod/sars/factsheet.htm.

UNIT 1, READING 3

Lee, Jennifer. 2003. Threats and responses: Identity documents. *New York Times*, February 12.
Leyden, Peter. 2006. UK extends airport iris scan scheme. *The Register*, March 10.
McGeever, J. 2006. Computer chips get under skin of enthusiasts. *Reuters*, January 6.
No Author (from Yomiuri Shimbun). 2009. South Korean woman tricked fingerprint scanner at Japanese airport. *Chicago Tribune*, January 2.
No Author. 2002. Schiphol backs eye scan security. *CNN.com/WORLD*, March 27.
No Author. 2009. Million dollar border security machines fooled with ten cent tape. *Findbiometrics*, January 8. http://www.findbiometrics.com/articles/i/6090/.
Seranno, R. 2010. High tech border fence is slow going. *Los Angeles Times*, February 22. http://articles. latimes.com/2010/feb/22/nation/la-na-border-fence22-2010feb22.

UNIT 2, SKILLS AND STRATEGIES 3

Top 10 Most Interesting Place Names. VirtualTourist.com. http://members.virtualtourist.com/ vt/t/1eb/.
Visit Paris Without Leaving the United States, http://hubpages.com/hub/UnitedStatesParis.

UNIT 2, READING 1

Lee, J. 2008. Barack a hot name for new babies. *New York Times*, November 10. http://www.nytimes. com/2008/11/10/world/americas/10iht-10babies.17670871.html.
Native American names. *Native Americans online*. http://www.native-americans-online.com/native- american-names.html.
Popular baby names. Social Security online. http://www.ssa.gov/OACT/babynames/decades/ names1910s.html.
Rieperoots, Surname geneology. http://www.rieperoots.com/pages/Names/customs.htm.

UNIT 2, READING 2

Ghosh, B. 2006. Where your name can be a death sentence. *Time.com*, July 10. http://www.time.com/ time/world/article/0,8599,1212291,00.html.
Jet Li. http://jetli.com/jet/index.php?s=life&ss=biography.
Sochaczewski, P. 1994. The guts of a name change. *International Herald Tribune*, March 24.
Wong, W. 2009. What's in a name? *Chicago Tribune*, August 9.
WuDunn, S. 1996. Korea's Romeos and Juliets, cursed by their name. *New York Times*, September 11.

UNIT 2, SKILLS AND STRATEGIES 4

Boring Oregon. http://www.oregoncities.us/boring/index.htm.
Inbar, M. 2009. Top 10 "bad boy" baby names. *Today Show*, July 17. http://www.msnbc.msn.com/
id/31960846/ns/today-parenting_and_family/.
Inbar, M. 2009. Top 10 "bad boy" baby names. *Today Show*, July 17. http://www.msnbc.msn.com/
id/31960846/ns/today-parenting_and_family/.
Should it be Burma or Myanmar? 2007. *BBC News*, September 26. http://news.bbc.co.uk/2/hi/uk_
news/magazine/7013943.stm.
Thompson, A. 2008. Your initials may spell success. *LiveScience*, January 11. http://www.livescience.
com/health/071210-name-letter.html.
Williams, J. *Interesting Stories of Brand Names*, http://www.brandophillic.com/brand-names/.

UNIT 2, READING 3

Altman, D. 2009. Renaming your way out of a swamp. *On the button*, June 15. http://onthebutton.
wordpress.com/2009/06/15/gm_renaming/.
Dahle, C. 2000. How to make a name for yourself. *Fast Company, 38*, August .
Deluzain, H. (no date). http://www.behindthename.com/articles/1.php.
Igor. (2009). *Naming the perfect beast: The Igor naming guide.*
Imperato, G. 1996. Make a name for yourself. *Fast Company, 5*, October.
Reebok history. http://corporate.reebok.com/en/reebok_history/default.asp.

UNIT 3, READING 1

A Harvest Gathered, exhibit at John Carter Brown Library, Brown University.
Coe, S. 1994. *America's first cuisines.* Austin: University of Texas.
Crosby, A. 1988. *The Columbian exchange.* New York: Greenwood.
Foster, N., & Cordell, L. 1992. *Chilies to chocolate: Food the Americas gave the world.* Tucson, AZ:
University of Arizona Press.
Sokolov, R. 1991. *Why we eat what we eat: How the encounter between the new world and the old
world changed the way everyone on the planet eats.* New York: Summit.

UNIT 3, READING 2

Adler, C. 2003. The long march of the Colonel. *Time.com*, November 17. http://www.time.com/time/
magazine/article/0,9171,543845,00.html.
Avila, O. 2005. Nostalgia served piping hot. *Chicago Tribune*, July 30.
Griffin, W. 2008. McDonalds has big appetite for China. *MSNBC*, August 15. http://www.msnbc.msn.
com/id/26226387/ns/business-cnbc_tv/.
Hoffman, O. 2006. August 11. http://www.euromonitor.com/Who_eats_the_most_fast_food.
Noreen. 2009. What you can and can't get at McDonalds India. *Indiamarks*, February 26. http://www.
indiamarks.com/guide/What-You-Can-and-Can-t-Get-at-McDonalds-India-/1739/.
Restaurant News. 2008. Study Says Fast Food Remains Popular. June 20. http://www.qsrmagazine.
com/articles/news/story.phtml?id=6789.
Schlosser, E. 2001. *Fast-Food Nation.* Boston: Houghton Mifflin.
Ruelas, R. 2009. Man brings Guatemalan fast-food favorite to Valley diners. *Arizona Living*, February
16. http://www.azcentral.com/arizonarepublic/arizonaliving/articles/2009/02/16/20090216chicken
man0216.html.
Workman, D. 2007. Top fast food countries. *Suite101.com*, August 29. http://internationaltrade.
suite101.com/article.cfm/top_fast_food_countries.

UNIT 3, SKILLS AND STRATEGIES 6

Davidson, J. 2009. Teacher's Ed. *America – History of Our Nation, Beginnings through 1877*, Prentice
Hall.
Divine, R., Breen, T., et al. 2010. *America Past and Present* AP Edition. 8th Ed. Pearson.
One Sweet Nation. 2005. *U.S. News and World Report*, March 3. http://health.usnews.com/usnews/
health/articles/050328/28sugar.b.htm.

UNIT 3, READING 3

Brown, L. 2007. Renaissance table manners: Changes in dining etiquette from the Middle Ages
through the 1500s. May 10. http://weuropeanhistory.suite101.com/article.cfm/renaissance_
table_manners.
Etiquette in China. *Travelettiquette.* http://www.traveletiquette.co.uk/EtiquetteChina.html.
Giblin, J. 1987. *From hand to mouth.* New York: Thomas Crowell.
Knife, fork, spoon. *The Book of Threes.* http://www.threes.com/index.php?option=com_content&view
=article&id=2333:knife-fork-spoon&catid=79:food-nutrition&Itemid=57.

Lauber, P. 1999. *What you never knew about fingers, forks and chopsticks*. New York: Simon and Schuster.

Mishima, S. Japanese table manners. *About.com*. http://gojapan.about.com/cs/tablemanners/a/tablemanner.htm.

Romagnoli, D. 1996. "Mind your manners" Etiquette at the table. In J-L. Flandrin & A. Sonnenfeld. *Food: A culinary history* (pp. 328–338). New York: Penguin.

UNIT 4, SKILLS AND STRATEGIES 7

New York Transit Museum. History of public transit in New York City. http://www.transitmuseumeducation.org/trc/background.

Wikipedia http://en.wikipedia.org/wiki/Metro_systems_by_annual_passenger_rides http://en.wikipedia.org/wiki/List_of_metro_systems.

World Almanac for Kids. http://www.worldalmanacforkids.com/WAKI-ViewArticle.aspx?pin=x-pu149500a&article_id=662&chapter_id=14&chapter_title=Technology&article_title=Public_Transportation.

UNIT 4, READING 1

Downie, A. 2008. The World's Worst Traffic Jams. *Time.com*, April 21. http://www.time.com/time/world/article/0,8599,1733872,00.html#ixzz0d0xbB2 ml.

Transitpeople. http://www.transitpeople.org.

UNIT 4, READING 2

Austen, I. 2009. Montreal inaugurates continent's most ambitious bike-sharing program. *New York Times*, May 13. http://greeninc.blogs.nytimes.com/2009/05/13/montreal-inaugurates-continents-most-ambitious-bike-sharing-program/.

Bicycle Helmet Safety Institute. http://www.bhsi.org/stats.htm.

Bicycles produced in the world. *Worldometers*. http://www.worldometers.info/bicycles/.

Bicycle statistics: Usage, production, sales, import, export. http://www.ibike.org/library/statistics.htm.

Fong, C. 2009. City bike-sharing picks up speed. *CNN.com*, April 26. http://edition.cnn.com/2009/TECH/04/15/eco.bikeshare/.

Gardner, G. 2008. Bicycle production reaches 130 million. *Vital Signs Online*. Worldwatch Institute.

Rosenthal, E. 2008. European support for bicycles promotes sharing of the wheels. *New York Times*, November 10. http://www.nytimes.com/2008/11/10/world/europe/10bike.html?_r=1.

UNIT 4, SKILLS AND STRATEGIES 8

Wikipedia. http://en.wikipedia.org/wiki/DeLorean_Motor_Company.

UNIT 4, READING 3

Associated Press. 2009. Technology to stop teens texting and driving flawed. January 20. http://www.foxnews.com/story/0,2933,480659,00.html.

Commission for Global Road Safety. Make Roads Safe. Decade of Action Report. http://www.makeroadssafe.org/Pages/home.aspx.

Grover, C. 2009. Asleep at the Wheel: New technologies to help drivers stay in control. *Thatcham Research News*, February.

Half a million road crashes 'caused by women drivers applying make-up'. 2009. *Daily Telegraph*, October 6. http://www.telegraph.co.uk/motoring/news/6252919/Half-a-million-road-crashes-caused-by-women-drivers-applying-make-up.html.

Locher, J., & Moritz, O. 2009. Eating while driving causes 80% of all car accidents, study shows. *New York Daily News*, July 19. http://www.nydailynews.com/ny_local/2009/07/19/2009-07-19_eatdrive_sure_recipe_for_a_crash.html.

Madden, M., & Lenhart, A. 2009. Teens and distracted driving. *Pew Internet and American Life Center*, November 16.

Mohin, T. 2009. Group warns of global road-death "epidemic." *New York Times*, September 22. http://wheels.blogs.nytimes.com/2009/09/22/group-warns-of-global-road-death-epidemic/.

Montana Department of Justice. http://www.doj.mt.gov/driving/drivingsafety.asp.

Richtel, M. 2009. Drivers and legislators dismiss cellphone risks. *New York Times*, July 19. http://www.nytimes.com/2009/07/19/technology/19distracted.html.

Richtel, M. 2009. U.S. withheld date on risks of distracted driving. *New York Times*, July 21. http://www.nytimes.com/2009/07/21/technology/21distracted.html.

Richtel, M. 2009. Truckers insist on keeping computers in the cab. *New York Times*, September 28. http://www.nytimes.com/2009/09/28/technology/28truckers.html.

Richtel, M. 2009. At 60 mph, office work is high risk. *New York Times*, October 1. http://www.nytimes.com/2009/10/01/technology/01distracted.html.

Stutts, J., Reinfurt, D, Staplin, L., & Rodgman, E. 2001. 'The role of driver distraction in traffic crashes.' AAA Foundation for Traffic Safety. May.

World Health Organization 2004. World report on road traffic injury prevention. http://www.who.int/ violence_injury_prevention/publications/road_traffic/world_report/en/index.html.

UNIT 5, READING 1

National Institutes of Health. Brain basics: Understanding sleep. http://www.ninds.nih.gov/disorders/ brain_basics/understanding_sleep.htm.

Neuroscience for Kids. What is sleep and why do we need it? http://faculty.washington.edu/chudler/ sleep.html.

University of Washington. How much do animals sleep? http://faculty.washington.edu/chudler/ chasleep.html.

UNIT 5, READING 2

APA online. Why sleep is important and what happens when you don't get enough. http://www.apa. org/topics/whysleep.html.

National Sleep Foundation. Napping. http://www.sleepfoundation.org/article/sleep-topics/napping.

Palmer, B. (2009). Can you die from lack of sleep? *Slate*, May 11. http://www.slate.com/id/2218092.

Roberts, S. 2009. A look at who naps. *New York Times*, July 29.

Taylor, I. 2009. Nap time. Pew Research Center. July 29. http://pewresearch.org/pubs/1296/americans- napping-habits.

UNIT 5, READING 3

Gross, M. 2003. Are you a lark or an owl? *Guardian*, December 4. http://www.guardian.co.uk/ science/2003/dec/04/lastword.health.

Kreizman, L. 2009. Larks, owls and hummingbirds. *New York Times*, April 21. http://judson.blogs. nytimes.com/2009/04/21/guest-column-larks-owls-and-hummingbirds/?emc=eta1.

National Sleep Foundation. Sleep drive and your body clock. http://www.sleepfoundation.org/article/ sleep-topics/sleep-drive-and-your-body-clock.

Park, A. 2009. Larks and owls: How sleep habits affect grades. *Time*, June 10. http://www.time.com/ time/health/article/0,8599,1903838,00.html?xid=rss-health.

Smolenksy, M., and Lamberg, L. 2001. The body clock guide to better health. New York: Henry Holt.

UNIT 6, READING 1

Cromie W. 1997. How your brain listens to music. *Harvard Gazette*, November 13.

Cromie, W. 2001. Music on the brain: Researchers explore the biology of music. *Harvard Gazette*, March 22.

Ghosh, P. 2009. "Oldest musical instrument" found. BBC News. June 25. http://news.bbc.co.uk/2/hi/ science/nature/8117915.stm.

Levitin, D. 2008. *The world in six songs*. New York: Dutton.

Levitin, D. 2006. *This is your brain on music*. New York: Dutton.

Lloyd, R. 2008. The amazing power of music revealed. Live Science. http://www.livescience.com/ health/081015-music-power.html.

Patel, A. 2008. *Music, language and the brain*. Oxford: Oxford University Press.

Shulman, M. 2008. Music as medicine for the brain. *U.S. News and World Report*, July 17. http:// health.usnews.com/articles/health/brain-and-behavior/2008/07/17/music-as-medicine-for-the-brain. html.

Spitzer, G. 2009. Researchers probe how music rewires brain. WBEZ radio. September 11. http://www. chicagopublicradio.org/Content.aspx?audioID=36705.

UNIT 6, READING 2

Alpert, J., & Alpert, M. 1990. Music influence on mood and purchase intentions. *Psychology and Marketing*, 7, 109–133.

Fisher, N. 2008. Classical music is a big hit on the London underground. *Times on line*, February 1. http://entertainment.timesonline.co.uk/tol/arts_and_entertainment/music/article3284419.ece.

LeTrent, S. 2010. Restaurants' table turnover tricks boost business. *CNN Living*, April 30. http://www. cnn.com/2010/LIVING/04/30/noisy.restaurant.business/index.html.

North, A., & Hargreaves, D. 2006. Music in business environments. In S. Brown & U. Volgsten (Eds.), *Music and manipulation* (pp.103-125). New York: Berhahn.

Timberg, S. 2005. Halt, or I'll play Vivaldi! *Los Angeles Times*, February 13. http://articles.latimes. com/2005/feb/13/entertainment/ca-musichurts13.

UNIT 6, SKILLS AND STRATEGIES 12

ABC Classic FM. Mad About Mozart: W.A. Mozart – a Timeline. http://www.abc.net.au/classic/mozart/timeline.htm.

Arizona opera. Wolfgang Amadeus Mozart. http://www.azopera.com/learn.php?subcat=composerbios&composer=Mozart

History of the piano. http://www.essortment.com/all/historypiano_resc.htm.

UNIT 6, READING 3

Blow, C. 2009. Swan songs? *New York Times*, August 1. http://www.nytimes.com/2009/08/01/opinion/01blow.html.

Michaels, S. 2008. Most music didn't sell a single copy in 2008. *Guardian.co.uk*, December 23. http://www.guardian.co.uk/music/2008/dec/23/music-sell-sales.

Pfanner, E. 2009. Music industry lures "casual" pirates to legal sites. *New York Times*, July 20. http://www.nytimes.com/2009/07/20/technology/internet/20stream.html.

Stone, B. 2009. The music streams that soothe an industry. *New York Times*, July 26. http://www.nytimes.com/2009/07/26/business/26stream.html.

Underhill, W. 2009. Music for free and it's legal. *Newsweek*, March 21. http://www.newsweek.com/id/190457.

UNIT 6, MAKING CONNECTIONS

BBC News. Compact disc hits 25th birthday. http://news.bbc.co.uk/2/hi/6950845.stm?lsm.

Wikipedia. http://en.wikipedia.org/wiki/The_Rolling_Stones.

UNIT 7, READING 1

Guiney, J., & Lawrence, M. 2000. Hurricane Mitch. National Hurricane Center. May 4. http://www.nhc.noaa.gov/1998mitch.html.

Karpilo, J. 2010. World's worst disasters. January 25. http://geography.about.com/od/hazardsanddisasters/a/worstworlddisasters.htm.

MCEER. Haiti Earthquake Facts 2010. http://mceer.buffalo.edu/infoservice/disasters/Haiti-Earthquake-2010.asp.

Zananas-Martinique : http://www.zananas-martinique.com/en-saint-pierre-martinique/pele-mount-eruption-1902.htm.

UNIT 7, READING 2

Mott, M. 2003. Can animals sense earthquakes? *National Geographic News*, November 11. http://news.nationalgeographic.com/news/2003/11/1111_031111_earthquakeanimals.html.

No author. 2005. British schoolgirl Tilly Smith saves hundreds of lives. *Yahoo Thailand News*, January 1. http://www.thaipro.com/thailand_00/320-tsunami-tilly-smith.htm.

UNIT 7, SKILLS AND STRATEGIES 14

2008 one of worst years for natural disasters this decade. 2009. *CBC News*, January 23. http://www.cbc.ca/world/story/2009/01/23/natural-disasters.html.

No author. 2009. Deadly earthquake deluges Taiwan, slams China. *CBS News*, August 10. http://www.cbsnews.com/stories/2009/08/10/world/main5228772.shtml.

Padgett, T. 2010. How to Survive an Earthquake: Two Schools of Thought. *Time.com*, February 1. http://www.time.com/time/specials/packages/article/0,28804,1953379_1953494_1958235,00.html.

Verma, S. 2005. *The Tunguska fireball: Solving one of the great mysteries of the 20th century*. Cambridge: Cambridge University Press.

UNIT 7, READING 3

Botzer, A. 2004. Yucatan asteroid didn't kill dinosaurs, study says. *National Geographic News*, http://news.nationalgeographic.com/news/2004/03/0309_040309_chicxulubdinos.html.

Cuk, M. 2002. How dangerous are asteroids? *Curious about Astronomy, How Stuff Works*, November http://www.howstuffworks.com/framed.htm?parent=peru-meteor.htm&url=http://curious.astro.cornell.edu/question.php?number=215.

Geologist Gets To The Bottom Of Chicxulub Impact Crater. 2007. *Science Daily*, January 22. http://www.sciencedaily.com/releases/2007/01/070118094039.htm.

The Great Dying. http://science.nasa.gov/headlines/y2002/28jan_extinction.htm.

Hecht, J. 2002. 2019 asteroid given all clear. *New Scientist*. http://www.newscientist.com/article/dn2606-2019-asteroid-given-all-clear.html.

Jet Propulsion Lab. http://neo.jpl.nasa.gov/images/yucatan.html.

Masters, K. 2004. Are there any asteroids on a collision course with Earth? *Curious about Astronomy, How Stuff Works*, April. http://www.howstuffworks.com/framed.htm?parent=peru-meteor. htm&url=http://curious.astro.cornell.edu/question.php?number=215.

Near Earth Object Program. NASA http://neo.jpl.nasa.gov/neo/life.html.

Owen, R. 2009. Who is responsible for averting an asteroid strike? *ABC News*, May 16. http://www. newscientist.com/article/dn2606-2019-asteroid-given-all-clear.html.

Smith, L. 2006. Huge meteor strike that gave birth to the dinosaur. June 3. http://www.timesonline.co.uk/tol/news/world/us_and_americas/article671126.ece.

What killed the dinosaurs? *Evolution, PBS*. http://www.pbs.org/wgbh/evolution/extinction/dinosaurs/ low_bandwidth.html.

Whitehouse, D. (2002). Space rock on "collision course." *BBC News*. http://news.bbc.co.uk/2/hi/sci/ tech/2147879.stm.

UNIT 8, READING 1

Espinoza, J. 2008. Eastern Europeans are "hardest working." *Forbes*, September 4. http://www.forbes. com/2008/09/04/working-hours-europe-markets-equity-cx_je_0904markets15.html.

Fleck, S. 2009. International comparison of hours worked. *Monthly Labor Review*, 132, May. http:// www.bls.gov/opub/mlr/2009/05/contents.htm.

UBS Prices and Earnings, 2009. http://www.ubs.com/1/e/wealthmanagement/wealth_management_ research/prices_earnings.html.

Veal, A. J. 2004. A brief history of work and its relationship to leisure. In J. Haworth & A. J. Veal (Eds.), *Work and leisure* (pp. 15–33). London: Routledge.

UNIT 8, READING 2

Barboza, D. 2010. For the Chinese, Web is the way to entertainment. *New York Times*, April 18. http://www.nytimes.com/2010/04/19/technology/19chinaweb.html.

Bronson, P. 2006. Just sit back and relax. *Time*, June 18. http://www.time.com/time/magazine/ article/0,9171,1205369,00.html.

Eldon, E. 2009. *Inside Facebook*. http://www.insidefacebook.com/2009/12/07/facebook-reaches-100-million-monthly-active-users-in-the-united-states/.

Facebook. 2010. February. http://www.facebook.com/press/info.php?timeline.

Fleming, R. May 7, 2010. http://www.digitaltrends.com/gaming/hardware-gaming/nintendo-wii-sales-begin-to-flatline/.

Gelber, S. 1999. *Hobbies: Leisure and the Culture of Work in America*. New York: Columbia University Press.

Hachman, M. 2009. More Time Spent Social Networking Than on Email. *PCMag.com*, March 10. http://www.pcmag.com/article2/0,2817,2342757,00.asp.

Legat, H. 2009. Time spent social networking up 93%. *Bizreport*, April 7. http://www.bizreport. com/2009/04/time_spent_social_networking_up_93.html.

McGuire, J. 2009. Volunteer vacations. *Time Magazine*, March 13. http://www.time.com/time/travel/ article/0,31542,1885136,00.html.

Patterson, T. 2009. Welcome to the "weisure" lifestyle. *CNN.com/living*, May 11. http://www.cnn. com/2009/LIVING/worklife/05/11/weisure/.

The serious leisure perspective. http://www.soci.ucalgary.ca/seriousleisure/

Social Networking and Blog Sites Capture More Internet Time and Advertising (September 24, 2009) http://blog.nielsen.com/nielsenwire/online_mobile/social-networking-and-blog-sites-capture-more-internet-time-and-advertisinga/.

Stebbins, R. 2004. *Between work and leisure: The common ground of two separate worlds*. New Brunswick, NJ: Transaction Publishers.

Stebbins, R. 2007. Serious leisure: A perspective for our time. New Brunswick, NJ: Transaction Publishers.

UNIT 8, SKILLS AND STRATEGIES 16

How do Americans spend their leisure time? http://www.libraryindex.com/pages/1947/How-Americans-Spend-Their-Time-HOW-DO-AMERICANS-LIKE-SPEND-THEIR-LEISURE-TIME.html.

Many Teens Spend 30 Hours A Week On "Screen Time" During High School. ScienceDaily 2008 March 14. http://www.sciencedaily.com/releases/2008/03/080312172614.htm.

Pong Story. http://www.pong-story.com/intro.htm.

UNIT 8, READING 3

Do us a favor, take a vacation. 2007. *Business Week*, May 21. http://www.businessweek.com/ magazine/content/07_21/b4035088.htm.

Does American culture frown on vacations? 2008. *Knowledge@Emory*, March 6. http://knowledge. emory.edu/article.cfm?articleid=1067.

Expedia.com – 2009 International Vacation Deprivation™ Survey Results. http://www.expedia.com/daily/promos/vacations/vacation_deprivation/default.asp.

Euromonitor 2008. http://www.euromonitor.com/_Euromonitor_Internationals_Top_City_Destinations_Ranking.

Stuever, H. 2000. What would Godzilla say? *Washington Post online*, February 14. http://www.washingtonpost.com/wp-srv/style/feed/a49427-2000feb14.htm.